EFFECTIVE DATA STORYTELLING

EFFECTIVE DATA STORYTELLING

How to *Drive Change* with Data, Narrative, and Visuals

Brent Dykes

WILEY

Library of Congress Cataloging-in-Publication Data:
Names: Dykes, Brent, author.
Title: Effective data storytelling : how to drive change with data, narrative and visuals / Brent Dykes.
Description: Hoboken, New Jersey : John Wiley and Sons, Inc., [2020] | Includes bibliographical references and index.
Identifiers: LCCN 2019032934 (print) | LCCN 2019032935 (ebook) | ISBN 9781119615712 (hardback) | ISBN 9781119615736 (adobe pdf) | ISBN 9781119615729 (epub)
Subjects: LCSH: Business communication. | Information visualization. | Storytelling.
Classification: LCC HF5718 .D95 2020 (print) | LCC HF5718 (ebook) | DDC 658.4/5—dc23
LC record available at https://lccn.loc.gov/2019032934
LC ebook record available at https://lccn.loc.gov/2019032935

To my family (and Jackson, who we miss dearly)

*To Dad, Stan, and Hans—thanks for sharing
the power of storytelling*

Contents

Foreword

Today, data has become one of the most valuable business assets. The companies that are best able to turn their data into insights, and their insights into knowledge, will outsmart and outperform their competition. In this data-driven world, storytelling is a vital enabler that will help organizations succeed.

We now live in a world with more data than ever before. Our data volumes are measured in zettabytes, which is an unimaginably vast quantity. One zettabyte is a number with 21 zeros at the end and contains one billion terabytes (one terabyte being the capacity of a state-of-the-art home computer). It is predicted that by 2025, we will have more than 175 zettabytes of data in the world, an exponential growth from the around 10 zettabytes we have in the world today. But all of that data is worthless unless businesses are able to gain insights from the data that allows them to act, make better decisions, and initiate change.

In order to make the most of the unprecedented opportunities presented by data, businesses and the individuals within them need the right skills—they need to be data literate. From my work helping companies all over the globe make better use of data, I know that the ability to tell a story from data is a core pillar of data literacy.

Storytelling has been ingrained in the human way of life for hundreds of thousands of years. Throughout history, humans have used stories as an essential tool to capture people's attention, engage them, ignite their imagination, and pass on knowledge—and that ability to tell stories is as important, if not more important, in today's data-driven world as it was when our ancestors dwelled in caves.

Those who use storytelling effectively don't just present facts, they present stories that will persuade, be remembered, and told and retold within an organization. The ability to tell stories from data is a skill that will become increasingly valuable in the job market of tomorrow.

Brent Dykes has done an outstanding job of creating a practical and engaging book that will help to improve your data storytelling skills. You will learn how to take the key ingredients of data, narratives, and visuals to help explain, enlighten, and engage people, leading to better decision making and initiating change.

I am sure that after you have finished reading *Effective Data Storytelling: How to Drive Change with Data, Narrative, and Visuals,* the book will remain on your shelf as an invaluable resource and reference guide to dive back into when you need a reminder of how to make better use of data and present data in a way that makes a real difference.

—Bernard Marr
Futurist and author of *The Intelligent Company*, *Big Data*, *Big Data in Practice,* and *Artificial Intelligence in Practice*

Preface

While many data visualization principles are covered in this book, *it is not a data visualization book*. I want to set that expectation upfront, or else you may be disappointed. However, if you're looking to communicate your insights more effectively to others, you've found the right book. If you want to better understand why data storytelling is so effective, again—this is the book. If you're seeking to drive positive change with data, this book will equip you with everything you'll need (at least, from a communication perspective). As you go through each chapter in this book, you'll notice I start each one with *a story*—because that's how much I believe in the power of storytelling. Let us begin this adventure together, *once upon an insight...*

★ ★ ★ ★

After more than two years of intense research and writing, I'm excited to share my perspective on data storytelling. My journey toward writing this book began in 2013 when I convinced Adobe's event team to let me deliver a breakout session on "data storytelling" at our upcoming customer conference. At the time, it was an emerging topic that resonated with me. Having worked with data for the better part of my career—over 15 years in enterprise analytics—I experienced daily how critical effective data communication was. This session was my first formal opportunity to share some of the early concepts and frameworks I had developed. When the presentation went extremely well and I was asked to repeat the session, I knew I was onto something.

Over the next few years, I continued to develop and hone my ideas on data storytelling and spoke at various business and technology conferences. Repeatedly, after I presented on how to tell stories with data, attendees would ask if I had a book or offered workshops—this was my next big signal. In 2016, I wrote a popular *Forbes* article titled "Data Storytelling: The Essential Data Science Skill Everyone Needs." It has generated more than 200,000 views and is consistently listed as Google's top search result for "data storytelling"—this was the final indication I needed to write this book.

With the growth in data usage across small and large organizations, people must increasingly be bilingual in data. However, my urgency to write this book increased when I realized how poorly understood the concept of data storytelling was and how the term was in danger of becoming just another empty buzzword. Despite its immense potential, it was frequently positioned as just an extension of data visualization. Furthermore, the narrative aspect of data storytelling was largely ignored or treated as simply a sidekick to the visuals. While many were advocating the virtues of data storytelling, very few people explained how and why it worked. If that weren't enough, during the course of writing this book, I've seen facts abused, twisted, and disparaged on a daily basis. Instead of using the rich levels of data to our benefit, we're sliding back to a time when facts didn't matter. Under these difficult circumstances, we need data storytellers more than ever before.

Acknowledgments

When you write a book, you realize how important it is to have the support of family, friends, and colleagues. I want to start by thanking my wife, Libby, and our five children (Lauren, Cassidy, Linden, Peter, and Josh). Without their love, support, and patience, this book wouldn't have been possible. I'm also grateful to my father, who has inspired me with his storytelling throughout my life, and to my mother, who endured all of my dad's stories.

I'm appreciative of all the people who offered me their feedback, expertise, experiences, and encouragement during the creation of this book. Right from the inception of this book, Chad Greenleaf and Tim Wilson have been great advisors at each stage of its development. I also want to thank Chris Haleua, Dylan Lewis, Maria Massei-Rosato, Andrea Henderson, Alan Wilson, Jason Krantz, Alex Abell, Sarah Chalupa, Dan Stubbs, Archie Baron, Dan Hillman, Chris Willis, Andrew Anderson, Jared Watson, Kristie Rowley, Jeremy Morris, John Stevens, and James Arrington. I'd like to recognize Jeri Larsen for her invaluable contributions with editing this book. Additionally, I'm grateful to Sheck Cho, Purvi Patel, and the entire Wiley team for making this book a reality.

Many people have inspired me in my data storytelling journey, and I would like to thank them as well: Hans Rosling, Chip and Dan Heath, Steve Denning, Stephen Few, Dona Wong, Alberto Cairo, Edward Tufte, and Daniel Kahneman. Lastly, I'm grateful to all of the people over the years who have attended my presentations and workshops on data storytelling, and who have read and shared my articles on this important topic. Your enthusiasm for this content has fueled my passion to complete this project, and I hope you enjoy reading what your interest inspired me to write.

Chapter 1

Introduction to Driving Change through Insight

Any powerful idea is absolutely fascinating and absolutely useless until we choose to use it.

—Richard Bach, author

A mildly traumatic experience taught me one of my first lessons about data storytelling. Early in my career, after completing the first year of my Master of Business Administration (MBA) program, I secured an internship at a well-known, multichannel retailer based in the Midwest. At the time, the economy was in the middle of a tough recession, and many US corporations weren't interested in hiring international students like me who would incur additional fees to sponsor. Fortunately, my online marketing experience in Canada appealed to this retailer, and I was offered an intern position in its acclaimed ecommerce department.

As one of several MBA interns vying for a job offer at the end of the summer, I had an important midpoint presentation coming up with the senior vice president (SVP) of ecommerce. It afforded me a crucial opportunity to ensure my project was heading in the right direction before my final presentation. With a pregnant wife and two young kids counting on me to secure a full-time position, I was feeling substantial pressure to make a good impression on this influential executive.

The SVP in question wasn't your typical business leader. He was a former military captain and special forces helicopter pilot. If his austere demeanor wasn't intimidating enough, he was also extremely sharp and had graduated from a top-tier business school. Over the years, many MBA interns saw their carefully crafted presentations shot to pieces in review sessions with this senior executive; it was not uncommon to see shell-shocked faces and tears after his meetings.

Not intending to become one of his many casualties, I worked diligently to prepare for my midpoint presentation. I was pleased with the progress I had made on my project, and I was confident in my ability to present what I had accomplished so far. However, during the course of my project, I had stumbled across an interesting data point while reviewing customer survey responses. The data indicated a commonly held practice related to order shipping wasn't as important to customers as the ecommerce team supposed. Even though this insight wasn't central to my project, I decided it was worth sharing because if the data turned out to be true, it could have a significant impact on the ecommerce team's approach.

When the day came for me to present, everything went well—until I got to the slide with the customer survey insight. It generated a reaction from the SVP . . . but not the one I expected. He leaned forward and blurted out "*Bullshit*"—not under his breath but forcefully for everyone in the room to hear. His emphatic response ensured no one in the room would challenge his authoritative opinion on the matter—including me. It felt like I had just stepped on a landmine—a cultural one. A paralyzing feeling of panic swept over me as I realized how ill-prepared and exposed I was at that exact moment. Luckily, a daring mentor jumped in to provide some needed cover fire so I could recover and stumble through my remaining slides. While my ego was a little shaken, I survived the meeting and left the boardroom with a valuable insight of my own.

As I reflected on the experience, I realized I had made a serious miscalculation. In my naive excitement to add value and contribute a potentially meaningful insight, I assumed the potential *merit* of the insight would ensure its acceptance and further investigation. Unfortunately, sheer merit alone wouldn't be enough to safeguard its adoption. Like so many other promising findings that have never seen the light of day, my insight was dismissed. It died in the boardroom that day. While noble and aspirational, the meritocracy I ascribed to was an illusion. People and organizations aren't always open to new findings—deliberately or unintentionally—that can better their performance or position.

Many factors contributed to the demise of my insight: my poor delivery, the executive's closed-mindedness, and cultural inertia. However, a key contributing factor that sealed the insight's fate was the level of change it would incite. Insight and change go hand-in-hand. Whenever we uncover an insight, it inescapably leads to changes if the data is acted upon.

Often, the potential value of a discovery is directly proportional to the level of resistance it will face. While we may want to believe insights are harmless gifts, they can have subtle-to-significant repercussions that may be difficult for people to accept. Generally, the bigger an insight is, the more disruptive it will be to the status quo. People can struggle with giving up what's routine and familiar. When a new insight isn't well understood and doesn't sound compelling, it will have no chance of overcoming resistance to change. After this experience, I discovered if you want to be insightful and introduce change, you can't just *inform* an audience; you must *engage* them.

Why Change Is Important

I cannot say whether things will get better if we change; what I can say is they must change if they are to get better.
—Georg C. Lichtenberg, scientist

The ancient Greek philosopher Heraclitus viewed change as being central to the universe and is attributed with the saying "change is the only constant in life." We live in a constantly evolving world that is more random, noisy, and unpredictable than we want to admit. It's important for individuals and organizations to be adept at adapting to shifting environments. As former General Electric CEO Jack Welch said, "Change before you have to." Instead of becoming stagnant or settling for less, we often search for new ways to improve ourselves and the world around us.

Throughout time, mankind's innovations have been driven by people seeking to *make things better*—faster, cheaper, safer, more efficient, more productive, and so on. Groundbreaking innovations such as the printing press, telephone, automobile, computer, and internet have introduced significant change. These scientific breakthroughs necessitated the tearing down of established beliefs, skill sets, and systems in order to replace them. Change becomes an unavoidable byproduct of progress. If you want to advance and improve, you must pursue new insights and implement new ideas that inevitably introduce change.

Not all change has to be massively disruptive. Post-war Japanese manufacturers developed the *kaizen philosophy* ("change for better"), where employees were encouraged to continuously introduce small, incremental improvements throughout their factories. Eventually, the culmination of these small process refinements over the years helped Japanese firms such as Toyota and Sony gain a major competitive advantage in terms of product quality and manufacturing efficiency. Today, most innovative startups and even large companies embrace a similar *lean methodology* that involves incremental experimentation and agile development.

An essential underpinning of both the kaizen and lean methodologies is data. Without data, companies using these approaches simply wouldn't know what to improve or whether their incremental changes were successful. Data provides the clarity and specificity that's often needed to drive *positive* change. The importance of having baselines, benchmarks, and targets isn't isolated to just business; it can transcend everything from personal development to social causes. The right insight can instill both the courage and confidence to forge a new direction— turning a leap of faith into an informed expedition.

Everyone Becomes an Analyst

Data helps solve problems.

—Anne Wojcicki, entrepreneur

For the greater part of the past 50 years, data has been primarily entrusted to only two privileged groups within most business organizations: an *executive* who required data to manage the business; or a *data specialist*—a business analyst, statistician, economist, or accountant—who gathered, analyzed, and reported the numbers for management. For everyone else, exposure to data has been fairly limited, indirect, or intermittent.

In today's digital age, data has become more pervasive, exposing more people to facts and figures than ever before. The volume of data is expected to grow 61% each year, reaching 175 zettabytes by 2025 (1 zettabyte is a trillion gigabytes) (Patrizio 2018). Much of this explosive growth can be attributed to the increasingly connected world in which we live and the additional data that is being created by machines—not just by humans or business entities.

Data has rapidly become a key strategic asset, shifting from being "nice-to-have" to essential at most organizations. For example, for tech giants such as Amazon, Google, Facebook, and Netflix, data has become an integral foundation of their business success—both in terms of how it powers their operations and the immense strategic value it offers. From the data-powered recommendation engines of Amazon and Netflix to the data-rich ad networks of Google and Facebook, these data-savvy companies have carved out formidable competitive advantages through data and technology. However, acumen with data is no longer just the domain of industry leaders—innovative companies of all sizes are reaping its benefits. For example, I met a small, Oregon-based home builder that was able to gain unparalleled data transparency into all of its approval and review processes, giving it a distinct advantage over local competitors that were saddled with inefficient paper-based processes.

In today's dynamic, fast-paced business environment, limiting information to a narrow set of executives and data specialists no longer makes sense. Forward-thinking organizations look to empower more of their workers with data so they can make better-informed decisions and respond more quickly to market opportunities and challenges. To democratize data and foster data-driven cultures, companies rely on various analytics technologies—everything from the ubiquitous spreadsheet to advanced data discovery tools.

You no longer need to have the words "data" or "analyst" in your job title to be immersed in numbers and be expected to use them on a regular basis. Data is now everyone's responsibility. In fact, the Achilles' heel of any analyst is a lack of context—something most business users have in spades. A sharp analyst can miss something in the data that is easily spotted by the seasoned eyes of a business user, who can draw on years of domain expertise. Data doesn't care who you are or what your analytical skill level is—it's willing to yield up insights to whoever is diligent and curious enough to find them. Greater data access means valuable insights can be discovered by people of all backgrounds—not just technical ones.

Outside of work, you may not realize how much analysis you're performing in your "free time" as data is increasingly integrated into various aspects of our lives. For example, when you plan a vacation or evaluate different products online, your decisions are most likely informed by a certain type of data—the recommendations and ratings of complete strangers. In fact, 89% of consumers indicated that online reviews influenced their buying decisions (PowerReviews 2018). If you're an avid sports fan, you're regularly consuming statistics throughout the season on your favorite team's performance (or in some cases, the lack thereof). Furthermore, you might be among the almost 60 million people in the United States and Canada who enjoy competing in fantasy sports that are powered entirely by data.

Closer to home, my wife never thought she would touch the world of analytics and data—until she started running marathons and competing in triathlons. Now, she is constantly analyzing her fitness level and training performance with her trusty Garmin GPS watch. Through hard work, determination, and data, she has been able to accomplish her fitness goals, including completing a full Ironman race and the well-known Boston Marathon. Whether we're pursuing personal fitness or business goals, the recent surge in digital data—along with its growing utility and importance—is pushing everyone to become more data savvy.

Data Literacy Is Essential in Today's Data Economy

> The ability to take data—to be able to understand it, to process it, to extract value from it, to visualize it, to communicate it—that's going to be a hugely important skill in the next decades.
> —Hal Varian, Chief Economist at Google

Even though data is being thrust on more people, it doesn't mean everyone is prepared to consume and use it effectively. As our dependence on data for guidance and insights increases, the need for greater data literacy also grows. If literacy is defined as the ability to *read and write*, data literacy can be defined as the ability to *understand and communicate data*. Today's advanced data tools can offer unparalleled insights, but they require capable operators who can understand and interpret data. Just as a library comprised of the finest literary works in the world will be relatively worthless to someone who can't read, the same applies to a rich repository of data in the hands of someone who doesn't know how to use it.

Fortunately, you don't need an advanced English degree to be literate in English. Similarly, to be data literate, you aren't required to have advanced statistical knowledge and programming skills in Python or R. However, you will need some basic numeracy skills such as being able to understand, process, and interpret a standard data table or chart. Because you're reading this book, I will assume you already possess the requisite numeracy skills to discover insights. Either through the good fortune of education, work experience, extracurricular activities, or just an innate curiosity, you've been able to develop this ability. Now, you're looking to improve the other half of being data literate—*the ability to communicate or share data effectively*.

As Google's Chief Economist Hal Varian has emphasized, the ability to find a valuable insight and then be able to share it effectively is going to be a "hugely important skill in the next decades" (McKinsey & Company 2009). In other words, much of the value that's going to be generated from data will depend on these essential skills. The potential value hidden within your data will remain dormant if you are unable to understand and interpret what the numbers mean. If you are able to find a valuable insight but are unable to communicate it effectively, there's still the possibility it won't deliver on its potential. As inventor Thomas A. Edison highlighted, "The value of an idea lies in the using of it." If your amazing finding is confusing or not compelling to others, they won't be motivated to act on it. The more people who are capable of driving action from their insights, the more positive change and value we'll see from data. Without action, insights are just empty numbers.

What Is an Insight?

> Intuition is the use of patterns they've already learned, whereas insight is the discovery of new patterns.
>
> —Gary Klein, psychologist

Throughout this book, I will repeatedly use the term *insight,* so it's important that we begin by clarifying its meaning. Starting with the origin of the word, insight comes from Middle English for "inner sight" or "sight with the 'eyes' of the mind" (Online Etymology Dictionary 2019). Psychologist Gary Klein defined an insight as "an unexpected shift in the way we understand things" (Gregoire 2013). These "unexpected shifts" in our knowledge can occur as we analyze and examine data. For example, we may uncover a new relationship, pattern, trend, or anomaly in the data that reshapes how we view things. While most insights are interesting, not all of them are valuable. This book will be centered around meaningful insights that offer some tangible promise of value—increased revenue, cost savings, reduced risk, and so on.

Entrepreneur Rama Ramakrishnan shared a simple example of an insight that his data science team uncovered at a large business-to-consumer (B2C) retailer. When they were analyzing the retailer's customer data by transaction amounts, they anticipated they would find a typical bell-curve distribution; however, they found an unanticipated second peak in the histogram (see Figure 1.1). The double-peaked histogram highlighted an interesting curiosity—an observation—but it quickly put his team on the path to discovering an insight.

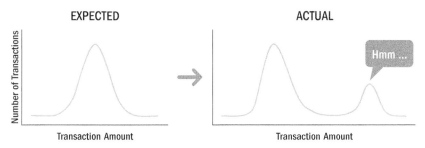

Figure 1.1   The data science team expected the transactions to be normally distributed (left), but to their surprise, there was an unexpected double peak in the histogram.

When they investigated the second peak (which Ramakrishnan referred to as the "hmm"), they discovered it was mainly comprised of international resellers—not the retailer's typical clientele of young mothers purchasing items for their children. Because this retailer didn't have a physical or digital presence outside of North America, these resellers "would travel to the US from abroad once a year, walk into a store, buy lots of items, take them back to their country and sell them in their own stores" (Ramakrishnan 2017). This simple shift in the understanding of its customer base spurred a slew of additional questions for the B2C retailer:

- What types of products were these resellers buying?
- At which store locations were they shopping?
- How could promotional campaigns better target these individuals?
- How could this transaction data inform global expansion plans?

As this example shows, a single insight can unlock a multitude of new opportunities (or challenges), impacting a wide variety of activities. Ideally, insights don't just shift our thinking but inspire us to do things differently. They convert data into direction that takes us to new, unforeseen places. For the B2C retailer, the discovery of the hidden segment of global resellers caused the retailer to re-examine how it would merchandise, promote, and expand internationally going forward. Key insights like this one can be true game changers, but only if we know how to share them effectively with the people who will decide their fate and help make them a reality.

Effective Communication Turns Insights into Actions

> The goal is to provide inspiring information that moves people to action.
>
> —Guy Kawasaki, author and venture capitalist

When you're analyzing data for your specific job or for personal matters (budgeting or dieting), you are the audience of your analysis. You know the data intimately and are most likely in a position to act on whatever insights you uncover, as they only affect you. However, in an organizational setting, the insights you uncover can often have a much broader impact beyond just you individually. They can affect people around you in different ways such as what they believe, how they work, and what they prioritize. You may also require their involvement and support to implement whatever changes each insight evokes. This people dynamic is also shaped by your position within the group as being perceived as an insider or outsider (see Table 1.1).

For example, you may need your manager's approval to spend money, time, and effort fixing a problem you've identified. To help resolve the issue, you may need support from peers and coworkers who may have different agendas and conflicting priorities. Additionally, you may have employees whom you need to adopt and implement the changes introduced by your insight. If these individuals are expected to embrace your insight, they will need to understand it sufficiently and be convinced of its importance. Effective communication becomes the vehicle for explaining your insight in a way so others understand it and are compelled to act on it.

Too often, communication is an afterthought rather than a critical step in the analytical process. While I have strived to communicate my insights effectively as an analyst, I too have underestimated the central role it

Table 1.1 Your Relationship with the Insight

Personal: When you analyze data for personal reasons, you don't need to worry about communicating your insight to anyone else. You are both the analyst and the audience.	
Insider: When you're sharing an insight with your team, you will have the advantage of added context and a more intimate knowledge of the audience. Because you are also impacted by the insight, you have a vested interest in it being understood and adopted. Authority, power, and position can also shape how influential your insight is to the group. For example, an executive will have more pull than an intern.	
Outsider: When you're sharing an insight with another team, you may be seen as more objective if you have nothing to gain from its adoption. In addition, the group may appreciate a fresh, external perspective. However, being an outsider can also be a disadvantage in terms of having less context and rapport with the audience.	

plays in deriving value from data. Through my years of experience in analytics, I have observed five key steps to driving value from analytics: *data*, *information*, *insight*, *decision*, and *action*. Like a line of dominos, each step plays a role in driving toward value (see Figure 1.2). It starts with

ANALYTICS PATH TO VALUE

Figure 1.2 To create value with analytics, like dominos, a sequential series of steps must occur (and be repeated over time).

collecting *raw data* to serve as the foundation for gaining knowledge on a subject. The data is organized and summarized in reports, turning raw data into *information* that's easier for more people to consume. When people examine and analyze these reports, they discover meaningful *insights* that inform *decisions* and drive *actions* that create *value*.

While on the surface these steps make sense, the diagram oversimplified the jump from finding an insight to influencing a decision. Facts alone will not influence decisions. As I learned from my ecommerce experience many years ago, other factors such as culture and tradition play an influential role in decision making. Only through skilled communication will an insight have any chance of persuading someone to re-evaluate their opinions and beliefs. Somehow you must figure out how your insights can break through cognitive, social, and organizational barriers to generate better decisions.

Data-driven Change Isn't Easy

Our dilemma is that we hate change and love it at the same time; what we really want is for things to remain the same but get better.
                    —Sydney J. Harris, journalist and author

Change is often hard—both for the ones expected to adopt the change and those advocating for it. The natural tendency for most people is to resist something new or different because it appears to be risky, uncertain, or threatening. Many individuals will be complacent with the way things are. Even though the status quo may be found wanting, it still represents "the devil they already know." Your findings may also encounter resistance if they make someone look bad. Nobody likes their poor performance, negligence, or bad decisions showcased for everyone to see. Even when your audience likes one of your insights, they may view acting on it as a lower priority or requiring more work than they can manage.

Navigating these concerns and issues adds complexity to the job of sharing insights. At times, you may even question whether it's worth the trouble to share a particular insight. You might have gone through a similar experience to what I shared at the beginning of this chapter. In these situations, you have a choice to make: keep the insight to yourself or embrace whatever communication challenges it will entail, knowing the insight will be more beneficial if it's shared. This decision will depend on how much you believe in the analysis or research. If you have any doubts about the insight's validity or usefulness, not sharing it may be the right option until you can strengthen your position. However, if you're confident in the quality of the analysis and convinced of its worth, you'll want to seize the opportunity to share your discovery with others. While you may not face the same jeopardy that whistleblowers face when reporting wrongdoing, courage and determination may be required for sharing insights that may be viewed as disruptive or unconventional.

Strive to Communicate, Not Just Inform

How well we communicate is determined not by how well we say things but how well we are understood.

—Andrew Grove, American businessman

If you are determined to have your insights understood and acted upon, you must shift your approach from simply *informing* to *communicating*. American journalist Sydney J. Harris said, "The two words 'information' and 'communication' are often used interchangeably, but they signify quite different things. Information is giving out; communication is getting through." Both approaches involve a sender (analyst) and a receiver (audience). However, there is a key difference between informing and communicating. While the goal of informing is to ensure the information is received, the purpose of communicating is to ensure the audience understands the meaning of the data (see Figure 1.3), which may often involve two-way communication between the sender and receiver to clarify the message.

When you inform someone, you're simply disseminating data in a passive, clinical manner. You expect the audience to interpret and comprehend the data for themselves. No overt message or interpretation

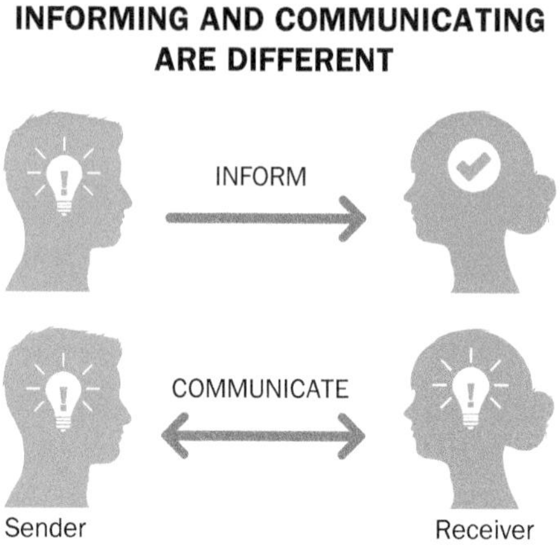

**INFORMING AND COMMUNICATING
ARE DIFFERENT**

INFORM

COMMUNICATE

Sender   Receiver

Figure 1.3 When you inform someone of something, you are just passing along information. However, when you communicate something to someone, you ensure they understand it as well.

of the data is passed along to the receiver—just the facts. On the other hand, communicating is about clarifying what the data means. When you communicate, you become an active, discernible participant in the delivery of the information rather than being a removed, neutral one if you are simply informing. When your goal is to "get through" to your audience, you must engage them by communicating in a way that guides them through the numbers and motivates them to act.

Storytelling is critical to effective communication. As an example, if you were to compare *informing* and *telling* someone about a recent vacation you took, you'd see a subtle difference in the two approaches. With informing, you'd just stick to the facts such as where you went, with whom you went, how long you were gone, and what you did. However, with telling (or communicating), you'd cover those same details but elaborate on why you chose to go on vacation, what you enjoyed the most, and how it made you feel. You may even motivate someone else to want to take a similar vacation based on your experiences. Where informing strives to connect with just the head, communicating seeks to touch the mind and heart.

If you're simply passing along information, and you aren't striving to make a specific point, a neutral, passive approach is fine. However, if your goal is to share a particular insight, then just informing your audience won't be an effective strategy. The act of informing doesn't focus on preparing your audience to interpret and understand the meaning and significance of your key findings. An insight must be transmitted to the receiver in a manner that will draw their attention, clarify what the data means, and persuade them to act. To convey your insights in an effective manner that influences decisions and drives action, you must embrace the familiar yet powerful approach of *storytelling*.

Telling the Story of Your Data

> Numbers have an important story to tell. They rely on you to give them a clear and convincing voice.
>
> —Stephen Few, data visualization expert

At the beginning of this chapter, I recounted how I shared what I thought was a valuable insight with a senior executive. When I attempted to inform him of how customers felt differently about one of the ecommerce team's core policies related to shipping, he abruptly rejected the data with a rude shout. In retrospect, I didn't do justice to my insight because I failed to communicate it properly. It deserved more focused attention in a separate, more targeted presentation—I needed to tell the story of those numbers. Simply presenting some information and hoping it would somehow resonate with the audience was very naive on my behalf. Sadly, I don't think I'm the only one who has stumbled across an interesting insight and then struggled to convey it in a meaningful way to others.

For change expert John Kotter, the first step in any change process is to create a *sense of urgency* that helps people understand why a change is necessary (Kotter 2013). When you have an opinion or feeling that something should change, it can be difficult to instill a sense of urgency without sufficient supporting information. However, by having unearthed or learned about an insight, you should already have all the raw materials—data—needed to clarify why a change must be made and what the potential repercussions will be if it isn't made. Storytelling can further amplify the power of your numbers, providing an engaging

ANALYTICS PATH TO VALUE (WITH DATA STORY)

Figure 1.4   When you present your insights as data stories, you're more likely to influence decisions and drive actions that lead to value creation.

narrative that connects the dots for your audience and compels them to act. When you craft your data insight into a data story, you have a powerful vehicle for conveying meaning, engaging your audience, and driving change (see Figure 1.4).

The goal of this book is to help you marry the *science of data* with the *art of storytelling*. I will attempt to impart a sound understanding of why data storytelling skills are essential to anyone who wishes to share insights with other people in a more effective manner. You will learn the core characteristics of a data story, and you'll be introduced to the three core pillars of data storytelling: *data*, *narrative*, and *visuals*. To prepare you for your journey toward becoming a more effective data storyteller and change agent, here's an overview of the chapters in this book:

Chapter 2: Why Tell Stories with Data?   You may not realize the influential and integral role stories play in your life. This chapter will explore the hidden power of stories and introduce a framework for harnessing the power of data storytelling. It will also examine the four key communication goals you should strive for when sharing data. This chapter will explore different empirical studies that reveal the unique advantages that narrative and visuals offer in terms of persuasion and memorability.

Chapter 3: The Psychology of Data Storytelling   You may expect facts to play a significant role in decision making. However, psychology and neuroscience research reveals emotion plays a more powerful role than logic and reason in decision making. In this chapter, you'll learn more about how the human mind processes both statistics and stories. It will explore the various ways in which stories maintain an unexpected advantage over facts.

Chapter 4: Anatomy of a Data Story Data storytelling has been associated with many different things—everything from data visualizations to data presentations to even marketing campaigns. In this chapter, you'll receive a clearer understanding of what a data story is and the six essential elements that comprise a data story. It will also examine your critical role as the data storyteller and the importance of understanding your audience.

Chapter 5: Data: The Foundation of Your Data Story Data forms the basic building blocks of your data stories. While this chapter doesn't focus on how to perform analysis, it will define the six attributes of an actionable insight—a key ingredient of any data story. It will examine the exploratory and explanatory steps in the analysis process that shape how stories are formed. The chapter will also discuss the discipline that's needed to develop sound insights and not overwhelm audiences with too much information.

Chapter 6: Narrative: The Structure of Your Data Story If data experts struggle in one area, it is how to create narratives for their insights. This chapter begins by examining the different narrative models that are available to us, and then shows you how to craft a data storytelling arc that is based on the familiar dramatic arc introduced by Gustav Freytag. The chapter then explores how to use storyboarding to organize your key points into this narrative structure. It also reveals how to insert characters and analogies into your data story to bring it to life.

Chapter 7: Visuals (Part 1): Setting Up the Scenes of Your Data Story This chapter explores the power of data visualization in relation to storytelling. It examines different visual perception theories to better understand how humans interpret graphical information. This chapter also focuses on the importance of facilitating comparisons for your audience. You'll learn the first three key principles of visual storytelling and how they help you establish the visual scenes of your data story.

Chapter 8: Visuals (Part 2): Polishing the Scenes of Your Data Story   After setting up the initial scenes of your data story, this chapter introduces the next four key principles of visual storytelling that help refine and enhance the visual power of your data stories. It will review various tactics on how you can remove unnecessary noise, draw attention to key data points, make your content more approachable, and instill trust in your numbers.

Chapter 9: Crafting Your Own Data Story   In this final chapter, you'll see how all the data storytelling elements come together in real-world examples. It will walk you through the different steps and strategies that go into crafting a compelling data story. From these real-world scenarios, you'll gain a deeper appreciation of how the concepts and principles in this book can be applied to your own insights so you can build compelling narratives that are both fact-based and visually impactful.

As everyone continues to be inundated with data, you are going to encounter more and more insights that will need their unique stories to be told. The responsibility for how well they are understood by others and whether they are acted upon falls on each of us. Maya Angelou, the American poet and civil rights activist, once said, "There is no greater agony than bearing an untold story inside you." Similarly, it can be burdensome to carry a critical insight with us and withhold its story from others when it deserves to be shared. Through reading this book, you will be equipped with all the data storytelling skills and knowledge you need to see your insights are understood, embraced, and adopted. None of your insights need be left behind ever again, and the world will be richer for it.

References

Gregoire, C. 2013. How to train your brain to see what others don't. *Huffington Post*, August 25. https://www.huffpost.com/entry/insights-brain_n_3795229.

Kotter, J. 2013. Leading change: establish a sense of urgency. YouTube, August 15. https://www.youtube.com/watch?v=2Yfrj2Y9IlI.

McKinsey & Company. 2009. Hal Varian on how the Web challenges managers. January. https://www.mckinsey.com/industries/high-tech/our-insights/hal-varian-on-how-the-web-challenges-managers.

Online Etymology Dictionary. 2019. Insight (n.). https://www.etymonline.com/word/insight (accessed May 26, 2016).

Patrizio, A. 2018. IDC: Expect 175 zettabytes of data worldwide by 2025. *Network World*, December 3. https://www.networkworld.com/article/3325397/idc-expect-175-zettabytes-of-data-worldwide-by-2025.html.

PowerReviews. 2018. The growing power of reviews: Understanding consumer purchase behaviors. https://www.powerreviews.com/insights/growing-power-of-reviews/.

Ramakrishnan, R. 2017. I have data, I need insights. Where do I start? *Towards Data Science*, July 2. https://towardsdatascience.com/i-have-data-i-need-insights-where-do-i-start-7ddc935ab365.

Chapter 2

Why Tell Stories with Data?

Sometimes reality is too complex. Stories give it form.
> —Jean-Luc Godard, film director, screenwriter,
> and film critic

B efore 1996, Steve Denning would have been skeptical of story-telling's effectiveness and importance. Like many other seasoned executives, he generally viewed analytical as *good* and anecdotal as *bad*. In his time at the World Bank—an international lending institution that provides funds for infrastructure projects in developing countries—Denning had climbed the corporate ranks to become the director of its Africa region and responsible for more than a thousand employees operating in 43 countries. However, in February 1996, shortly after his boss retired, he was unexpectedly displaced from his position and pushed aside—the unfortunate victim of political maneu-vering, a situation that is far too common in large organizations.

As Denning discussed career options with a dismissive superior, it became apparent that the new regime within the organization had no plans for him despite his past contributions. When he pushed this leader for a meaningful assignment, he was told he could try focusing on "information." At that point, Denning knew he was being com-pletely marginalized. Rather than resigning and restarting his career elsewhere, intellectual curiosity drove him to look into the topic of knowledge management. While the World Bank had development experts in a variety of fields—agriculture, health, education, transpor-tation, and so on—it was extremely difficult to tap into this diverse knowledge on a consistent and efficient basis. However, with the recent advances in information technology, Denning found the bank had a massive opportunity to better consolidate, share, and leverage its wealth of information—both internally and externally (Denning 2007).

The challenge he then faced was how to convince a change-resistant lending organization that it needed to pivot its focus toward informa-tion sharing. When Denning decided to get involved with knowledge management, he was essentially starting from nothing; the financial institution had no strategy, budget, or technology in place to support his new assignment. For weeks, Denning attempted to generate interest for his plans within the organization, but he wasn't able to make much progress.

> I used the traditional methods of communicating with no success. I gave people reasons why the idea was important but they didn't listen. I showed them charts and they just looked dazed. In my desperation, I was willing to try anything and eventually I stumbled on the power of a story. (Denning 2000)

His unexpected discovery came during a 10-minute presentation to a group of skeptical senior managers. Denning started his presentation by covering the problems the organization was facing with knowledge management, and then he shared a brief anecdote from Zambia to add color to what the future might look like. The Zambia story was about how, in 1995, a health worker from a remote village in Zambia—one of the poorest countries in the world—found information on how to treat malaria from the Centers for Disease Control (CDC) website, which was no small feat considering how relatively new the Internet was. The World Bank had equally useful know-how on a variety of poverty-related topics, but its knowledge was scattered and mostly inaccessible—even from inside the organization.

The short anecdote from Zambia ignited his audience's imagination for exciting new possibilities at the World Bank in terms of sharing its information more effectively. Through the process of storytelling, *Denning's* idea became *theirs*. After his presentation, he had senior managers racing up to him to better understand how they could help drive the initiative forward. Shortly thereafter, he was invited to present to the entire senior management team, and later that same year, his castoff assignment became an official corporate priority sanctioned by the organization's president. Initially, Denning thought the senior executives had just come around to what was (in his mind) a good idea, but then he started to recognize the influential effects of stories.

Even though Denning was able to win the support of several senior managers at the World Bank with the Zambia story, change was still hard. His ideas still faced strong resistance from the coalition of managers who had originally banished Denning to what they had supposed would be an inconsequential, fruitless assignment. While the Zambia story alone wouldn't sustain all his change efforts, it had begun to open Denning's eyes to the power of storytelling. In 1998, two years into the knowledge management initiative, his opponents orchestrated a program review meeting with the senior management team, hoping that support for his program could be redirected into other areas. However, being wise to their intentions, Denning came prepared with another impactful tale—this time from Pakistan.

His new story focused on a recent request made to a World Bank field office by the Pakistan government, which was having widespread issues with its highways. The Pakistan highway authority was investigating a new pavement technology and was looking for quick advice—in a few days—on how to best proceed. Traditionally, the World Bank would not have been able to respond in such a short timeframe, as it would have taken months to research and assemble a formal report. Instead, the Pakistan field office reached out to the World

Bank's community of internal and external highway experts. In less than 48 hours, they received guidance on the new pavement technology from experts in Jordan, Argentina, South Africa, and New Zealand, including insights from the head of another highways authority and a researcher writing a book on the pavement technology (Denning 2001).

The Pakistan story struck a chord with the senior management team—they recognized the tremendous potential of being able to respond quickly to requests from the remote corners of the bank's operations. The leadership team was determined to replicate and extend what had been done for its highways community to the rest of the bank's areas of expertise. To the chagrin of Denning's detractors (who expected a court martial–type hearing), the Pakistan story further galvanized the bank's desire to become an agile, knowledge-sharing organization. Soon, Denning began hearing the same Pakistan story being passionately repeated by others in meetings, even by the World Bank's president.

Denning was able to take the World Bank from having no budget, no strategy, and no technology for knowledge management in 1996 to being recognized as a world leader in information sharing by 2000 with over 100 communities of practice. He attributed much of his success to stumbling into the power of storytelling. Denning stated, "When it comes to inspiring people to embrace some strange new change in behavior, storytelling isn't just better than the other tools. It's the only thing that works" (Denning 2012). This insight inspired him to leave the international financial institution in 2000 so he could evangelize what he had learned about storytelling as a leadership consultant and author.

If I asked you to stop reading and reflect on what you're read so far, what do you remember? Do you recall how many countries Denning was responsible for when he was the director of the Africa region? Probably not. However, I'm fairly confident you could retell the Zambia story or the Pakistan story to a friend or colleague. That's just a small taste of the power of stories. When we recognize how storytelling has advanced our human civilization and how it continues to influence us each day, we begin to understand the immense utility it offers us as we seek to communicate important insights.

Humans Are Storytelling Creatures

After nourishment, shelter, and companionship, stories are the thing
we need the most in the world.

—Philip Pullman, author

For thousands of years, storytelling has been an integral part of our
humanity. When humans gained their mastery of fire over 400,000
years ago, the campfire soon became a focal point of early storytelling.
A 1970s study of the Ju/'hoan people of Namibia and Botswana—one
of the last remaining hunter-gatherer societies—found 81% of their
firelight conversations centered around telling stories (Balter 2014).
While storytelling is commonly associated with entertainment, stories
served a more foundational purpose for human society—*learning*.
Storytelling became an effective way of passing along life-saving
knowledge, reinforcing cultural standards, instilling moral values, and
building social bonds—all essential to communal living.

Storytelling methods evolved significantly over the millennia, though
they began as just spoken words shared around a campfire. Over 30,000
years ago, prehistoric hunters painted beautifully detailed depictions of
various animals such as bison and deer on the walls of the Chauvet Cave
in southern France. It represented a significant milestone in storytelling,
as oral stories could be enhanced with visual images. Another milestone occurred when the ancient Sumerians in southern Mesopotamia
introduced the first written language, Cuneiform, in 3500–3000 BCE.
Oral stories such as *The Epic of Gilgamesh*—the earliest surviving work
of literature—could be recorded and shared in a consistent manner and
reach a far greater audience than was previously possible.

Today in our digital age, stories continue to appeal to us just as
much as they did to our ancient ancestors. Stories play a vibrant role
in our daily lives—and yet we may not realize how much they do.
A 2017 study estimated that US adults spend more than 12 hours per
day consuming major media (eMarketer 2017). Stories form the backbone of the news, books, television shows, and movies we consume.
With the growth of social media, we have all become storytellers,

sharing our struggles and victories with friends and family. One of the most popular features on Instagram and Snapchat is the stories feature that lets users post photos or videos for 24 hours. Instagram Stories is credited with adding 200 million users in its first year—160% growth (Kastrenakes 2017).

We've also seen the rapid rise of the global TED Talks phenomenon. Much of TED Talks' success can be attributed to new-age storytelling that is both free and easily accessible online. Analysis of the 500 most popular TED Talk presentations found that stories made up at least 65% of their content (Gallo 2014). Modern-day storytelling is also poised to be further transformed as virtual reality becomes mainstream, and people are able to fully immerse themselves in the narrative as full participants.

Aside from our media consumption, our daily interactions with work colleagues, classmates, friends, and family members are also heavily centered around stories. Throughout your workday, you may recount different experiences you've had to coworkers in and between meetings. Interestingly, 65% of our daily conversations are comprised of social topics or gossip, which are essentially stories about people (Dunbar 2004). When you get home from work, the storytelling continues as you interact with your spouse, children, and friends. For example, as a parent, you might console a child who is struggling in school by sharing a similar experience you had when you were his or her age.

After a long day of telling and listening to stories, your narrative-hungry brain still isn't completely satisfied. When we lay down to rest each night, our brains conjure up new adventures to feed our need for narrative in the form of dreams—at least four to six times per night (Schneider and Domhoff 2019). Even when we're awake the next day (or somewhat awake, if we spent the prior night binge-watching a new TV series), we are constantly daydreaming, essentially fantasizing about the mundane and important matters we encounter. For example, on your commute to work, you may wonder what it would be like to own a luxury car like the guy in front of you, or in the first meeting of your day, what it would be like to stand up to a belligerent coworker. It's estimated that we spend about 14 seconds per daydream and generate about two thousand daydreams each day—almost a third of each day (Gottschall 2012).

As human beings, our brains are inescapably hardwired for stories. Unless you're presenting your insights to robot overlords—let's hope you're not—your human audience will be innately receptive to storytelling. If you wish to convey your insights more effectively, it's essential that you learn how to tap into the power of storytelling.

Stories Beat Statistics

Storytelling is the most powerful way to put ideas into the world today.
—Robert McKee, screenwriting expert and author

Despite our natural inclination for stories, analytically minded individuals and organizations may find it difficult to see how stories could be more powerful than statistics. While facts are seen as hard and objective, stories are often viewed as soft and subjective. Left-brained people may inadvertently look down on storytelling as a creative exercise that is reserved for their right-brained peers. As a result, we can underestimate the power stories wield over us that numbers alone can't match. In fact, when statistics are pitted against stories, it's not even a fair fight—statistics don't even last the first minute of the opening round.

Time and time again, storytelling has proven to be a powerful delivery mechanism for sharing insights and ideas in a way that is more memorable and persuasive than just pure facts. Stanford professor and *Made to Stick* coauthor Chip Heath routinely highlights the memorability advantage that stories possess over statistics in one of his university courses on communication. For an exercise in his course, he divides his classroom into groups of six to eight students and provides them with various crime data. He then has the students in each group deliver a one-minute persuasive pitch to their group on why nonviolent crime is or isn't a serious problem. After each student has presented their argument to their group, the other students rate each individual's performance. When the students are invited to watch a short movie clip, they think the classroom activity is over.

However, Professor Heath then abruptly asks the students to write down every idea they can remember from their peers' speeches. Even though no more than 10 minutes have passed, the students often struggle to recall one or two ideas from the pitches they heard—many of them aren't able to remember a single thing from some of the speeches they heard only moments earlier.

> In the average one-minute speech, the typical student uses 2.5 statistics. Only one student in ten tells a story. Those are the speaking statistics. The "remembering" statistics, on the other hand, are almost a mirror image: When students are asked to recall the speeches, 63% remember the stories. Only 5% remember any individual statistic. (Heath and Heath 2008)

Regardless of how highly some of the students were rated by their peers, the articulate speakers' ideas were no more memorable than those of the poorly rated ones. In the moment, the other students enjoyed their eloquent pitches, but their ideas evaporated and were easily forgotten without a story to anchor them. Even though statistics were an integral part of the students' pitches, they are nowhere near as memorable as stories.

When you're looking to drive certain behaviors or actions, stories have also proven to be more persuasive than statistics. In 2004, researchers at Carnegie Mellon University created an experiment in which people were given five one-dollar bills for completing a survey, as well as a pamphlet for Save the Children, a charity focused on the welfare of children worldwide. The researchers asked the participants to read the pamphlet and offer a donation if they wished in an envelope that was provided. There were two variations of the charity pamphlet. One version was loaded with statistics on how people in different African countries were being impacted by food shortages and droughts. For example, it highlighted how severe rainfall deficits in Zambia had resulted in a 42% drop in maize production, leaving 3 million Zambians with insufficient food. The second version of the pamphlet took a story-based approach. It focused on the challenging circumstances of a seven-year-old girl named Rokia from Mali, Africa, whose family was desperately poor and facing starvation.

On average, the participants who received the statistics-based version donated $1.14. The individuals who were given the Rokia pamphlet contributed $2.38—more than double the donations generated by the numbers-based pamphlet. The researchers found people responded better to identifiable victims than statistical ones. The story about a representative but fictional Malian girl proved to be more relatable and personal than the faceless statistics on millions of people suffering in Africa. This study shows how a simple story can connect emotionally with an audience and be far more persuasive than a litany of statistics (Heath and Heath 2008).

While stories clearly dominate statistics from both a memorability and persuasiveness perspective, it's rarely a battle between facts and anecdotes—or even facts and other facts. The real clash is actually *between stories*: the prevailing incumbent and a new challenger. As storytelling creatures, we routinely form narratives to help us understand the world around us. When we experience different events or encounter various facts, our minds seek to make sense of them by forming stories around them. For example, if you have had some bad experiences with graduates from a particular university, you may create a negative narrative in your mind about people who went to that school. Suddenly, you judge everyone from the university by what you've experienced on just a few unfortunate occasions. Sometimes these internal narratives we form not only shape our beliefs and opinions but also become deeply rooted in our identity. For example, the narratives you have formed around gun control or climate change are most likely aligned with your political ideology—who you are as an individual.

When your insight runs into resistance, it is because the new information you're sharing challenges or disrupts the prevailing story in your audience's minds. It's never as simple as replacing an outdated or incorrect fact with a new, better one. When you dislodge a particular key fact, you can also dislodge or break the narrative that surrounds and encompasses it. As *Putting Stories to Work* author Shawn Callahan said, "You can't beat a story with fact. You can only beat it with a better story" (Callahan 2016). In the next chapter, I'll explore this topic in more depth, but for now it's important to realize that when you're introducing a new set of facts, you also need to consider the new narrative that will accompany them. Understanding your intended audience's existing narrative about a topic should inform how you position your new insight. *The Story Factor* author Annette Simmons stated, "Resistance always has a story. Understanding the unique story of resistance to your new idea enables you to successfully negotiate a new story that is more attractive than the old one" (Simmons 2006).

For example, a new business executive at a multinational company was forced to confront a misleading narrative that was impeding the progress of a Japanese ecommerce division. He inherited a struggling department that was experiencing declining year-over-year online revenue. As the new leader met with the existing team, he recognized they attributed their falling revenue performance to currency fluctuations between the Japanese yen and US dollar—something the team was powerless to control. With the help of a sharp analyst, he was able to confirm the currency differences had almost no effect on their sliding online sales—*the prevailing story turned out to be a myth.*

Armed with this new insight, he set about debunking the faulty currency story and introducing a *better* narrative that the ecommerce team wasn't helpless at all, let alone at the mercy of currency fluctuations—it could shape its own destiny. Shortly thereafter, his re-energized team was able to identify an optimization to its email marketing practices that generated over $300,000 per week in incremental revenue alone. Subsequent improvements to their revenue performance would never have been possible without reframing his team's circumstances with a better narrative. Rather than seeing stories and statistics as two competing forces, it's better to seek confluence between them. Ultimately, when data and stories work together, your insights can help form a better narrative that can chart a new direction.

Three Essential Elements of Data Stories

> Maybe stories are just data with a soul.
> —Brene Brown, research professor and author

Data storytelling involves the skillful combination of three key elements: *data*, *narrative*, and *visuals*. Data is the primary building block of every data story. It may sound simple, but a data story should always find its origin in data (more on this in Chapter 4), and data should serve as the foundation for the narrative and visual elements of your story. Figure 2.1 highlights the unique, complementary relationship between these three elements as they contribute in distinct ways to the telling of a data story.

THE THREE DATA STORY ELEMENTS
COMPLEMENT EACH OTHER

Figure 2.1 In data storytelling, all of the different elements—data, narrative, and visuals—complement each other in different ways.

Explain. When narrative is coupled with data, it helps to *explain* to your audience what's happening in the data and why a particular insight is important. Ample context and commentary are often needed to fully appreciate an analysis finding. The narrative element adds structure to the data and helps to guide the audience through the meaning of what's being shared.

Enlighten. When visuals are applied to data, they can *enlighten* the audience to insights that they wouldn't see without charts or graphs. Many interesting patterns and outliers in the data would remain hidden in the rows and columns of data tables without the help of data visualizations. They connect with our visual nature as human beings and impart knowledge that couldn't be obtained as easily using other approaches that involve just words or numbers.

Engage. Finally, when narrative and visuals are merged together, they can *engage* or even entertain an audience. From an early age, much of our learning and entertainment is based on a combination of narrative and visuals in the form of illustrated story books and animated television shows. Even as adults, we collectively spend billions of dollars each year at the movies to continually immerse ourselves in different lives, worlds, and adventures. While the cutting-edge special effects capture our interest, a good story is what holds our attention and transports us to other places and perspectives.

Whether you're working with data, narrative, or visuals, each element can be powerful individually. You can achieve some level of success with a thought-provoking statistic, a compelling narrative, or stunning data visualization. However, it's the skilled blend of data, narrative, and visuals in a data story that can harness the unique contributions of all three elements. When you combine the *right* visuals and narrative with the *right* data, you have a data story that can influence and drive *change* (see Figure 2.2).

EFFECTIVE DATA STORIES CAN DRIVE CHANGE

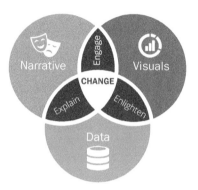

Figure 2.2 When you combine the right data with the right narrative and visuals, you have a data story that can drive change.

Essentially, data storytelling is a form of persuasion. It employs data, narrative, and visuals to help an audience see something in a new light and to convince them to act. In his treatise *Rhetoric*, the ancient Greek philosopher Aristotle outlined three key modes of persuasion—ethos, logos, and pathos—which are known as the rhetorical triangle. However, he also mentioned two other forms of persuasion you should be aware of:

- **Ethos**—an appeal to credibility
- **Logos**—an appeal to logic or reason
- **Pathos**—an appeal to emotion
- *Telos*—*an appeal to purpose*
- *Kairos*—*an appeal to timeliness (opportune moment)*

While some forms of communication may only rely on a few of these persuasive appeals, a data story depends on all five. As Figure 2.3 shows, a data story closely aligns to each of Aristotle's appeals, making it one of the most powerful forms of communication available to us.

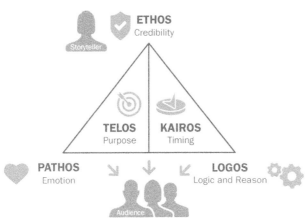

ARISTOTLE'S
RHETORICAL TRIANGLE

Figure 2.3 If we expand the traditional rhetorical triangle to include *telos* and *kairos*, we can see how all of these persuasive appeals can come together in a data story, starting at the top with the *ethos* of the speaker and moving down to the *pathos* (narrative) and *logos* (data) appeals to the audience.

First, from an *ethos* perspective, the success of your data story will be shaped by your own credibility and the trustworthiness of your data. Second, because your data story is based on facts and figures, the *logos* appeal will be integral to your message. Third, as you weave the data into a convincing narrative, the *pathos* or emotional appeal makes your message more engaging. Fourth, having a visualized insight at the core of your message adds the *telos* appeal, as it sharpens the focus and purpose of your communication. Fifth, when you share a relevant data story with the right audience *at the right time (kairos)*, your message can be a powerful catalyst for change. I believe Aristotle would have been impressed by the persuasiveness of data storytelling.

Driving Action with Data Stories

If you wish to influence an individual or a group to embrace a particular value in their daily lives, tell them a compelling story.
—Annette Simmons, storyteller and author

Several years ago, I got an unexpected taste of the power of data storytelling and its potential for influencing change when I worked with a business-to-business marketing department for a large technology company. Each month, as an external consultant, I would prepare and deliver a monthly analysis of their online marketing sites and campaigns. After reviewing their key metrics for the previous month, I would then share the results of a couple of exploratory analyses. Because I had never met this marketing team in person and our interactions were mainly limited to the monthly call, it was difficult to gauge their interest in the findings I shared each month.

On a particular monthly review, I examined a web page on their site that directed prospective leads to either phone a call center or complete an online lead form. Whenever the call center was closed, the page's content would direct people to just the online form. As I analyzed the traffic to this page on an hourly basis, I noticed a decent number of unique visitors were visiting the lead page before and after the call center's office hours (see Figure 2.4). Based on a simple data story, I recommended expanding their call center hours to capture more of these potential leads with a live sales representative.

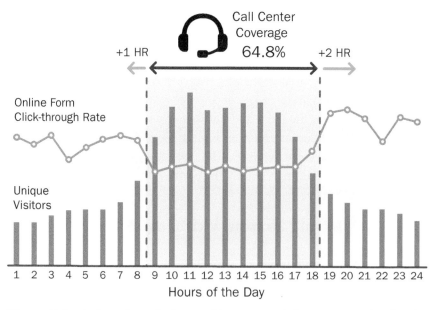

Figure 2.4 A data chart similar to this one revealed an opportunity for the technology company to extend its call center hours to capture more leads with its telephone sales agents.

After I shared this insight, I didn't get any reaction from the customer. However, on a subsequent call a few weeks later, the marketing director mentioned in passing at the end of the call that they had tested my theory about extending the call center hours. She said they had run a short trial with extended hours, but it didn't deliver a significant return, so they decided to stick with their existing call center hours.

After the call ended, I was flabbergasted they had implemented my suggestion. As an outsider to this organization, it was no small feat that I had persuaded such a large technology company to change something. While my insight hadn't uncovered a large amount of incremental leads or revenue, it did trigger a decision to test my idea. To incur the costs of testing such an idea with their call center wasn't insignificant. Although I wish I could say my recommendation generated a significant positive return for this company, it did drive a change—even if it was only a temporary assessment. All that an insight can offer is *potential* value. There's no guarantee that an insight will deliver on its promise when it is acted on. However, getting an organization to experiment and explore an insight's potential is a major accomplishment. Even when an insight fails to reach its full potential, you still gain additional knowledge from taking action, which may eventually lead a related enhancement in the future.

When you uncover a new insight you want to share with others, you have four key objectives for your communication. In the strongman game known as high striker, you prove your strength by hitting a lever with a large hammer to ring a bell suspended at the top of a tower. Similarly, the strength of your message can be judged by how many communication levels it can reach (Figure 2.5). At the first, basic level, you want your insight to catch and hold the *attention* of your audience. In today's fast-paced work environment, it can be difficult to catalyze interest in a new insight and ensure it receives the proper attention it deserves. There's always a lot of noise that can obscure important signals. If your insight fails to capture an audience's attention in its limited window of opportunity, other competing information and distractions will draw away their focus, and your insight will go nowhere.

**HOW STRONG IS YOUR DATA
COMMUNICATION?**

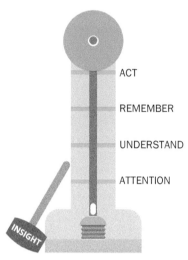

ACT

REMEMBER

UNDERSTAND

ATTENTION

Figure 2.5   The strength of how you communicate an insight can be measured by what effect it has on your audience. Driving an action is the ultimate goal, as your insight will then have the potential to create value.

Once you have their attention, you want your audience to *understand* your insight. While your audience may give you their attention, that doesn't mean they also fully grasp what your insight means. If they misinterpret what you're sharing with them, it could lead to the wrong decision and outcome. When your idea is concrete and clear in the minds of your audience members, you have a shared understanding to build on—whether or not they agree with your findings.

On the third level, you would like your audience to *remember* your insight. A majority of the information we receive is understandable, but it is also transitory and disposable. It can be shocking how much information is never retained more than a few moments before being cast off as unimportant. You want your insight to resonate enough to be recalled by your audience. If your audience goes on to share your insight with others, you know it has been retained in their memories. Narrative will be critical to ensuring your insights take root in the minds of your audience and are not easily forgotten and lost.

The bell at the top of this scale represents the highest level that can be achieved: to have your audience *act* on your insight. While it is nice to have an insight understood and remembered, it won't drive any value if it never leads to any form of action. Your data communication must be persuasive if it's going to inspire or motivate people to act. It will require a skilled blend of both narrative and visuals to propel your insight up to this final level. An effective data story will pass all four rungs, striking the action bell at the top. Less effective attempts at communication may rise up to a certain level but fail to ring this essential bell. Where facts struggle to be memorable and persuasive, it's something that narrative does with ease. Merging your evidence with narrative seems only—logical.

The act of combining narrative with data is not always as straightforward as it sounds. In the Carnegie Mellon study where the story pamphlet outperformed the statistical version, the researchers also tested what would happen when the participants received *both* of the pamphlets. They were curious to see whether the combination of an emotional story and rational evidence would produce even better results through the wealth of information being shared. While this merged experiment outperformed the statistics version ($1.43 vs. $1.14), it didn't come close to challenging the pure story-based approach ($2.38).

Based on this outcome, some may question the need to craft data stories when narrative alone appears to work best. However, rather than just appending a story to a bunch of statistics, the most success will come from *weaving both elements into a cohesive data story*. The mere presence of narrative will have a positive halo effect on your insights. However, the more integrated they are, the more potent they will be together. In Chapter 6, you'll learn how to build narrative structures around your key insights so you can strike the action bell with your audiences.

Why Your Insights Need Narrative and Visuals

Stories change people while statistics give them something to argue about.
—Bernie Siegel, author and surgeon

The right fact at the right moment may catch your attention, but it may not speak as well to other people as it does to you. On its own, data often doesn't possess the inherent strength needed to be more than just noise—let alone to drive action. Without the right context and explanation, it can easily be misunderstood, forgotten, or dismissed. Fortunately, data doesn't have to go it alone. It can lean on the complementary abilities of narrative and visuals to convey its message in a memorable and persuasive way.

The combination of narrative and data can help etch facts into your audience's memory and encourage them to act on your ideas. In 1969, researchers at Stanford University conducted an experiment to test the influence of narrative on memory. In the trial, two groups of students were asked to study and remember words from 12 sets of words—each containing 10 random nouns. The control group studied the words using rote learning and rehearsal. Meanwhile, the rest of the students were told to construct a meaningful story around the words in each list. When the students were asked to recall the words from each of the 12 lists, the narrative group were able to recall *six to seven times* as much as the control group could (Bower and Clark 1969). The Stanford professors believed the thematic organization of the narrative assisted the students' memory of the words. While this study focused on lists of words, a similar effect could happen with the key statistics within a well-constructed data story.

Lawyers are often faced with the difficult challenge of assembling a story or narrative from a set of facts. In the late 1980s, researchers at the University of Colorado wanted to explore how storytelling influences how juries perceive presented evidence. The focus of their study was a real 1983 criminal case involving a Boston bar fight that resulted in a stabbing death. There was some debate as to whether the smaller man was simply defending himself from a much larger, aggressive bully or if it was homicide. When the study's participants heard the evidence from both sides as it was presented at the actual murder trial, 63% agreed it was murder. However, when the prosecuting attorneys presented the same evidence in a story format, 78% were convinced of his guilt. On the other hand, when the defending attorneys shared their evidence in a story format, only 31% felt the man was guilty of murder (see Figure 2.6) (Pennington and Hastie 1988). This mock trial showed how the combination of data and story can have a powerful persuasive effect—strengthening the argument *for or against* the defendant. Ultimately, you want narrative on the side of your insight.

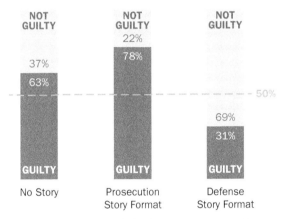

Figure 2.6   When the prosecuting or defending attorneys used a story format for presenting their evidence, it had a significant influential effect on the mock trial decision.

While we're just beginning to see data being combined with narrative with more regularity, it's not uncommon for us to see data accompanied by visuals. Data can be complex to process and cumbersome to share. However, visual representations of the data in the form of charts and diagrams can be used to convey the essence or meaning of an insight in a more effective manner than what would be possible with text or speech alone. By adding relevant visuals to a data story, you tap into the most effective method for transmitting information to other human beings. Stanford Professor Robert E.

Horn noted that when visual elements are closely intertwined with words, they offer "the potential for increasing human 'bandwidth,' or the capacity to take in, comprehend, and more efficiently synthesize large amounts of new information" (Horn 2001). For this reason, data visualizations play an integral role in the sharing of data insights and the formation of data stories.

The most dominant sense that we have as human beings is vision. It's estimated more than 50% of the brain is focused on processing visual stimuli—outpacing the processing spent on our other four senses combined (Hagen 2012). As early as 1894, Professor E.A. Kirkpatrick shared a study where students had a higher recall rate of 10 common objects (bird, door, pencil) after three days when they were shown the objects (6.35 items) compared to when they only read or heard the names of objects (2.23 and 1.25 items respectively) (Kirkpatrick 1894). After publishing his findings in the first volume of the *Psychological Review*, multiple researchers have since confirmed the *Picture Superiority Effect*, in which pictures are more easily recalled than words. For example, in 1970, researchers at the University of Rochester studied the recall of pictures by exposing study participants to more than 2,500 pictures for 5–10 seconds at a time. Up to three days later, the participants could recall over 90% of the images (Standing, Conezio, and Haber 1970).

While pictures have proven to be more memorable than text, the benefits of visuals extend beyond just recall and recognition. In 1996, researchers at Michigan State University examined the effects that pictures had on health-related communications. In their experiment, the researchers gave either full text or illustrated instructions on wound care to 400 patients who visited an emergency room for lacerations. They discovered the illustrated instructions outperformed the text-based ones in multiple ways. As shown in Figure 2.7, the patients who received the illustrated instructions were more likely to have read the instructions (98% vs. 79%), comprehended the content (46% vs. 6%), and acted on the wound care advice (77% vs. 54%). In addition, the patients with less than a high school education (24%) saw an even larger positive difference between the two formats in terms of comprehension and compliance (Delp and Jones 1996).

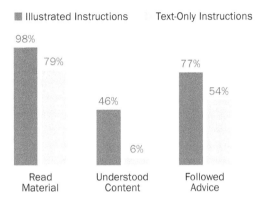

Figure 2.7 In each key area of focus, the illustrated instructions outperformed the text-based instructions.

Along with drawing attention and assisting with comprehension and recall, visuals can also be persuasive. While there is still limited research into the persuasive power of data visualizations, two recent studies shed some light on their potential influence. In 2014, researchers at the New York University performed an experiment in which they evaluated the attitudes of people on one of three topics: incarceration, corporate income tax, and video games. Using a Likert scale, they determined how much each individual agreed with a particular stance on the subject matter before and after they were exposed to additional information via data tables or data charts. They found data charts to be persuasive when an individual didn't already possess a strong opposing opinion. For example, if you had a neutral or weak position on whether incarceration reduces crime rates, you will be more likely to be persuaded by charts that show mass imprisonment doesn't decrease crime than someone who already has a strong counter opinion. The study showed the data charts had a modest but consistent persuasive effect (8% increase) when compared to data tables (Pandey, Manivannan, Nov, Satterthwaite, and Bertini 2014).

In another 2014 study, researchers at Cornell University tested the influence of trivial graphs on the persuasiveness of information. In one of their experiments, they tested the acceptance of a scientific claim for a made-up drug that could enhance immune function and significantly reduce the chances of catching a cold. For one version of the claim, they used only text to share the information; another version included both text and a graph. The inclusion of the data visualization had a dramatic persuasive effect: 97% who saw the graph believed the drug would work, compared to 68% who received the text-only version (43% difference) (Tal and Wansink 2016). While these different empirical studies highlight the influence of narrative and visuals, I'd like to share a real-world example in which these two elements helped to drive action where facts alone couldn't.

In late 2014, California experienced a serious measles outbreak that was traced back to people who had visited the Disney theme park during four days in December. The Disney measles exposure led to 125 measles cases, 110 of which were based in California. Of the 49 California individuals who were not vaccinated, 28 were unprotected due to their personal beliefs against vaccination (CDC 2015). The measles virus is so contagious that if someone who is infected with measles entered a room filled with 10 unvaccinated people, nine of them would immediately contract the virus. Anyone entering that same room in the next two hours could also be infected (University of Pittsburgh 2015). Fortunately, the measles, mumps, rubella (MMR) vaccine is very effective at preventing infection, but only if there's a high concentration of immune people to impede the spread of the disease to unprotected people such as young infants and others with compromised immune systems.

When pediatrician and state senator Richard Pan introduced Senate Bill 277 in 2015, he needed a way to convince fellow legislators of the need for mandatory vaccinations. While studying medicine at the University of Pittsburgh, Pan gained first-hand experience with the devastating effects of a measles outbreak in Philadelphia in 1991, which sickened 900 people and killed nine children (Bay Area News Group 2017). He faced two significant challenges. First, it is difficult for many people to fully grasp the abstract concepts of herd immunity and exponential growth. Second, some of his fellow politicians were concerned about making vaccination a prerequisite for attending public school, thereby limiting access to education. Allowing some people to opt out of vaccination based on personal or religious beliefs was often viewed as inconsequential and a minor concession to individual rights.

In his research to help demonstrate the potential danger of not achieving herd immunity (approximately 92–95% vaccination rate for measles), senator Pan discovered an outbreak simulator called FRED Measles. This tool, developed at his alma mater, the University of Pittsburgh, was designed to visually depict the spread of contagion if an outbreak occurred. With this new modeling tool, he could visually show fellow senators how an epidemic could quickly erupt within their respective county if 20 percent of the school-children were not vaccinated (see Figure 2.8). Former state senator Marty Block was initially skeptical of the bill, but after watching a measles outbreak simulation for his constituency, he recognized the bill was important to protecting his state's public health. The former senator stated,

> If people decide to put themselves in harm's way as a knowing decision, it bothers me still, but that may be their right. When I saw the simulation, it was clear that they were putting others in harm's way. That's when it became to me a very important thing for the government to legislate. (Hare 2017)

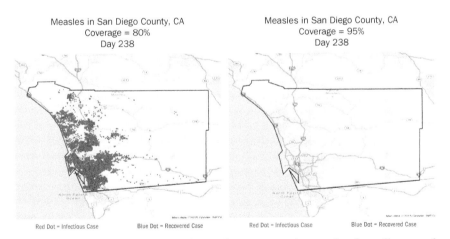

Figure 2.8 FRED Measles shows how a measles outbreak will expand exponentially within a county if there is only an 80% vaccination rate.
Source: Public Health Dynamics Laboratory, University of Pittsburgh.

Despite the compelling evidence supporting the need for mandatory vaccinations, the bill faced stiff opposition from antivaccine advocates—even resulting in death threats being made to Pan and his coauthor, senator Ben Allen. However, in June 2015, Pan's Senate Bill 277 was successfully signed into law, and California's kindergarten vaccination rate rose to 96% in 2016—the highest rate since 2001. With the help of the FRED Measles tool, Pan and other provaccine advocates were able to build a data story for the importance of MMR vaccinations and what could happen without the life-saving herd immunity.

As the different empirical studies and this real-life example have shown, both narrative and visuals can make valuable contributions to the effectiveness of your insight-related communications. Yes, it may take some effort to craft an insight into a data story; however, the potential payoff will be worth the investment. In fact, it may be the only effective means for conveying your insight to an audience that may be initially skeptical of your facts and figures. Data storytelling gives your insight the best opportunity to capture *attention*, be *understood*, be *remembered*, and be *acted on*. An effective data story helps your insight reach its full potential: inspiring others to act and drive change. That's all anyone who has uncovered a meaningful insight can ask for—especially when it can save lives.

References

Balter, M. 2014. Ancient campfires led to the rise of storytelling. *Science*, September 14. http://www.sciencemag.org/news/2014/09/ancient-campfires-led-rise-storytelling.

Bay Area News Group. 2017. State Sen. Richard Pan praised by colleagues over vaccine bill. *Daily News*, July 4. http://www.dailynews.com/2015/07/04/state-sen-richard-pan-praised-by-colleagues-over-vaccine-bill/.

Bower, G.H., and Clark, M.C. 1969. Narrative stories as mediators for serial learning. *Psychonomic Science* 14:181–182.

Callahan, S. 2016. The role of stories in data storytelling. *Anecdote*, August 4. http://www.anecdote.com/2016/08/stories-data-storytelling/.

Centers for Disease Control and Prevention. 2015. Measles Outbreak—California, December 2014–February 2015. *Morbidity and Mortality Report*, February 20. https://www.cdc.gov/mmwr/preview/mmwrhtml/mm6406a5.htm.

Delp, C., and Jones, J. 1996. Communicating information to patients: The use of cartoon illustrations to improve comprehension of instructions. *Academic Emergency Medicine* 3:264–270.

Denning, S. 2000. *The Springboard: How Storytelling Ignites Action in Knowledge-Era Organizations.* New York, NY: Butterworth-Heinemann.

———— 2001. Storytelling to ignite change: Steve Denning—The Pakistan story. http://www.creatingthe21stcentury.org/Steve6-Pakistan.html.

———— 2007. *The Secret Language of Leadership: How Leaders Inspire Action Through Narrative.* San Francisco, CA: John Wiley & Sons.

———— 2012. The science of storytelling. https://www.forbes.com/sites/stevedenning/2012/03/09/the-science-of-storytelling/#3be796732d8a.

Dunbar, R.I.M. 2004. Gossip in evolutionary perspective. *Review of General Psychology* 8 (2): 100–110.

eMarketer. 2017. US adults now spend 12 hours 7 minutes a day consuming media. *eMarketer*, May 1. https://www.emarketer.com/Article/US-Adults-Now-Spend-12-Hours-7-Minutes-Day-Consuming-Media/1015775.

Gallo, C. 2014. How Sheryl Sandberg's last-minute addition to her TED talk sparked a movement. *Forbes*, February 28. https://www.forbes.com/sites/carminegallo/2014/02/28/how-sheryl-sandbergs-last-minute-addition-to-her-ted-talk-sparked-a-movement/#3871d1a365c2.

Gottschall, J. 2012. *The Storytelling Animal: How Stories Make Us Human.* Boston, MA: Mariner Books.

Hagen, S. 2012. The mind's eye. *Rochester Review* 74 (4). http://www.rochester.edu/pr/Review/V74N4/0402_brainscience.html.

Hare, E. 2017. Facts alone won't convince people to vaccinate their kids. *FiveThirtyEight*, June 12. https://fivethirtyeight.com/features/facts-alone-wont-convince-people-to-vaccinate-their-kids/.

Heath, C., and Heath, D. 2008. *Made to Stick: Why Some Ideas Survive and Others Die*. New York, NY: Random House.

Horn, R. 2001. Visual language and converging technologies in the next 10–15 years (and beyond). National Science Foundation Conference on Converging Technologies (Nano-Bio-Info-Cogno) for Improving Human Performance (December 3–4, 2001).

Kastrenakes, J. 2017. Instagram added 200 million daily users a year after launching Stories. *The Verge*, September 25. https://www.theverge.com/2017/9/25/16361356/instagram-500-million-daily-active-users.

Kirkpatrick, E.A. 1894. "An Experimental Study of Memory." *Psychological Review* 1: 602–609.

Pandey, A., Manivannan, A., Nov, O., Satterthwaite, M., and Bertini, E. 2014. The persuasive power of data visualization. *Visualization and Computer Graphics, IEEE Transactions* 20 (12): 2211–2220.

Pennington, N., and Hastie, R. 1988. Explanation-based decision-making: Effects of memory structure on judgment. *Journal of Experimental Psychology: Learning, Memory & Cognition* 14 (3): 521–533.

Schneider, A., and Domhoff, G. W. 2019. The quantitative study of dreams. http://www.dreamresearch.net/ (accessed May 14, 2019).

Simmons, A. 2006. *The Story Factor: Secrets of Influence from the Art of Storytelling*. New York, NY: Basic Books.

Standing, L., Conezio, J., and Haber, R.N. 1970. Perception and memory for pictures: Single-trial learning of 2500 visual stimuli. *Psychonomic Science* 19 (2): 73–74. https://doi.org/10.3758/BF03337426.

Tal, A., and Wansink, B. 2016. Blinded with science: Trivial graphs and formulas increase ad persuasiveness and belief in product efficacy. *Public Understanding of Science* 25 (1): 117–125.

University of Pittsburgh. 2015. Simulation brings facts to measles outbreak and vaccination debate. *Globe Newswire*, February 17. https://globenewswire.com/news-release/2015/02/17/707021/10120524/en/Simulation-Brings-Facts-to-Measles-Outbreak-and-Vaccination-Debate.html.

Chapter 3

The Psychology of Data Storytelling

Stories not only give us a much-needed practice on figuring out what makes people tick, they give us insight into how we tick.

—Lisa Cron, story analyst and author

When you work with data on a regular basis, it can be difficult to see why solid evidence can't be compelling in its own right—without the need for storytelling. When we're convinced of the strength of our findings, we say "the facts speak for themselves." In other words, if people are simply exposed to the same numbers as we were, they will be equally enlightened. In these situations, we expect rational human beings to appreciate the soundness of our well-founded insights, arrive at the same conclusions, and be equally motivated to pursue a logical course of action. However, we often discover—*to our disappointment*—that the facts don't seem to stand on their own. In attempting to pass along our discoveries, something is somehow lost in translation. When an audience fails to grasp the significance of our findings, we are left wondering how this could happen when the numbers spoke so clearly and forcefully to us.

A Hungarian doctor named Ignaz Semmelweis (1818–1865) found himself in this predicament after making a significant lifesaving discovery in the field of obstetrics. In 1846, Semmelweis was appointed as the first assistant to the professor of obstetrics at a large Vienna-based maternity hospital that had two clinics for training doctors and midwives. Similar to other hospitals around the world at this time, many maternity patients were dying of a mysterious illness called puerperal or childbed fever. Healthy, expecting women would suddenly become ill and die shortly after giving birth to their children—less than a day or two later.

Figure 3.1   Ignaz Semmelweis (1818–1865)

Source: https://commons.wikimedia.org/wiki/File:Ignaz_Semmelweis_1860.jpg. Public domain.

Employing his statistical training (see Figure 3.2), Semmelweis made an alarming discovery: the doctors' clinic in his hospital had an average mortality rate of 9.9%, which was significantly higher than that of the midwives' clinic (3.9%). He became curious as to why there was a noticeable difference between the two clinics and was determined to identify the cause. At the time, there was no notion of germs or infections, so the hospital staff had considered a variety of potential causes such as bad air (miasma), overcrowding, cold temperature, and delivery methods—all to no avail.

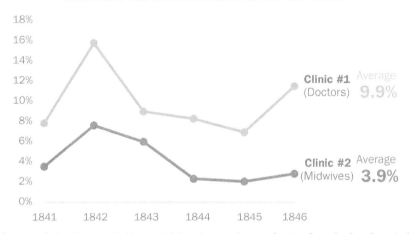

CHILDBED FEVER MORTALITY RATES BY CLINIC

Figure 3.2 From 1841 to 1846, Ignaz Semmelweis found the hospital's maternity clinic for student doctors (Clinic #1) had a childbed fever mortality rate that was more than double that of its midwife clinic (Clinic #2).

The high mortality rate in the first clinic weighed heavily on Semmelweis's mind when an unexpected breakthrough came from a tragic accident. A friend and teacher whom Semmelweis admired was conducting an autopsy when he was inadvertently poked by a student's scalpel. The professor died shortly after receiving this minor injury. As Semmelweis performed the difficult post-mortem examination, he noticed a strong similarity in the pathology of his friend's illness and that of the women who died of childbed fever. From this unexpected observation, Semmelweis began to form an interesting hypothesis.

At the Vienna hospital, it was common for the student doctors to perform autopsies in the morning and then spend the rest of their day attending to patients in the first clinic—without ever properly disinfecting their hands. Unlike the doctors, the midwives performed no autopsy work and were not routinely in contact with any corpses. Semmelweis hypothesized that some kind of poisonous particles were being transferred by the doctors from the cadavers to the patients in the first maternity clinic. He found a chlorinated lime solution was strong enough to remove the putrid smell of the autopsy tissue from the doctors' hands and determined it would be ideal for removing these deadly contaminants.

Two months after the death of his friend, he introduced a new handwashing policy for the doctors to use the chlorinated lime solution after autopsies. When he launched the new policy, the monthly mortality rate was 12.2% in the doctors' clinic (see Figure 3.3). Semmelweis's new policy had an immediate impact, and the death rate was lowered to 2.2% (an 82% decrease). After several months of significantly lower mortality rates, he still observed student doctors who were not following the policy. After introducing stricter controls on the negligent doctors, Semmelweis was able to lower the mortality rate even further, including two months where *no mothers died of childbed fever.*

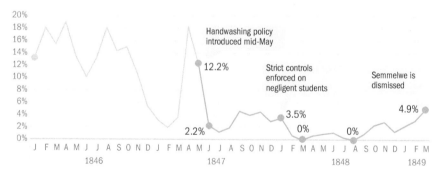

CHILDBED FEVER MORTALITY RATES IN CLINIC #1

Figure 3.3   After introducing his handwashing policy, Clinic #1's childbed fever mortality rate dropped from 12.2% to 2.2% (82% decrease). Semmelweis was able to reduce the mortality rate to 0% in two separate months (March 1848 and August 1848) before his unfortunate dismissal in March 1849.

Semmelweis couldn't scientifically prove why his handwashing policy worked; that wouldn't happen until the French chemist Louis Pasteur (1822–1895) discovered the germ theory of disease in the mid-1860s. What the doctor had was more than 18 months of statistical data showing his handwashing approach worked and that such practices could save the lives of thousands of expectant mothers. He had uncovered an important truth about childbed fever. But was it enough?

Semmelweis believed he had made a major breakthrough for obstetrics and "expected that the truth and the importance of his work would lead to its ultimate acceptance without further effort on his part" (Semmelweis 1861). Essentially, he felt the facts should speak for themselves and left it to his medical students and colleagues to share this new knowledge. However, rather than lauding Semmelweis's valuable discovery and adopting his methods, the established medical community criticized, ridiculed, and resisted his ideas. None of the doctors could agree with Semmelweis that he had uncovered the single source of childbed fever. To them, his discovery was just one of 30 possible causes of the illness. More important, his medical peers couldn't accept their hands were the primary harbingers of these deaths, and that better hygiene could save lives.

The famous French philosopher Voltaire once said, "It is dangerous to be right in matters on which the established authorities are wrong." Semmelweis paid dearly for his untraditional ideas about handwashing. In 1849, he was unable to renew his position in the maternity ward and was blocked from obtaining similar positions in Vienna. A frustrated and demoralized Semmelweis moved back to Budapest. After waiting more than 10 years for his handwashing practices to catch on, he finally published his life's work, entitled *The Etiology, Concept, and Prophylaxis of Childbed Fever* in 1861. Half of his lengthy 500-page book was devoted to his childbed fever research, and the other half focused on angrily disputing arguments made by his many critics. Unfortunately, his book ended up being refuted and openly attacked in medical lecture halls and medical publications throughout Europe. In response to unfavorable reviews, he wrote increasingly irate letters to prominent European obstetricians denouncing them as irresponsible murderers and ignoramuses. The rejection of his lifesaving insights affected him so greatly that he eventually had some kind of mental breakdown, and he was committed to a mental institution in 1865. Two weeks later, he was dead at the age of 47—succumbing to an infected wound inflicted by the asylum's guards.

Semmelweis's data met three key criteria—his insight was *truthful, valuable,* and *actionable.* From a *truth* perspective, while he didn't discover the actual microbes that were infecting women with childbed fever, he did introduce a preventive solution with credible data to support its effectiveness. From a *value* viewpoint, if his handwashing practices were widely adopted, they could have saved the lives of countless women who died needlessly at the contaminated hands of their obstetricians—not just in Austria but throughout Europe and the world. Finally, from an *actionability* standpoint, hospitals only had to implement a simple, low-cost procedure to quell the deadly curse of childbed fever.

Despite a strong *logos* appeal (per Aristotle's model from the previous chapter), Semmelweis's findings couldn't stand on their own. They weren't enough to persuade a stubborn medical community to change its ways or admit any fault. He stated, "I believed that I could leave it to time to break a path for the truth." But time wasn't enough, either. Unfortunately, the Hungarian physician failed to see his handwashing practices adopted in his lifetime. Seduced by his own statistics, Semmelweis stumbled when it came to the communication of his lifesaving insight. If he had a better appreciation of how people process facts and data, he might have taken a different approach with sharing his insight. Today, he would be remembered for what he accomplished rather than for what he might have achieved.

Even though this data tragedy occurred more than 150 years ago, the same challenges that Semmelweis faced with human nature persist today. This chapter will give you with a clearer appreciation of how data storytelling can help your insights navigate the human mind.

Most Decisions Are Not Based on Logic

It has been said that man is a rational animal. All my life I have been searching for evidence which could support this.
—Bertrand Russell, philosopher

One of the traps that analytical people fall into is the assumption that decisions are shaped primarily by logic and reason. As someone who has worked with data for more than 20 years, I'm familiar with this pitfall. I've made the mistake of assuming that if I could simply provide someone with the critical data or facts they were missing, they would be able to formulate a logical decision. My view reflected a common misconception known as the *information deficit model,* where an audience is simply lacking the information they need to fully understand a problem. Ignaz Semmelweis fell victim to this same false hope. He felt his peers in the medical community—most of whom were well-educated and scientifically minded—would embrace the promising results he generated with his unconventional handwashing practices. He was shocked when they didn't. In these situations, it's actually less about *what* people think, and more about *how* they think that really matters. Even analytical audiences are still subject to another powerful force that can lead to unanticipated outcomes: emotion.

When it comes to decision making, we often look down on emotions. We view them as something that can cloud our judgment and lead us to make rash or unwise decisions. When we share our findings, we don't want them to be tainted by any emotional entrapments. As a result, we often take a clinical, detached approach when we share our insights as we attempt to "just stick to the facts." In many ways, we end up sharing our insights like Mr. Spock from the popular science fiction TV series and movie franchise *Star Trek.* If you're not familiar with the Star Trek universe, Spock is the chief science officer and second-in-command on the starship *USS Enterprise.* More notably, being half Vulcan, he strives to suppress his emotions and live by his people's strict code of logic and reason.

Whenever the starship crew faced some new threat or crisis, Spock would provide his commanding officer, Captain James T. Kirk, with a cold, analytical assessment of each situation and the crew's tactical options. While Captain Kirk valued Spock's facts and probabilities, he also sought out the more emotional opinion of his fiery Chief Medical Officer, Doctor Leonard McCoy (a.k.a. Bones). Inevitably, the Captain relied on an intuition-based synthesis of the two perspectives when making decisions (see Figure 3.4). Even though analytical people like to pretend emotion can be checked or removed from decision making, it's always present and a highly influential aspect of the process.

TWO KEY FACTORS IN DECISION MAKING

Figure 3.4   Like *Star Trek*'s Mr. Spock, we may like to believe that decisions should only be based on logic and reason. However, emotion has a bigger influence on decision making than we care to admit.

USC professor and neuroscientist António Damásio made a groundbreaking discovery into emotion's critical role in decision making. When he was working with patients who had brain trauma in an area that processes emotions (prefrontal cortex), Damásio discovered many of these seemingly normal individuals struggled to make basic decisions when choosing between a set of alternatives. Deciding on where to eat or when to schedule an appointment turned into lengthy cost-benefit debates for these emotionless individuals. In short, they resembled real-life Vulcans.

For example, when choosing which restaurant to visit, one of his patients might deliberate back and forth on various factors such as the menu selection, wait times, parking availability, server friendliness, and so on. A simple decision about where to have lunch could take these individuals 30 minutes or more to make (Damásio 2009). Damásio found emotion actually assists the reasoning process and plays an essential role in helping our brains to navigate through alternatives and arrive at timely decisions. He made the following observation about emotion and decision making: "I continue to be fascinated by the fact that feelings are not just the shady side of reason, but that they help us to reach decisions as well" (Damásio 2009).

Data science isn't the first analytical discipline to underestimate the role that emotions have on the decision-making process. Centuries of economic theory have been based on the principle that an individual will make a *rational* decision based on what will generate the greatest personal utility or benefit. Not until the late 1960s did psychologists such as Daniel Kahneman and Amos Tversky begin to question whether people always make rational choices. Their research gave birth to the field of behavioral economics by highlighting how decision making is influenced by heuristics—mental shortcuts—and cognitive biases that lead fallible individuals to not always behave rationally or in their own best interests.

In his best-selling, Nobel Prize–winning book *Thinking, Fast and Slow*, Kahneman (2011) shares the results into how the human brain processes information. He popularized the theory that the human mind is comprised of two cognitive subsystems (see Figure 3.5). *System 1* is fast, intuitive, emotional, automatic, and subconscious. It acts as a sort of *autopilot* that uses heuristics or mental shortcuts to make rapid but sometimes rough interpretations, which are then passed along to the next system. *System 2* is slow, analytical, logical, effortful, and conscious. It acts as the *pilot* that monitors and evaluates the quality of the information coming from System 1 and, as needed, evaluates it more thoroughly. While System 2 is often perceived to be running the show as the pilot, it is actually a lazy controller. System 2 doesn't want to exert a lot of effort and will depend on System 1 to provide feelings and impressions that become the sources of its explicit beliefs and choices. In the end, Kahneman views System 1—the more emotional, intuitive system—as the real star of the cognitive show.

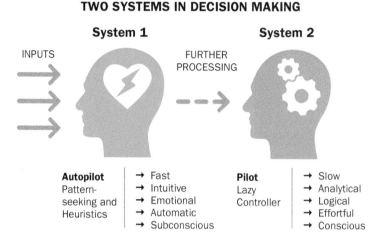

Figure 3.5 Daniel Kahneman popularized the notion that the human mind has two subsystems that work together to process information.

With System 1 serving as our intuition, we often underestimate its influence over our decision making. Kahneman developed a simple bat-and-ball puzzle to illustrate its effect on how our minds process information. Rather than trying to solve the following puzzle, listen to what your intuition tells you:

A bat and ball cost $1.10.
The bat costs one dollar more than the ball.
How much does the ball cost?

Most people will automatically assume the ball costs 10 cents. Even though this answer comes easily to our minds, it's wrong. If the ball costs 10 cents, and the bat is worth one dollar more ($1.10), the total cost would then be $1.20—not $1.10. If you were able to identify the correct cost of five cents, you are in the minority that was able to resist the intuitive response suggested by System 1. When Kahneman presented university students at Harvard, MIT, and Princeton with the bat-and-ball puzzle, he found more than 50% of them thought the ball would cost 10 cents. At other less prestigious universities, he discovered more than 80% of the students reached the same incorrect conclusion (Kahneman 2011). This simple puzzle highlights how systematic errors can be introduced into our thought processes based on our reliance on System 1. While it is an imperfect system and can occasionally introduce cognitive biases, it is essential to our ability to process vast amounts of information very quickly.

One of the unique talents of the System 1 is its ability to weave scattered fragments of information into stories to help give them meaning. To illustrate how quickly your mind can generate narrative with only a limited amount of information, take a moment to consider each of the following lines individually:

1. For sale: Baby shoes, never worn.
2. Our bedroom. Two voices. I knock.
3. Paramedics finished her text, ". . . love you."

Each of these short phrases is an example of a "six-word story." The urban legend is that someone dared the famous American novelist Ernest Hemingway to tell a story in six words, so he wrote the first example (which isn't true). Interestingly, each set of six words is not really a story. The short phrases are transformed into narratives by our brains, which automatically fill in the missing pieces. From just six words, a rough narrative emerges in our minds that is populated with a background, setting, plot, and characters. All of this processing happens without any conscious effort on our part.

Similarly, in everyday situations, System 1 searches for causality to explain what's happening in our environment—even when none may exist. The foremost concern of the intuitive mind is to assemble the different pieces of data it receives into unified, coherent stories. Kahneman observed through his research that,

> The measure of success for System 1 is the coherence of the story it manages to create. The amount and quality of the data on which the story is based are largely irrelevant. When information is scarce, which is a common occurrence, System 1 operates as a machine for jumping to conclusions. (Kahneman 2011)

GEOMETRIC SHAPES FROM HEIDER
AND SIMMEL'S SHORT FILM

Figure 3.6 The three scenes above are representative of different moments in Heider and Simmel's 1944 animated film. All but one of the participants used a narrative to describe the movements of the three objects after watching the short movie.

In their 1944 landmark study, psychologists Fritz Heider and Marianne Simmel displayed our dogged desire to form coherent narratives (Heider and Simmel 1944). They asked 34 students to observe a short, animated movie (see Figure 3.6) and then describe what happened. The film consisted of three geometric shapes—a large triangle, a small triangle, and a small circle—moving around a rectangle at various speeds and in different directions. All but one of the participants ended up describing the scene that unfolded as a story involving animated characters—not simply geometric shapes. They ascribed humanlike emotions, personalities, and motivations to the objects in the film to explain their movements such as the large triangle bullying and chasing the other shapes. In attempting to understand a diverse set of events, System 1 attempts to connect everything together into tidy, plausible narratives.

Incorrect or missing information will not impede our brain's attempts at jumping to conclusions and seeking to assemble coherent narratives. In 1994, psychologists Hollyn Johnson and Colleen Seifert conducted an experiment in which subjects were given a series of messages that described a warehouse fire (Johnson and Seifert 1994). At one point, they were told a short circuit occurred near a closet allegedly containing volatile materials such as paint cans and pressurized gas cylinders. Later on, they were informed that there had been a mistake, and the closet had actually been empty. When these subjects were asked a series of questions about the fire, most of the participants inferred the warehouse

WAREHOUSE FIRE SCENARIO #1
(WITH MISINFORMATION)

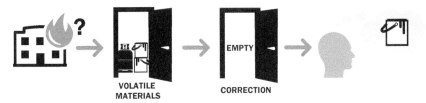

Figure 3.7 Even though the subjects were informed that the closet did not contain volatile materials, they still relied on this misinformation to build an explanatory narrative for the warehouse fire.

owners had been negligent due to the volatile materials—even though it was clarified they never existed (see Figure 3.7). Without a better explanation, the subjects inadvertently relied on the misinformation to form a narrative to explain what happened.

In a second experiment by Johnson and Seifert, after being informed of the mistake, the subjects were told gas-soaked rags had been found in a suspicious location. For this second group, when they were questioned about the fire, they no longer clung to the misinformation about the volatile materials (see Figure 3.8). They had a causal alternative to form a new narrative—arson instead of negligence—and the misinformation was discarded. Rather than simply trying to correct facts, this study shows we must help an audience to assemble a plausible story with the new data. When key information is discounted or disproven, people will revert to the original narrative if it offers them more coherence.

WAREHOUSE FIRE SCENARIO #2
(WITH MISINFORMATION AND ALTERNATE CAUSE)

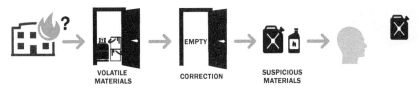

Figure 3.8 When an alternative cause was presented (suspicious materials), the subjects were able to let go of the misinformation related to the volatile materials.

Our need for causality is deeply engrained in our DNA. Researchers have found we are capable of seeing a sequence of events as a cause-and-effect scenario as early as six months old (Leslie and Keeble 1987). If we were to resist this emotional tendency for narrative interpretation, we would be fighting human nature. Emotions are an inescapable, innate part of decision making that can't be ignored or downplayed. Instead of trying to remove or marginalize emotions, we must acknowledge their presence and use them to better connect with others. Going back to the *Star Trek* analogy, over time, Mr. Spock eventually learned to balance logic and emotion—and we must do the same with our communications.

How We React to Facts

There are no facts, only interpretations.
—Friedrich Nietzsche, philosopher

Depending on our existing knowledge and beliefs, we are primed to react differently to new information. When we receive new evidence that aligns with our current viewpoint, we are less skeptical and more accepting of it. In fact, we may even experience a rush of dopamine—a neurotransmitter associated with our reward and pleasure system—when we encounter confirming data. However, when we encounter facts that challenge our current beliefs or knowledge, our System 2 engages, and we become more critical and suspicious of the new data. Psychologist Daniel Gilbert used an illustrative example for how we respond differently to data depending on whether we agree or disagree with what's being shared.

> When our bathroom scale delivers bad news, we hop off and then on again, just to make sure we didn't misread the display or put too much pressure on one foot. When our scale delivers good news, we smile and head for the shower. By uncritically accepting evidence when it pleases us, and insisting on more when it doesn't, we subtly tip the scales in our favor. (Gilbert 2006)

In 1992, psychologists Peter Ditto and David Lopez studied this behavior with an experiment where students were told they would be tested for the presence of an enzyme in their saliva that would turn a piece of paper from yellow to green if it was present (Ditto and Lopez 1992). Half of the participants were told the enzyme meant they were 10 times *less likely* to develop pancreatic disease, and the other half were told they were 10 times *more likely* to have pancreatic disorders in their lifetime. The subjects who received the unfavorable diagnosis were more likely to question the accuracy of the test and suggest irregularities such as diet, stress, or sleep pattern issues that might have affected the test result. The study showed we are less skeptical when information supports a preferable conclusion—such as being healthy instead of potentially unhealthy. Only when the facts are inconsistent with our preferred judgments do we question their accuracy or demand more data.

Now, not all of our beliefs are equally important to us. In some situations, we are open to new information when we recognize our knowledge is incorrect or outdated. For example, it has been a longstanding belief that Napoleon Bonaparte, the nineteenth-century French military leader, was short in stature. After he died, doctors reported his height to be 5 feet 2 inches. However, this measurement was in French units and not the smaller English units. His height would be about 5 feet 7 inches (1.70 m) in the English or Imperial units, which would make him slightly taller than the average Frenchman of his time (5 feet 5 inches or 1.65 m) (Rodenberg 2013). The myth of Napoleon's short stature was an early form of trolling by political cartoonists in England, who enjoyed portraying him as a short-tempered child, to the great annoyance of the French leader (Figure 3.9). This simple misconception has persisted for over two hundred years.

For most of us, it's easy to adjust our perception of Napoleon's height once we're presented with new data. No one is too emotionally attached to how tall the French general was. However, the same can't be said for data that conflicts with our worldview or core beliefs, which are often shaped by strongly held cultural, religious, or political views. In fact, researchers found that in these cases, we may view disagreeing data as we would a threat to our physical safety (Kaplan, Gimbel, and

Figure 3.9 This illustration by English caricaturist James Gillray (1756–1815) shows how Napoleon was portrayed in unflattering ways as short and childlike, to the French emperor's chagrin.

Source: https://commons.wikimedia.org/wiki/File:Caricature_gillray_plumpudding.jpg. Public domain.

Harris 2016). Just as our System 1 alerts us to potential danger when we hear a potential intruder in the house or encounter an animal in the wild, our brain can view counterevidence as a similarly imposing threat. In these cases, our mind is prepared to defend itself from conflicting information that could disrupt or harm our belief system.

In 2004, psychologist Drew Westen conducted an interesting study with 30 subjects who identified themselves as committed Republicans or Democrats (Westen, Blagov, Harenski, Kilts, and Hamann 2007). As their brain activity was being scanned using a functional magnetic resonance imaging (fMRI) machine, each participant was presented with a series of contradictory statements made by leading politicians from each party. The subjects could easily spot the contradictions in the opposing candidate's message; however, they didn't see nearly the same inconsistency in their own candidate's messaging. For example, a Democrat supporter could clearly see the contradiction in a conflicting comment made by Republican President George W. Bush but failed to see anything as incongruous in the inconsistent remarks made by Democratic Senator John Kerry. While their partisan reaction may not be too surprising, what the neural scans revealed about their reasoning process was.

After initially feeling some distress due to the conflicting data, their minds quickly sought to rationalize the new information and regulate the flow of negative emotions. None of the areas that are associated with conscious reasoning were activated (System 2)—everything occurred in the unconscious, emotional centers (System 1). Their brains not only suppressed the flow of negative emotions but also triggered the reward circuits to positively reinforce their false, biased conclusions. This process is known as *motivated reasoning*. In today's polarized political environment, it's becoming increasingly difficult for people to accept facts that don't align with their personal beliefs, moral values, or group identity. Motivated reasoning fuels conspiracy theories and drives the emergence of "alternative facts" to support dubious conclusions. It also explains the unfortunate rise in cries of "fake news" when hard facts are difficult to swallow.

In these situations, our tendency is to throw more facts and evidence at people who have strongly held opposing viewpoints and beliefs. However, instead of weakening their position, we can inadvertently reinforce it with our conflicting evidence. Psychologists have labeled this phenomenon as the *backfire effect*. In their 2010 study, political scientists Brendan Nyhan and Jason Reifler presented different individuals with the false claims that weapons of mass destruction (WMD) were found in Iraq and that President Bush–era tax cuts led to increased treasury revenues. They were then exposed to corrective information such as the WMDs were never found in Iraq and the nominal tax revenues actually declined sharply as a proportion of national GDP after Bush's tax cuts. Depending on the political leaning of the participants, they either agreed or disagreed with the misleading and corrective statements along partisan lines. Interestingly, the corrections backfired when the conservatives became even more convinced that the original misconceptions were true (Nyhan and Reifler 2010).

While Nyhan and Reifler's concept of the backfire effect has gained popularity, other researchers have since found this cognitive bias may be more of a rare occurrence than a common one (Wood and Porter 2017). Regardless, the backfire effect represents just one of many landmines you must navigate when you attempt to correct misinformation that could be connected to someone's core beliefs or identity.

In other research by Nyhan and Reifler, they uncovered one strategy that was able to consistently reduce misperceptions—*the use of charts or graphs* (Nyhan and Reifler 2018). In three experiments, they identified situations in which individuals might be "unwilling to acknowledge factual information that contradicts their preexisting beliefs." In two of the studies, data charts were created to highlight potential misperceptions surrounding actions taken by US Presidents George W. Bush (Iraq troop surge in 2006) and Barack Obama (job creation in 2010). When compared to the control groups, the graphs had a significant impact on correcting misinformed viewpoints. For example, for the Obama disapprovers in the control group, more than 80% believed Obama failed to create jobs in 2010. However, less than 30% of the Obama disapprovers who saw the data chart felt the same way.

In a third experiment, the political scientists wanted to compare the effectiveness of presenting data graphically versus textually. When they shared a graph showing the change in global average temperatures and a paragraph describing the same temperature variation, only the data chart was able to decrease false or unsupported beliefs.

While visualizing your data isn't going to correct everyone's false beliefs, it can be effective at reducing some of the information deficits. While data visualizations can be helpful to your message, it is important to recognize that not all charts are equally effective. In Chapters 7 and 8, we'll explore in more detail how to create visuals that will convey your key points and resonate with an audience. Now that you better understand how an audience instinctively reacts to data, let's examine how they respond to narrative.

How We React to Stories

The human mind is a story processor, not a logic processor.
—Jonathan Haidt, social psychologist

Something extraordinary happens to us when we hear those simple words "once upon a time . . . ." When someone shares a story with us, our brains react differently than they do to facts. If you were to receive a set of factual information, a scan of your brain would reveal activity in two key areas of the brain: the *Broca's* and *Wernicke's* areas. Both of these regions of the brain work together to produce and process language. Our brains receive the facts as words and numbers that are decoded into meaning—and nothing more. However, a story has the power to activate more than just these two regions of the brain. Various studies found narrative engages other regions of the brain besides the language processing centers—such as those associated with smell, touch, and movement (see Figure 3.10). For example, words like "coffee" or "perfume" will activate your olfactory cortex. Phrases such as "he had leathery hands" will light up the sensory region of your brain. Sentences such as "Mary kicked the ball" will engage parts of your motor cortex linked to leg movements (Paul 2012). Essentially, we *hear* statistics, but we *feel* stories. A narrative offers an opportunity to engage the minds of your audience at a deeper and more encompassing level than facts ever can.

COMMUNICATION FORMATS AND BRAIN ACTIVATION

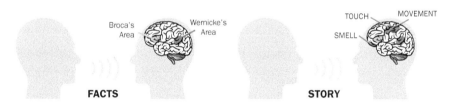

Figure 3.10 Facts will only activate the Broca's and Wernicke's areas that are associated with language processing. However, a story can light up multiple sensory-related areas of the brain.

When a story is shared, an interesting pattern emerges in the brains of the storyteller and the listeners—*they synchronize*. Neuroscientist Uri Hasson conducted an experiment with 12 subjects who were connected to fMRI machines as they listened to a woman's 15-minute story about her high school prom disaster that involved jealous boyfriends, a fistfight, and a car crash. Hasson discovered the storyteller and listeners shared very similar brain activity even though the woman was

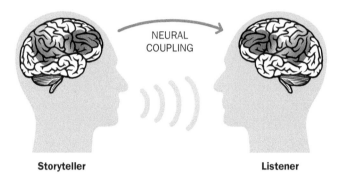

NEURAL COUPLING SYNCHRONIZES THE LISTENER WITH THE STORYTELLER

Storyteller   Listener

Figure 3.11 Uri Hasson discovered when we share stories with others, neural coupling occurs in which the listener's brain activity mirrors that of the storyteller's. Storytelling enables us to connect with an audience and transmit ideas to them more effectively.

producing language and the listeners were processing it. He described this phenomenon as *neural coupling*, where the minds of the storyteller and their audience align or meld (see Figure 3.11). Hasson found the stronger the coupling between the two parties, the better the communication and the deeper the audience's understanding (Stephens, Silbert, and Hasson 2010). Establishing common ground is important for the coupling to occur, as contextual differences can interfere with the effective transmission of ideas through storytelling (Hasson 2016). However, when you are able to connect with your audience through stories, you open a pathway to shared comprehension.

Stories also have the power to change brain chemistry. Neuroeconomist Paul Zak conducted research into what happens to the molecules in the brain when we hear a story (Zak 2012). Using blood tests and fMRI scans, he analyzed how subjects in his studies reacted to a short film about a two-year-old boy named Ben and his father. Ben is depicted as a happy, playful toddler, but you see Ben's father struggling with the fact that he knows a brain tumor will take his young son's life in a matter of months. As participants watched the film, Zak found that their brains produced two chemicals: *cortisol* and *oxytocin*. Cortisol has been referred to as the "stress hormone" due to it being released when we feel distress. Flowing with the tension in a story, it serves a valuable role in focusing and maintaining the audience's attention. Oxytocin is a hormone that is associated with empathy and trust. Through higher levels of oxytocin, your audience becomes more empathetic and connected with you and your ideas. With 80% accuracy, Zak could predict who would donate to a charity at the end of the study based on their oxytocin levels. The hormone is instrumental in motivating people to work with others and take action.

Under the influence of these two powerful hormones, an audience can enter into a psychological state where they are "transported"— becoming immersed in the narrative and less connected to reality. In 2000, research by psychologists Melanie Green and Timothy Brock showed that the more individuals were transported or absorbed in a story, the more their beliefs aligned with those expressed in the story— regardless of their prior beliefs. They also saw that highly transported participants were less likely to see "false notes"—contradictory facts or inaccuracies—in the story. Rather than nitpicking the details, they were engaged in following the story's protagonist and plot. In addition, narrative transportation appeared whether the story was positioned as fiction or nonfiction (Green and Brock 2000). Other researchers have since discovered narrative transportation has a sleeper effect: it becomes more persuasive over time as the story's ideas and facts are integrated into people's working knowledge and belief systems (Appel and Richter 2007). Clearly, stories can navigate through the human brain in ways that can cause facts to trip and stumble. They offer a potent, persuasive delivery approach that is designed to engage minds that are already primed to seek and respond to narrative.

Stories can also help an audience make sense of logic that may be difficult to follow or comprehend. In 1966, English psychologist Peter Wason developed a four-card selection task that tested people's deductive reasoning abilities. A variation of the task instructions is as follows:

> A set of four cards is placed on a table (see Figure 3.12). Each card has a number on one side and a color on the other side. Which card(s) must you turn over in order to test the truth of the proposition that if a card shows an even number on one side, then its opposite side is red?

WASON SELECTION TASK

Figure 3.12 Most people don't know which card(s) to turn over in this example of the Wason Selection Task.

Wason discovered only 10% of participants could ascertain the correct cards to turn over. While turning over the "8" card is fairly obvious to proving the proposition, turning over the "blue" card isn't as intuitive, even though discovering an even number on the opposite side would disprove the proposed proposition. However, when the Wason Selection Test was put into the context of a relevant narrative, 65–75% of participants were able to pinpoint the right cards to flip over (Badcock 2012). For example, in the example below, the majority of participants were able to identify which two cards definitely needed to be turned over to ensure only people over 21 years old were drinking alcohol in a bar (in this case 16, beer).

> As a bartender, you must enforce the rule that if someone is drinking beer, they must be at least 21 years of age. Each of the four cards represents a person sitting at a table. Each card shows you their age and what beverage they're drinking (see Figure 3.13). Which card(s) must you turn over to verify if the rule is being violated?

WASON SELECTION TASK IN STORY FORM

Figure 3.13 The Wason Selection Task became easier for people to comprehend when it was framed as a relevant story.

Putting complex or difficult concepts into a story format can help people to more easily grasp their meaning and make better sense of the numbers. While storytelling can be helpful in facilitating better reasoning, simply adding any story isn't sufficient. The story must be relevant to the topic, as researchers found a nonsensical, irrelevant narrative didn't help participants to succeed with the Wason Selection Test. When used wisely, stories can help abstract or complex insights seem more concrete and approachable for your audience.

Table 3.1   Summary: How We React to Facts versus Stories

Reaction to Facts
1. **We mainly scrutinize facts we don't like.** When facts align with an audience's current viewpoint, the audience will be less skeptical and more accepting of the data.
2. **We may fight conflicting facts like a physical threat.** Data that challenges an audience's worldviews is often treated by the brain like a threat to their physical safety.
3. **Our brains may bend or break facts to support our existing biases.** Motivated reasoning leads the brain to positively reinforce false, biased conclusions.
4. **Corrective facts can potentially strengthen our misinformed position.** The backfire effect can occur when corrective information actually reinforces, rather than weakens, an individual's misinformed beliefs.
5. **When facts are visualized, it is harder for us to reject them.** Data visualizations are effective at reducing information deficits for some people.

Reaction to Stories
1. **Stories engage more of our brain.** Stories engage more sensory areas in the brain besides the two associated with producing and processing language (Broca's and Wernicke's).
2. **Stories form a unique connection between the storyteller and listener.** Neural coupling can occur when the minds of the storyteller and audience mirror similar brain activity.
3. **Stories increase our attention and empathy.** Stories cause audience members' brains to release two hormones—cortisol and oxytocin—that increase attention, empathy, and the desire to act.
4. **Stories make us less skeptical and more open to change.** Narrative transportation leads to less criticism of the story details and modifies beliefs to align with those of the story.
5. **Stories enhance our comprehension.** Stories can help the audience to better comprehend difficult or complex concepts.

Data Stories Bridge Logic and Emotion

A story is a fact, wrapped in an emotion that compels us to take an action that transforms our world.

—TV writer/producer Richard Maxwell and
executive coach Robert Dickman

When you find and share important insights, you want them to be understood and embraced by your intended audience. However, no matter how strong or sound your data is, there's no guarantee it will resonate in their minds. When you share new facts with an audience, the data must traverse through both systems of the brain. You are not just engaging with the reasoning side of the brain (System 2) but also the emotional one (System 1). It's possible that your findings could be dismissed unconsciously by the emotional, intuitive System 1. Alternatively, they may be passed to a skeptical System 2 to be analytically picked apart and flatly rejected. When you have a deeper appreciation for how the brain processes facts and stories, you begin to see how combining them can positively impact how your insights are heard, understood, and adopted. With storytelling being so deeply connected with how people process and remember information, it affords salient advantages that are not available to facts alone.

Data storytelling provides a bridge between the worlds of logic and emotion. A data story offers a safe passage for your insights to travel around emotional pitfalls and through analytical resistance that typically impede facts. Rather than working *against* System 1, stories work *with* the emotional, intuitive side of the brain to assist System 2 in considering new insights. *The Storytelling Animal* author, Jonathan Gottschall, underscored the unique influence stories have over us in the following statement:

> When we read dry, factual arguments, we read with our dukes up. We are critical and skeptical. But when we are absorbed in a story we drop our intellectual guard. We are moved emotionally and this seems to leave us defenseless. (Gottschall 2012)

To rephrase what Gottschall observed, when people are approached with facts, they respond by raising their shields to protect their viewpoints and not be misled. However, the presence of a story causes people to reflexively lower these shields and not assume a defensive posture that can make conveying new information more difficult. Some people have compared the hidden persuasive power of stories (*pathos* appeal) to a Trojan horse (Guber 2013). While a story can act as a powerful delivery agent for sharing facts, *the intent of data storytelling should never be to deceive an audience.* Just like falsifying data is unacceptable, using narrative in a manipulative manner is similarly irresponsible. Instead, data storytelling should be viewed as a means of making insights more compatible with the human mind and more conducive to comprehension and retention.

Rather than comparing storytelling to a negative Greek tale of lies and deception, I prefer to relate it to a high occupancy vehicle (HOV) express lane in a major city. If you were responsible for transporting goods across a busy, gridlocked city, you would jump at the chance to use the express lanes as often as you could to avoid congested, slow-moving roadways. Not only would the travel times be reduced, but your trips would be far less stressful. The human brain resembles a large city—with a network of interconnecting routes that handle a steady, heavy flow of signals moving between different systems. Because people are naturally conditioned to respond to stories, special pathways are available to stories that facilitate the transportation of knowledge. When you have important insights to share, you want to access these cognitive express lanes by telling a story with your data (see Figure 3.14). Without data storytelling, your insights are left to

A DATA STORY TAKES ADVANTAGE OF THE BRAIN'S EXPRESS LANE FOR NARRATIVE

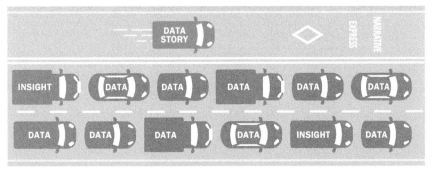

Figure 3.14 When you share insights with data stories, you're able to take advantage of the special express lane that the brain reserves for narrative.

the whims of how Systems 1 and 2 typically process unfamiliar infor-mation, which can lead to unwanted delays, detours, and road closures for your ideas.

In 2011, the Skeptical Science website's John Cook and psy-chologist Stephan Lewandowsky published a short, practical guide on how to counter misinformation and the backfire effect called *The Debunker's Handbook* (Cook and Lewandowsky 2011). In the guide, they explore why people don't always process information rationally, and why it can be difficult for people to modify their existing knowl-edge. Although the book's original intent was to help address climate change denial, its concepts can be applied to any number of myths or misperceptions.

Two key tools in their handbook underline the importance of tell-ing stories with data. First, when you seek to correct a myth or miscon-ception, you must be mindful to craft an alternative narrative around your new facts (see Figure 3.15). Otherwise, the audience will be left with a gap in their mental model where the myth was debunked with nothing to fill it. Because an audience will prefer an incorrect model over an incomplete one, data storytelling can help by organizing new facts into a plausible narrative to fill the cognitive gap in your audience's

FACTS MUST BE ACCOMPANIED BY A SUPPORTING NARRATIVE

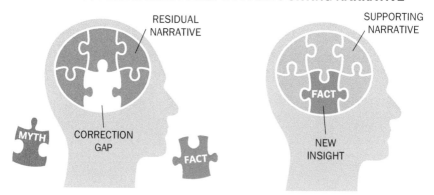

Figure 3.15 When you correct and dislodge a myth, the residual narrative can still be problematic. Therefore, you must also provide a new supporting narrative with your new insight.

reasoning. In this case, "mind the gap" doesn't just apply to the London Underground, it also relates to sharing new insights.

Second, Cook and Lewandowsky highlighted the important role graphics play in addressing misinformation over other approaches such as text or speech. In their handbook, they state:

> When people read a refutation that conflicts with their beliefs, they seize on ambiguities to construct an alternative interpretation. Graphics provide more clarity and less opportunity for misinterpretation. (Cook and Lewandowsky 2011)

When you use visuals to tell your data story, your insights become clearer and more concrete for your audience. While individuals can attempt to interpret the visualized data in various ways, there's usually less wriggle room for them to draw misguided conclusions. For example, in a study by Lewandowsky, he found that when surface temperature data was visualized, subjects correctly judged a warming trend regardless of their personal attitudes toward global warming (Lewandowsky 2011). When you harness the power of data storytelling through data, narrative, *and* visuals, you give your insights the best chance at overcoming resistance and driving change. A data story has a greater possibility of reaching people's hearts—not just their minds—to stir them to act.

What Could Semmelweis Have Done Differently?

All great truths begin as blasphemies.
                                        —George Bernard Shaw, playwright

At the beginning of the chapter, we saw how Ignaz Semmelweis's ideas about handwashing were rejected by the nineteenth-century medical establishment. While his passion and determination to help expectant mothers earned him the posthumous title of "Savior of Mothers," he was unable to convince his peers to embrace his lifesaving hygiene practices. One of the lessons we can learn from Semmelweis's challenge is the need to communicate insights effectively. Hindsight makes it easy to criticize mistakes that he made more than 150 years ago. With the passage of time, we certainly lose context for the political struggles and professional egos the Hungarian doctor faced in the Viennese medical community. However, I believe the principles of data storytelling could have helped him in his attempts to change the dangerous medical practices that were costing the lives of so many young mothers.

From a narrative perspective, Semmelweis could have attempted to humanize his data for his audience because insightful statistics alone won't persuade skeptical minds. The data-savvy doctor missed an opportunity to weave his handwashing results into a compelling data story that could have connected with his medical colleagues on an emotional level (*pathos* appeal). He could have shared the story of Sophie, a poor but healthy, young mother of two small children who arrived at the hospital expecting her third child. Rather than returning home with her beautiful, newborn daughter two days later, Sophie's and her infant's lifeless bodies were reminders of the daily cost being inflicted by childbed fever. Sophie could be a real patient that Semmelweis's team of student doctors encountered at the Vienna maternity clinic or a representative persona that embodied the many women who were needlessly losing their lives to this preventable disease.

Rather than viewing the women's deaths as an unfortunate but natural consequence of their labors, he could have admonished his fellow obstetricians to remember the poor women behind the cold, faceless statistics. Sophie wasn't just another victim of childbed fever but a mother, wife, and daughter who had others to care for and love. Sophie's story might have touched the male doctors as they contemplated what it would be like to unexpectedly lose their own wife, sister, or daughter to this ugly illness. With his data on childbed fever deaths (1841–1846), Semmelweis could have extrapolated how many lives would have been saved if the doctors' clinic had the same mortality rate as the midwives' clinic (3.9%, not 9.9%)—more than 1,200 women! Only the coldest and most desensitized of physicians would feel no interest in exploring Semmelweis's ideas and their potential to save women's lives. Some people may question using a narrative approach with more technical content such as medical findings. However, in a study of over 700 scientific journal articles, researchers found a narrative style was more influential (cited more often) than those that relied on a more traditional expository approach (Hillier, Kelly, and Klinger 2016).

From a visuals perspective, Semmelweis missed an opportunity to help bring his insights to life through data visualizations. When the Hungarian doctor published his book, it included more than 60 data tables—*without a single data chart*. Rather than participating in what was considered the "Golden Age" of modern statistical graphics in the mid-to-late 1800s, Semmelweis stuck with traditional data tables for conveying his findings (Friendly 2008). While he had the raw material for many powerful visuals, he settled for what was familiar and easy to produce. He failed to realize how a well-designed chart could make his insights even more salient than what he could achieve with rows and columns of data.

For example, Semmelweis used a detailed data table to compare the childbed fever mortality rates of his Vienna maternity clinic to a similar one in Dublin over a 65-year period (see Figure 3.16). He wanted to highlight the impact that introducing the practice of pathological autopsies in 1823 had on increasing the mortality rates at the Vienna hospital. The Dublin maternity hospital did not follow a similar training practice with its obstetricians, and its mortality rate exceeded 3% on only one occasion (1826). While his data table showed the mortality rate at the Vienna maternity clinic spiked as high as 15.8% in 1842, the stark difference between the two hospitals isn't as clear without the aid of a time-series chart (see Figure 3.17). Even though the data table contains all of the relevant data points, the visual representation of the data is what helps to tell the lethal tale of unhygienic obstetric practices. In most situations, data charts should take center stage in your data stories, and complex data tables should only appear in the appendices to be called on as needed.

Semmelweis had compiled a compelling array of evidence to support his argument that proper handwashing practices could significantly reduce the occurrence of childbed fever. Unfortunately, his efforts to persuade a skeptical medical community were ineffective. With few supporters, Semmelweis went largely ignored and was forgotten by the field of obstetrics. In contrast, it was the British surgeon Joseph Lister (1827–1912) who ushered in the age of antiseptic medicine in the late 1870s. Inspired and supported by the germ theory discoveries of Louis Pasteur, Lister's antisepsis ideas faced similar skepticism and resistance by the traditional medical community. However, his ideas began to gain

	Dublin Maternity Hospital			Viennese Maternity Hospital		
	Births	Deaths	Rate	Births	Deaths	Rate
				BEFORE SEPARATION OF CLINICS		
				Before Pathological Anatomy		
1784	1,261	11	0.87	284	6	2.11
1785	1,292	8	0.61	899	13	1.44
1786	1,351	8	0.59	1,151	5	0.43
1787	1,347	10	0.74	1,407	5	0.35
1788	1,469	23	1.56	1,425	5	0.35
1789	1,435	25	1.74	1,246	7	0.56
1790	1,546	12	0.77	1,326	10	0.75
1791	1,602	25	1.56	1,395	8	0.57
1792	1,631	10	0.61	1,579	14	0.88
1793	1,747	19	1.08	1,684	44	2.61
1794	1,543	20	1.29	1,768	7	0.39
1795	1,503	7	0.46	1,798	38	2.11
1796	1,621	10	0.61	1,904	22	1.15
1797	1,712	13	0.75	2,012	5	0.24
1798	1,604	8	0.49	2,046	5	0.24
1799	1,537	10	0.65	2,067	20	0.96
1800	1,837	18	0.97	2,070	41	1.98
1801	1,725	30	1.73	2,106	17	0.80
1802	1,985	26	1.30	2,346	9	0.38
1803	2,028	44	2.16	2,215	16	0.72
1804	1,915	16	0.83	2,022	8	0.39
1805	2,220	12	0.54	2,112	9	0.42
1806	2,406	23	0.95	1,875	13	0.69
1807	2,511	12	0.47	925	6	0.64
1808	2,665	13	0.48	855	7	0.81
1809	2,889	21	0.72	912	13	1.42
1810	2,854	29	1.01	744	6	0.80
1811	2,561	24	0.93	1,050	20	1.90
1812	2,676	43	1.60	1,419	9	0.63
1813	2,484	62	2.49	1,945	21	1.07
1814	2,508	25	0.99	2,062	66	3.20
1815	3,075	17	0.55	2,591	19	0.73
1816	3,314	18	0.54	2,410	12	0.49
1817	3,473	32	0.92	2,735	25	0.91
1818	3,539	56	1.58	2,568	56	2.18
1819	3,197	94	2.94	3,089	154	4.98
1820	2,458	70	2.84	2,998	75	2.50
1821	2,849	22	0.77	3,294	55	1.66
1822	2,675	12	0.44	3,066	26	0.84

	Dublin Maternity Hospital			Viennese Maternity Hospital		
	Births	Deaths	Rate	Births	Deaths	Rate
				After Pathological Anatomy		
1823	2,584	59	2.28	2,872	214	7.45
1824	2,446	20	0.81	2,911	144	4.94
1825	2,740	26	0.94	2,594	229	8.82
1826	2,440	81	3.31	2,359	192	8.13
1827	2,550	33	1.29	2,367	51	2.15
1828	2,856	43	1.50	2,833	101	3.56
1829	2,141	34	1.58	3,012	140	4.64
1830	2,288	12	0.52	2,797	111	3.96
1831	2,176	12	0.55	3,353	222	6.62
1832	2,242	12	0.53	3,331	105	3.15
				AFTER SEPARATION OF CLINICS		
				Males and Females in Both		
1833	2,138	12	0.56	3,737	197	5.27
1834	2,024	34	1.67	2,657	205	7.71
1835	1,902	34	1.78	2,573	143	5.55
1836	1,810	36	1.98	2,677	200	7.47
1837	1,833	24	1.30	2,765	251	9.07
1838	2,126	45	2.11	2,987	91	3.04
1839	1,951	25	1.28	2,781	151	5.42
1840	1,521	26	1.70	2,889	267	9.24
				Males in First Clinic Only		
1841	2,003	23	1.14	3,036	237	7.80
1842	2,171	21	0.96	3,287	518	15.75
1843	2,210	22	0.99	3,060	274	8.95
1844	2,288	14	0.61	3,157	260	8.23
1845	1,411	35	2.48	3,492	241	6.90
1846	2,025	17	0.83	4,010	459	11.44
				Chlorine Washings Used in Physicians' Clinic		
1847	1,703	47	2.75	3,490	176	5.04
1848	1,816	35	1.92	3,556	45	1.26
1849	2,063	38	1.84	3,858	103	2.66
Total	141,903	1,758		153,841	6,224	
Avg.			1.21			4.04

Figure 3.16 Semmelweis relied heavily on data tables such as this one to support his arguments. This data table compares the mortality rates of the Dublin Maternity Hospital and Viennese Maternity Hospital over a 65-year period.

Source: Adapted from Semmelweis 1861.

acceptance when other surgeons in Germany and Denmark realized remarkable results from following his techniques. In Munich, a hospital was able to dramatically reduce its 80% post-surgery infection rate to almost zero (Schlich 2013). After patiently and consistently promoting his ideas for more than a decade, Lister was able to witness their wide acceptance in his lifetime—an outcome that sadly eluded Semmelweis.

Some people may attribute the Hungarian doctor's failure to never discovering the actual agent (bacteria) behind what was causing child-bed fever. However, not understanding how or why something works doesn't necessarily impede promising ideas from being adopted. For example, even though the drug known as acetaminophen—or Tylenol by its brand name—has been one of the most popular painkillers since the 1950s, drug experts still don't understand how it actually works

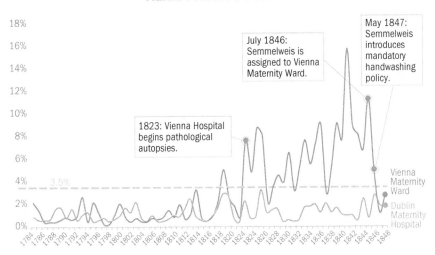

CHILDBED FEVER MORTALITY RATES: VIENNA VERSUS DUBLIN

Figure 3.17 Up until 1823, when the Vienna hospital introduced the practice of pathological autopsies, the two hospitals had similar childbed fever mortality rates. When compared to the tabular presentation of the data in Figure 3.16, this visual representation better supports Semmelweis's conclusion that the university's autopsy focus was a contributing factor in the childbed fever deaths at the Vienna Hospital.

(Drahl 2014). The new frontier of artificial intelligence (AI) is already presenting situations in which developers can't fully explain how their AI models work. For instance, a deep learning application—aptly named Deep Patient—developed at the Mount Sinai Hospital in New York was "trained" on 700,000 patient records and became adept at predicting disease in new patients. In particular, its creators found it could inexplicably anticipate psychiatric disorders such as schizophrenia, which are "notoriously difficult for physicians to predict" (Knight 2017). While it's reassuring to fully understand why something works, positive outcomes often matter more.

Unfortunately, poor communication was a key reason why Semmelweis's ideas were never embraced. Despite the strength of his empirical evidence and the positive results of his handwashing practices, he wasn't able to convince fellow obstetricians to adopt or even test his findings. If Semmelweis had been able to tell a more persuasive story with his numbers, who knows how many lives he could have saved—including maybe even his own?

Whenever we are fortunate enough to come across a valuable insight, we have a responsibility as its steward or guardian to see it realize its full potential. However, an insight in the mind of one person can accomplish very little; in most cases, it must be shared with others and embraced by them to reach its potential. When you combine data with narrative and visuals, you prepare your insight for the difficult journey through the human mind—both Systems 1 and 2. Data storytelling not only presents information in a way that is congruous with the narrative-seeking brain, but it can also ignite a desire in your audience to act. The Greek philosopher Plutarch observed, "The mind is not a vessel to be filled but a fire to be kindled." A well-crafted data story may be the very spark or psychological catalyst you need to drive the change you seek.

References

Appel, M., and Richter, T. 2007. Persuasive effects of fictional narratives increase over time. *Media Psychology* 10 (1): 113–134.

Badcock, C. 2012. Making sense of Wason. *Psychology Today*, May 5. https://www.psychologytoday.com/us/blog/the-imprinted-brain/201205/making-sense-wason.

Cook, J., and Lewandowsky, S. 2011. *The Debunking Handbook.* St. Lucia, Australia: University of Queensland.

Damásio, A. 2009. When emotions make better decisions. Interview at Aspen Ideas Festival in Aspen, CO (July 4). https://www.youtube.com/watch?v=1wup_K2WN0I.

Ditto, P.H., and Lopez, D.F. 1992. Motivated skepticism: Use of differential decision criteria for preferred and nonpreferred conclusions. *Journal of Personality and Social Psychology* 63 (4): 568–584.

Drahl, C. 2014. How does acetaminophen work? Researchers still aren't sure. *Chemical & Engineering News* 92 (29): 31–32. https://cen.acs.org/articles/92/i29/Does-Acetaminophen-Work-Researchers-Still.html.

Emory University Health Sciences Center. 2006. Emory study lights up the political brain. *Science Daily*, January 31. https://www.sciencedaily.com/releases/2006/01/060131092225.htm.

Friendly, M. 2008. A brief history of data visualization. In *Handbook of Data Visualization*. Berlin Heidelberg: Springer-Verlag.

Gilbert, D. 2006. I'm O.K., you're biased. *New York Times*, April 16. https://www.nytimes.com/2006/04/16/opinion/im-ok-youre-biased.html.

Gottschall, J. 2012. Why storytelling is the ultimate weapon. *Fast Company*, May 2. https://www.fastcompany.com/1680581/why-storytelling-is-the-ultimate-weapon.

Green, M.C., and Brock, T.C. 2000. The role of transportation in the persuasiveness of public narratives. *Journal of Personality and Social Psychology* 79 (5): 701–721.

Guber, P. 2013. *Tell to Win: Connect, Persuade, and Triumph with the Hidden Power of Story*. New York: Crown.

Hasson, U. 2016. This is your brain on communication. https://www.ted.com/talks/uri_hasson_this_is_your_brain_on_communication/transcript#t-3558 (accessed May 16, 2019).

Heider, F., and Simmel, M. 1944. An experimental study of apparent behaviour. *American Journal of Psychology* 57:243–259.

Hillier, A., Kelly, R.P., and Klinger, T. 2016. Narrative style influences citation frequency in climate change science. *PLoS ONE* 11 (12). https://doi.org/10.1371/journal.pone.0167983.

Johnson, H.M., and Seifert, C.M. 1994. Sources of the continued influence effect: When misinformation in memory affects later inferences. *Journal of Experimental Psychology: Learning, Memory, and Cognition* 20 (6): 1420–1436.

Kahneman, D. 2011. *Thinking, Fast and Slow*. New York: Farrar, Straus and Giroux.

Kaplan, J.T., Gimbel, S.I., and Harris, S. 2016. Neural correlates of maintaining one's political beliefs in the face of counterevidence. *Scientific Reports*, December 6. doi: 10.1038/srep39589

Knight, W. 2017. The dark secret at the heart of AI. *MIT Technology Review*, April 11. https://www.technologyreview.com/s/604087/the-dark-secret-at-the-heart-of-ai/.

Leslie, A.M., and Keeble, S. 1987. Do six-month-old infants perceive causality? *Cognition* 25 (3): 265–288.

Lewandowsky, S. 2011. Popular consensus: Climate change set to continue. *Psychological Science* 22: 460–463.

Nyhan, B., and Reifler, J. 2010. When corrections fail: The persistence of political misperceptions. *Political Behavior* 32 (2): 303–330.

———— 2018. The roles of information deficits and identity threat in the prevalence of misperceptions. *Journal of Elections Public Opinion and Parties* 29 (2): 1–23.

Paul, A. 2012. Your brain on fiction. *New York Times*, March 18. https://www.nytimes.com/2012/03/18/opinion/sunday/the-neuroscience-of-your-brain-on-fiction.html.

Rodenberg, M. 2013. How tall (short) was Napoleon Bonaparte? *Finding Napoleon*, October 24. http://www.mrodenberg.com/2013/10/24/how-tall-short-was-napoleon-bonaparte/.

Schlich, T. 2013. Farmer to industrialist: Lister's antisepsis and the making of modern surgery in Germany. *The Royal Society Journal of the History of Science*, May 29. http://rsnr.royalsocietypublishing.org/content/67/3/245.

Semmelweis, I. 1861. *The Etiology, Concept, and Prophylaxis of Childbed Fever* (trans. C. Carter). Madison, WI: University of Wisconsin Press.

Stephens, G.J., Silbert, L.J., and Hasson, U. 2010. Speaker-listener neural coupling underlies successful communication. *Proceedings of the National Academy of Sciences of the United States of America* 107: 14425–14430. doi: 10.1073/pnas.1008662107.

Westen, D., Blagov, P.S., Harenski, K., Kilts, C., and Hamann, S. 2007. The neural basis of motivated reasoning: An fMRI study of emotional constraints on political judgment during the US Presidential Election of 2004. *Journal of Cognitive Neuroscience* 18: 1947–1958.

Wood, T., and Porter, E. 2019. The elusive backfire effect: Mass attitudes' steadfast factual adherence. *Political Behavior* 41 (1): 135. https://doi.org/10.1007/s11109-018-9443-y.

Zak, P. 2012. Empathy, neurochemistry, and the dramatic arc: Paul Zak at the Future of Storytelling 2012. https://www.youtube.com/watch?v=q1a7tiA1Qzo (accessed May 16, 2019).

Chapter 4

The Anatomy
of a Data Story

Data stories combine visualizations with narrative flow. This combination can breach the barriers between people and data, engaging the former and delving deeper into the latter.

—James Richardson, Research Director at Gartner

An ancient Jewish folktale dating back to the eleventh century captures the essence of why we must tell stories with our insights.

Truth, naked and cold, had been turned away from every door in the village. Her nakedness frightened the people. When Parable found her she was huddled in a corner, shivering and hungry. Taking pity on her, Parable gathered her up and took her home. There, she dressed Truth in story, warmed her and sent her out again. Clothed in story, Truth knocked again at the villagers' doors and was readily welcomed into the people's houses. They invited her to eat at their table and warm herself by their fire. (Simmons 2009)

Just like *Truth* in this allegory, cold, hard facts are often dismissed or ignored. However, similar to how *Parable* helped *Truth* gain access to the villagers' homes, stories can help insights enter into the minds of your audience. Truly, narrative and visuals help your data go places it can't go alone.

In the first few chapters, I've explored *why* the combination of data and narrative is so powerful. Now, I want to shift the focus to *what* exactly a data story is before I dive into *how* to tell stories with data. Without a clear understanding of what a data story is, you'll have a more challenging time crafting an effective one. As data storytelling has grown in popularity, so has the misuse of the term, which can be an obstacle to comprehending what a data story really is. All too often, data storytelling is positioned by various technology vendors and experts as being synonymous with data visualization. This flawed perspective on data storytelling means any data communication that involves data being visualized in some graphical or pictorial manner becomes a data story. We then find ourselves surrounded by "data stories" as visualized data is increasingly shared with us in a multitude of ways: data presentations, reports, dashboards, infographics, interactive apps, standalone data charts, alerts, and so on. However, the mere presence of a data visualization doesn't mean a data story is being told or even that one was intended. *Data visualization alone is not data storytelling.*

While visuals are an essential part of data storytelling, data visualizations can serve a variety of purposes from analysis to communication to even art. Most data charts are designed to disseminate information in a visual manner. Only a subset of data compositions is focused on presenting specific insights as opposed to just general information. When most data compositions combine both visualizations and text, it can be difficult to discern whether a particular scenario falls into the realm of data storytelling or not. The following continuum (see Figure 4.1) introduces five key attribute pairings that

THE DATA STORYTELLING CONTINUUM

Figure 4.1 If a data communication bears more attributes from the right side of the data storytelling continuum, it will likely be a better fit for telling a data story. If it has more attributes from the left side, then it may not be as well-suited for data storytelling.

can help you to identify situations in which data storytelling does or doesn't make sense:

- **Informative versus insightful.** Many people view these two words as synonyms and use them interchangeably. However, when you examine their definitions, you discover they're complementary but mean different things. *Informative* is defined as providing interesting or useful information. However, *insightful* goes beyond just being informative and is defined as exhibiting a clear, deep perception or understanding. Your data communication can be very informative—packed with lots of fascinating or helpful information—but that doesn't mean it will yield any specific insights. With informative content, you're choosing breadth over depth. In contrast, when you have a clear, distinct insight, your message can be more focused and more easily formed into an engaging data story.
- **Exploratory versus explanatory.** In some cases, you may provide your audience with interactive data visualizations that enable them to explore the data for themselves. Rather than providing them with a predetermined set of findings, you give the audience the freedom to filter and interact with the data to discover their own insights. When the end users control how they

view the data, you can't anticipate what specific insights they'll discover. While exploratory use cases are often compared to the children's "Choose Your Own Adventure" gamebooks, it's a false analogy that implies storytelling is occurring. The audience is not choosing between alternate data narratives—just differing slices or cuts of a dataset. On the other hand, when you have a particular insight in mind, it's much easier to explain—in the form of a data story—what your insight is and why it's important.

- **Abstract versus concrete.** In some cases, you may decide to share a wide array of information but not wish to steer your audience in a particular direction or toward a specific conclusion. When you keep the data more abstract, it frees up the data to be interpreted in a variety of ways. However, by leaving the possibility of having multiple interpretations, you forego the ability to tell a specific data story. In some situations, this tradeoff may be desirable because you don't want to limit the ways in which the data can be interpreted. In contrast, when the insights in your data composition are more concrete and specific, it is much easier to build a coherent data story because you are highlighting a particular view of the data.

- **Continuous versus finite.** Many data communications, such as automated dashboards, are set up to constantly refresh with new information as it becomes available. Similar to a CCTV camera or TV channel that's always on, they are constantly streaming new information. The data visualizations are constantly shifting to reflect the latest trends. As a result, interesting results can come and go. The transient nature of the data makes it difficult to tell stories. At any particular moment, you may have several potential insights begging for further attention and exploration—or none at all. In order to capture an insight before it disappears, you often need to take snapshots of the data like you might do with a camera. By capturing these fixed moments, you're able to break down what's happening and examine an insight at a much deeper level.

- **Automated versus curated.** Increasingly, we are becoming dependent on automated reports and dashboards to manage and navigate the vast amount of data permeating our daily lives. While these automated data compositions attempt to display information in meaningful ways, they can often miss or not fully comprehend the significance of certain insights. While innovations in artificial intelligence continually advance what computers can do, most of the responsibility for identifying key signals in the noise of information still falls to us humans. In order to bring out a story and tailor it for a specific audience, the data often needs to be curated by human hands. *To curate* means to "select, organize, and present information or content, typically using professional or expert knowledge" (Oxford 2019). While technology can easily handle the automated detection of anomalies in the data as well as the automated dissemination of information, it can struggle with the identification and communication of truly meaningful insights. Skilled human intervention is often required to assemble and weave together meaningful visual narratives for important insights.

Data storytelling represents one aspect of a larger analysis process that we go through to convert data into action. Obviously, before you can communicate an insight, you must find one. Many of the data compositions we create help us—or others—analyze data and pinpoint meaningful insights. Most of the items on the left side of the data storytelling continuum are associated with this initial step of *storyframing* (see Figure 4.1). With storyframing, you distill down the vast amount of data to a more targeted set of key metrics and dimensions (see Figure 4.2).

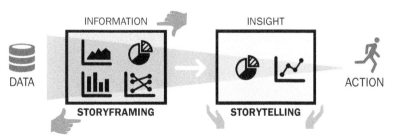

THE ANALYSIS JOURNEY: FROM STORYFRAMING TO STORYTELLING

Figure 4.2 While they may appear to be similar because they both leverage data visualizations, *storyframing* serves a different purpose than storytelling does. It attempts to create a window into the key information so potential insights can emerge from the data. *Storytelling* is appropriate when you want to explain a specific insight to an audience.

By limiting what data is focused on and choosing how it is visualized, you *frame* the potential stories that can emerge from the data. For example, if you built an infographic that compared the prices of various vehicles by fuel economy and safety rating data, it would lead people to different insights than if it focused on acceleration and horsepower data. Storyframing is primarily focused on providing useful information to an audience—which may or may not translate into meaningful findings.

However, once you have a key discovery you need to explain to others, you move beyond storyframing to storytelling. A different approach is needed for storytelling that gives the intended audience a solid understanding of the insight in question and compels them to act on it. *Data storytelling* can be defined as a structured approach for communicating data insights using narrative elements and explanatory visuals. Based on this understanding and definition of data storytelling, let's take a closer look at the anatomy of a data story.

The Six Essential Elements of a Data Story

> A story is not an accumulation of information strung into a narrative, but a design of events to carry us to a meaningful climax.
> —Robert McKee, screenwriting expert and author

When you are surrounded by all kinds of stories and consuming them on a constant basis, it may be difficult to pause and think about what makes a story . . . a story. People often turn to literary and news stories as frames of reference for what a story is. However, these two forms of stories can actually contrast sharply with each other. While narrative journalism found in *The New Yorker* magazine or on CBS's *60 Minutes* program can mirror many aspects of literary stories, most news stories are focused on *informing* an audience with a top-down, fact-based approach that typically follows the *inverted pyramid method*. For the past century, journalists placed the most newsworthy information (the lede) at the beginning of an article, followed by the next most important information down to the least important details at the end (see Figure 4.3). This method enables news articles to quickly grab a reader's attention

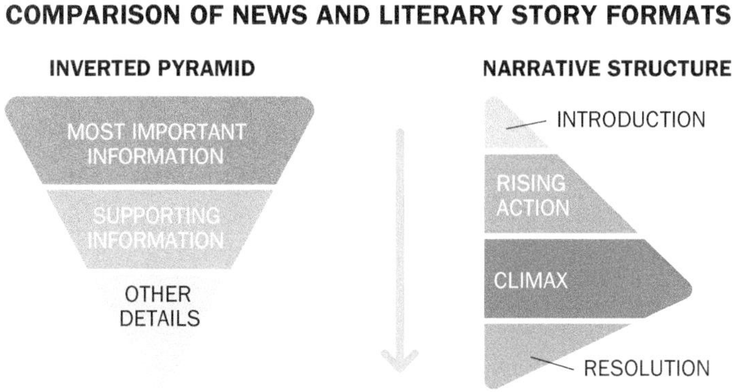

COMPARISON OF NEWS AND LITERARY STORY FORMATS

INVERTED PYRAMID

NARRATIVE STRUCTURE

MOST IMPORTANT INFORMATION

SUPPORTING INFORMATION

OTHER DETAILS

INTRODUCTION

RISING ACTION

CLIMAX

RESOLUTION

Figure 4.3 The inverted pyramid approach features the most important information at the beginning while a traditional narrative structure builds up to the most important information with a climax.

and make it easier for editors to trim less important details to fit an article into a smaller space if needed.

When this approach is applied to data, the audience will have the most salient information upfront at the outset of the communication. This format can make it easier for a busy, impatient audience to quickly scan the facts to determine if there's anything relevant or meaningful to them. In contrast, with the traditional narrative structure, the audience has to wait for the story to build up to a meaningful climax before they know what they have. While journalism's inverted pyramid approach may sound like a great idea, it comes at a price. By not following the traditional narrative structure, you forego the emotional power that can be gained from telling a story in this familiar manner. Essentially, you have the opposite of a story—you have *an antistory*.

If your goal is to quickly pass along information such as in storyframing situations, the inverted pyramid approach can be effective. It summarizes the critical information at the beginning, and then the audience can decide whether it wants to spend time combing through the supporting details or not. However, if the main intent is to explain your insight and engage your audience, the inverted pyramid approach cannot compete with the power of the traditional narrative structure. When your content engages the audience, they will better retain the information and will be more likely to act on it. Accordingly, rather than using a news story as the archetype for defining what a data story is, I will rely on the literary story as our model.

Before jumping into the specific elements of a data story, we must clarify the definition of a typical literary story. Wikipedia defines a narrative or story as "a report of connected events, real or imaginary, presented in a sequence of written or spoken words, or still or moving images, or both" (Wikipedia 2019). When you consider the books of J.K. Rowling, the plays of William Shakespeare, or the movies of Steven Spielberg, some may question whether stories based on data can even be equated with these types of works. However, data stories have more in common with these other forms of stories than you may realize. Many of the attributes found in works of literature, film, and theater can also be present in data stories. You'll see common traits in the following six essential elements that define a data story.

Figure 4.4   There are six essential elements to a data story.

Element 1: Data Foundation

The one unique characteristic that separates a data story from other types of stories is its fundamental basis in data. Although other stories may have various facts scattered throughout them, only data stories are derived entirely from data. While I don't boast about too many things, I do make a mean batch of chocolate-chip cookies. Just like the quality of a good chocolate-chip cookie depends on the concentration and quality of its chocolate content, a data story hinges on having a fact-based foundation. The building blocks of every data story are quantitative or qualitative data, which are frequently the results of an analysis or insightful observation. Because each data story is formed from a collection of facts, each one represents a work of nonfiction. While some creativity may be used in how the story is structured and delivered, a true data story won't stray too far from its factual underpinnings. In addition, the quality and trustworthiness of the data will determine how credible and powerful the data story is. In the next chapter, I'll take a deeper look at how data serves as the foundation of your data story.

Element 2: Main Point

In the classic John Hughes comedy *Planes, Trains, and Automobiles* (1987), actor Steve Martin plays a harried business executive who is stranded during his trip home before Thanksgiving. His character is stuck with an unwanted travel companion—a chatty traveling salesman played by John Candy. At one point, Martin's character gives pointed feedback to Candy's character about his penchant for sharing useless anecdotes:

> You know everything is not an anecdote. You have to discriminate. You choose things that are funny or mildly amusing or interesting. You're a miracle! Your stories have none of that. They're not even amusing accidentally! . . . When you're telling these little stories, here's a good idea—have a point. It makes it so much more interesting for the listener!

Similarly, a data story must have a central insight or idea—*it must have a main point*. While you can certainly share different facts in a data story, they should all support an overarching insight. By focusing on a main point, you ensure your data story has a clear purpose (*telos* appeal).

A random collection of interesting but disconnected facts will lack the unifying theme to become a data story—it may be informative, but it won't be insightful. For example, you may have uncovered a number of flaws in your company's hiring processes. All of these observations can tie into an overall insight that these faulty hiring procedures will end up stalling your company's growth this year if they're not addressed. Any additional insights that don't relate to this central message will only detract from it.

The American writer Mark Twain once said, "A tale shall accomplish something and arrive somewhere." The intended endpoint or destination of a data story is to guide an audience toward a better understanding and appreciation of your main point or insight, which hopefully leads to discussion, action, and change. However, if you have several divergent findings and try to combine them into a single data story, you may run the risk of confusing your audience or overwhelming them with too much information. To tell a cohesive data story, you must prioritize and limit what you focus on. Sometimes an insight deserves its own data story rather than being appended to the narrative of another insight.

Element 3: Explanatory Focus

Every data story should have an explanatory emphasis. Frequently, people make the mistake of just describing the data or insights. Being *descriptive* is not, however, the same as being *explanatory*. If you look more closely at the definitions of *describe* and *explain* there is a subtle but important difference.

> *To describe: To represent or give an account of in words or pictures.*
>
> *To explain: To make plain or clear; render understandable or intelligible.*

When you describe something, you provide details of its features or characteristics, especially related to *who, what, when,* and *where*. However, when you explain something, you go a step further to clarify the insight and ensure it is understood by your audience. An explanatory focus will often mean helping the audience to interpret the data by drilling into aspects such as *how* and *why*. For example, at the end of each mystery novel, private investigators such as Sherlock Holmes or Hercule Poirot don't just unveil who committed the crime, they reveal the perpetrators' methods (how) and motivations (why).

Likewise, a data story must go beyond just the descriptive details and seek to clarify how and why something occurred (or will occur). For instance, learning that sales were down 35% year-over-year in the last quarter is informative but not insightful. When you explain how recent marketing mistakes and aggressive moves by competitors contributed to this 35% drop in sales, you're helping the audience to better understand contextually what's behind the sales slump and how they can fix it. A data story will be based on deeper analytical reasoning than just presenting the surface-level details.

It's also significantly more challenging to be explanatory than just descriptive. We don't always have neat and tidy explanations for why or how things happened a certain way. There's going to be some degree of uncertainty and speculation. As a data storyteller, you need to be comfortable with sharing a point of view based on the best information that's available to you.

Element 4: Linear Sequence

Every data story follows a linear sequence in which supporting data points build on each other until a main point or conclusion is reached. The general definition of a *story* is "an account of a causally related or connected series of events." In a story, something notable happens, which triggers an effect on someone or something else—cause and effect. For example, in the popular children's story *The Wizard of Oz*, the protagonist Dorothy Gale encounters an interesting sequence of events—a tornado transports her to a strange land; she is given a pair of magical shoes; she meets some traveling companions while journeying down the Yellow Brick Road; a wizard sends her and her friends on a mission; and they melt a wicked witch with a pail of water (see Figure 4.5). Independently, these interesting events wouldn't amount to much, but sequentially, they create a powerful tale that is loved by multiple generations.

STORY: A LINEAR SEQUENCE OF EVENTS

Figure 4.5 Most literary stories such as *The Wizard of Oz*, written by L. Frank Baum, feature a linear sequence of events. Similarly, your key data points should be introduced in a sequential fashion and build support for your central insight.

In the case of data stories, you are unfolding a series of supporting data points that lead to a central insight. Instead of unloading all of the information on the audience at the same time, the data is exposed to them in stages. Each new detail should build on the previous ones, and through this sequential process the audience steadily gains an appreciation of the central issue or opportunity. Depending on how you share the data, the layout or presentation flow should provide a clear, sequential path for the audience to follow your points. If you are using a presentation to share your insights, you control how the data is revealed to your audience. With an emailed report, you lean more on the formatting, hierarchy, and other layout aspects to guide the recipients through the story sequence.

Element 5: Dramatic Elements

The beginning of the 2009 Pixar animated movie *Up* features a masterfully constructed montage that shows the loving relationship between the main character, Carl, and his wife, Ellie. In five minutes, we learn a great deal about Carl's life through a series of heartwarming scenes that span 60 years. By using various dramatic techniques—including music with no dialogue—*Up*'s directors Pete Docter and Bob Peterson set the stage for the audience to care about someone who would otherwise be dismissed as a grouchy old man (see Figure 4.6).

PIXAR'S *UP*'S MEMORABLE OPENING MONTAGE

1 Childhood Romance	2 Renovated Dream Home	3 Unfulfilled Desire for Family	4 Saving for Dream Vacation
5 Financial Setbacks	6 Grow Old Together	7 Bucket List Trip	8 Grieving Widower

Figure 4.6 In Pixar's movie *Up*, a short, five-minute montage at the beginning introduces us to the main character, Carl. Without this background information about the relationship with his wife, Ellie, we may have a much different opinion of Carl. Providing context or background information around your insights can help your audience to fully appreciate their value.

Data stories share similar dramatic fundamentals—setting, plot, characters, and so on—to those used in literature and film. In data stories, the application of these elements may not be the same or as obvious, but they are equally important. Just as the *Up* directors established the setting for their story with ample background information, you must also provide sufficient contextual details in order for your audience to properly grasp your insights. To set up a data story, you may need the audience to understand the time frame, data sources, past performance, and other details for context. For example, $2 million in sales in the last quarter may be bad or great depending on what the sales results were like in the same quarter last year.

From a plot perspective, *good* writers and directors never include random, unrelated events in their stories. Each event serves a purpose in advancing the story and developing the characters. Similarly, how you structure and sequence the information forms the backbone of your data story. Sometimes, what is left out is just as critical to the story's success as what is included. Although you may not believe a data story can have characters, the data that's being analyzed is often about people: customers, prospects, employees, partners, students, patients, voters, and so on. By highlighting the people behind the numbers, you add a more relatable human perspective to your data story. The more you incorporate dramatic elements into your data story, the more engaging it becomes for an audience on an emotional level. In Chapter 6, I will explore the different ways in which these dramatic elements come together to form a narrative structure for your data story.

Element 6: Visual Anchors

In the late 1920s, the film industry transitioned from silent films to talking pictures. Many people don't realize the influential English filmmaker Alfred Hitchcock's first 10 movies were actually silent pictures in which he was able to hone his visual storytelling skills. Hitchcock believed "silent pictures were the purest form of cinema" because the filmmakers were forced to rely solely on images—not sound—to develop their narratives. While not all literary forms of story require visual imagery, data stories must often be visually anchored. Because human beings are visual creatures, the visual depictions of the data end up being more powerful than just words or numbers.

Mark Twain offered advice to other writers when he said, "Don't say the old lady screamed—bring her on and let her scream." While data charts are frequently used in the analysis process to discover the insights, they can play an integral role in explaining them as well. With raw statistics being complex and difficult to comprehend, visualizing the numbers can make them more approachable and consumable for an audience (see Figure 4.7). The data visualizations can help people to see patterns, trends, and anomalies in the data that they would miss without them. In addition, other forms of imagery can also be used to complement and enhance the storytelling. For example, icons can be used to create mental shortcuts for your audience, or photos can add emotional emphasis to key data points. In Chapters 7 and 8, I will show how visuals shape the critical scenes of your data story.

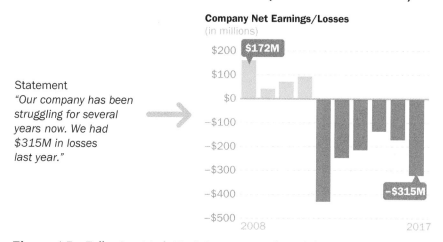

VISUALS CAN HELP YOUR DATA SPEAK (MAYBE EVEN SCREAM)

Figure 4.7 Following Mark Twain's argument that it's better to bring on the old lady and "let her scream" than to state "the old lady screamed," it's also often far more compelling to visualize the data than to merely state it.

All six of these elements are essential to creating an effective data story. If you ignore any of the components—no matter how compelling or interesting your data is—your analysis results end up being just information and you miss out on the many benefits that can be gained when the data is woven into a story. Now, some data stories will adhere more closely and deeply to the six elements than others. The more comprehensive ones will look and feel more like literary stories, whereas others with a lighter dose of the six elements may benefit simply from being more "storylike" in their delivery.

Data Stories Come in All Shapes and Sizes

Stories are memory aids, instruction manuals, and moral compasses.
—Aleks Krotoski, psychologist and journalist

Just as every insight will be slightly different, each data story will be unique. There is no set length for how long a data story will be, as it will depend on the information that is to be shared. Ideally, you should strive to tell the data story as concisely and clearly as possible, but the nature of your discovery and its intended audience will ultimately shape the breadth and depth of the narrative.

Frequently, the delivery method you choose can shape and influence how well you are able to tell a story with your data. Although we have many different ways of sharing information, they are not all equally well-suited to data storytelling and could potentially be geared more toward storyframing. Using the framework outlined above, you can see how certain types of data communications struggle to meet all of the essential criteria (Figure 4.8).

DATA COMMUNICATION METHODS BY USAGE OF SIX DATA STORY ELEMENTS

	DATA FOUNDATION	MAIN POINT	EXPLANATORY FOCUS	LINEAR SEQUENCE	DRAMATIC ELEMENTS	VISUAL ANCHORS	
Data Presentations	Yes	Maybe	Often	Often	Maybe	Yes	Curated
Curated Reports and Dashboards	Yes	Maybe	Often	Maybe	Maybe	Yes	
Infographics	Yes	Maybe	Maybe	Maybe	Maybe	Yes	
Data Visualizations	Yes	Maybe	Maybe	Maybe	Maybe	Yes	
Automated Reports	Yes	No	No	No	No	Yes	
Automated Dashboards	Yes	No	No	No	No	Yes	
Alerts	Yes	Yes	No	No	No	Maybe	Automated

Figure 4.8   All of these communications are based on data, but not all of them are equally conducive to data storytelling.

Currently, the automated forms of data communication (near the bottom of the table) can't support many of the essential elements of a data story. In the future, we will see an influx of artificial intelligence and machine learning attempting to bridge this gap, but it will be some time before storytelling can be fully automated in a significant way—if ever. While technology can make significant inroads into enhancing storyframing, it's too early to say what role it will play in actual data storytelling. For example, an automated dashboard can highlight random anomalies in the data, but no narrative really emerges until someone (or some intelligent agent) connects the dots and interprets what's happening.

In the field of data journalism, new interactive forms of data storytelling have emerged in the form of scrollers and steppers. Scrollers—sometimes referred to as scrollytelling—reveal the content as the user scrolls down a page. The digital publication *The Pudding* (https://pudding.cool), features a variety of scrollers or "visual essays" on a wide array of cultural topics. Steppers require the user to click through the steps or scenes of a story and are quite popular with major media sites such as the *New York Times, Wall Street Journal,* and *Vox*. Both of these interactive formats maintain a linear sequence, which is essential to a data story, but they can be challenging to design and execute.

In the case of data visualizations and infographics, the limited depth and sometimes static nature of the content can make it more challenging to meet all of the criteria. One of the most famous examples of an effective infographic is Charles Joseph Minard's map of Napoleon's Russian campaign of 1812 (Figure 4.9). The retired French civil engineer produced a vivid depiction of the French general's disastrous march into Russia. His thematic map has been referred to as "the best statistical graphic ever drawn" by acclaimed information designer Edward Tufte (2001). Minard skillfully combined multiple types of data—geography, time, temperature, distance, troop movement, and army size—in a single, two-dimensional graphic. The sequential flow and rich context of the visualization helps to tell the story of Napoleon's costly military mistake of invading Russia. While not all subjects demand intricate data visualizations such as this one, telling a multifaceted data story requires planning and skill to accomplish. Many modern data visualizations and infographics are laden with information but fail to achieve what Minard did in 1869—one year before his death at 89 years old!

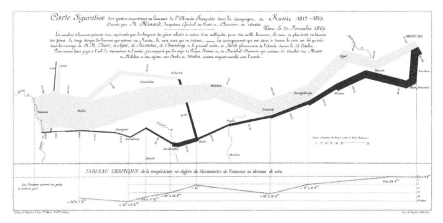

Figure 4.9 In 1869, retired French civil engineer Charles Joseph Minard produced this thematic map of Napoleon's infamous 1812 Russian campaign that highlights the French army's catastrophic loss of life.

Source: https://en.wikipedia.org/wiki/File:Minard.png. Public domain.

The more human-curated options such as data presentations or manual reports offer more potential to align with the data story elements. They are less confined in terms of space and offer more flexibility to sequence and annotate the insights as needed. However, despite these inherent advantages for storytelling, these data communications rarely end up resembling stories. Instead, their ability to convey rich levels of information is often misused or abused, resulting in unwanted data dumps. A simple insight may not require more than just a straightforward, clean data visualization to tell a story. Data visualization experts like Minard may be able to squeeze elaborate data stories into more confined spaces. However, in most cases, complex insights will require more robust approaches to form compelling stories. Ultimately, the data story and its delivery are heavily influenced by two key factors: the *storyteller* and the *audience*.

Every Data Story Needs a Storyteller

Every story is complicated until it finds the right storyteller.
—Anonymous

In the previous chapter, we saw how the Hungarian physician Ignaz Semmelweis failed to turn his life-saving discovery into a compelling data story. Nobody can question his dedication to the medical profession nor his passion to help save the lives of young mothers. However, he did fail in understanding how to effectively communicate his insights to others. During this same time period, two English medical practitioners were seeking to promote their own life-saving findings. Like Semmelweis, each of these individuals displayed an aptitude for statistics and applied these analytical skills to their medical profession. However, unlike Semmelweis, they identified ways in which they could share their ideas visually with others in order to see them embraced and adopted. These two individuals ended up becoming early pioneers in the use of data visualizations—rather than just the typical data tables—to explain their critical insights. They were both able to effect significant change in their respective fields, and much of their success can be attributed to their ability to tell a compelling story with their data.

One of these early data storytellers was Florence Nightingale (1820–1910), who is regarded as the founder of modern nursing and was also a skilled statistician. During the outset of the Crimean War (1853–1856), news reports of the horrendous treatment of wounded soldiers had stirred up public outrage, and the British government was eager to address the issue. Nightingale was asked to lead a group of 38 female nurses to improve the poor conditions at a British army hospital in Scutari, Turkey. Her nursing team encountered what Nightingale referred to as "the kingdom of hell"—an overcrowded, filthy hospital that lacked basic medical supplies, proper sanitation, and reliable record keeping. Despite some initial resistance from the overworked male medical staff, Nightingale and her nurses set in motion various changes to cleanliness, sanitation, ventilation, nutrition, and so on that eventually reduced the mortality rate from 42% to 2% (Wikipedia 2019).

Figure 4.10 Florence Nightingale (1820–1910)
Source: Florence Nightingale. Engraving, 1872, after A. Chappel. Credit: Wellcome Collection. CC BY.

In 1856, Nightingale returned to England as a national heroine and was touted as "the lady with the lamp" in English press coverage. Her newfound fame granted her an audience with Queen Victoria; in that meeting, she was able to secure a Royal Commission in 1857 to examine the health of the British army. Working with England's leading statistician William Farr, she discovered peacetime British soldiers aged between 20 and 35 had a mortality rate that was double that of the civilian rate due to unsanitary living conditions. In Crimea, Nightingale witnessed firsthand the ravages of unsanitary conditions as soldiers were 10 times more likely to die from contagious illnesses such as typhoid, cholera, and dysentery than from battle injuries. To introduce sanitation reforms, she needed to be able to convince army officers, government officials, and the general public of their merits.

To help audiences who were generally less data literate, Nightingale created a series of data visualizations—including her famous polar area diagram (Figure 4.11) that outlines the causes of death for British soldiers fighting in the Crimean War. Nightingale knew a visual representation of the statistics could be more persuasive, and the data charts could "affect through the eyes what we fail to convey to the brains of the public through their word-proof ears" (Bostridge 2015). In order to combat resistance to her proposed sanitary reforms, she distributed her polar area diagram through various pamphlets and reports, as well as having it featured as a fold-out in the front of Harriet Martineau's book *England and Her Soldiers* (1859).

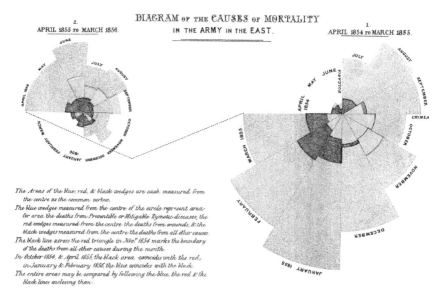

Figure 4.11 Nightingale's polar area charts (also called Nightingale Rose or Coxcomb charts) are divided into 12 wedges of equal size corresponding to a 12-month period. The height or radius of each color section is measured from the center and indicates the number of deaths from different factors: battle wounds (red), preventable contagious diseases (blue), and all other causes (black). Starting with the chart on the right (April 1854–March 1855), it shows the disproportionate number of deaths due to infectious diseases rather than battle injuries.

Source: https://edspace.american.edu/visualwar/nightingale/#gallery-1 Public domain.

Nightingale's efforts eventually convinced the British army's leaders that they needed to adopt better sanitary measures. Her sanitary reforms ended up saving the lives of countless soldiers during peacetime and in subsequent military conflicts. In an 1869 letter, Nightingale celebrated how sanitary reforms had, by her estimates, saved the lives of 729 soldiers and kept 5,184 men from being bedridden each year (McDonald 2012). While "the lady with the lamp" is well-known for her contributions to modern nursing, Nightingale was also a light to the field of statistics. In recognition of her contributions, she was fittingly recognized as the first female Fellow of the Royal Statistical Society in 1858. While she wasn't the first person to create statistical graphics, historian Hugh Small considers her to be "the first to use them for persuading people of the need for change"—making her a pioneering data storyteller and change agent (Small 1998).

The second data storyteller is Dr. John Snow (1813–1858), who is considered to be the father of modern epidemiology, which deals with the incidence, distribution, and potential control of infectious diseases in a population. Despite coming from a poor, working-class family, Snow had established a successful anesthesia practice and had even administered chloroform to Queen Victoria during her last two childbirths. At his time, most of Victorian society adhered to the *miasma theory* (including Nightingale) that diseases such as cholera or typhoid were caused by bad air or noxious odors from decaying organic matter. At the forefront of the industrial age, London became one of the most densely populated cities in the world with 2.5 million people. Most of the human waste went into a disorganized, antiquated system of cesspools and sewers that dumped into the River Thames—the main source of the city's drinking water.

Figure 4.12 Dr. John Snow (1813–1858)

Source: http://resource.nlm.nih.gov/101429151. Public domain.

When major cholera outbreaks occurred in 1832 and 1848, it was easy for government leaders and the medical community to associate these health crises with miasma due to the city's increasingly foul stench. However, Dr. Snow's experience and research led him to believe the diseases were not transmitted through the air but through the water. When he published a pamphlet titled "On the Mode of Communication of Cholera" in 1849, his supposition that cholera was spread through contaminated water fell on deaf ears. Notwithstanding this disappointing response, Snow remained unwavering in his belief that cholera was a waterborne disease, and he was undeterred in amassing more evidence to support his unorthodox position.

In the summer of 1854, the next cholera outbreak occurred right at Snow's doorstep within his Soho neighborhood. As families scrambled to escape the fast-moving, deadly disease, Snow went in the opposite direction toward what appeared to be the epicenter of the outbreak—the neighborhood surrounding the Broad Street water pump. While he could find very few visible impurities when he examined the water, Snow could see no other "common agent" that could explain the cholera outbreak. When he reviewed the initial list of 83 registered deaths in the first few days of the outbreak, Snow discovered "nearly all the deaths had taken place within a short distance of the pump," and he noted that only 10 of the fatalities were in closer proximity to a different street pump (Snow 1855). Through his investigative efforts, he was able to ascertain that five of these 10 individuals preferred the water of the Broad Street pump, and three more of the remaining outliers were children who may have drunk from the pump on the way to school. As he mapped the cholera deaths, he noticed a couple of interesting anomalies: A local brewery with 70 employees and a workhouse with 535 inmates were relatively unscathed during the outbreak even though they were closely situated to the water pump. It turned out that each had a private well, so they didn't rely on water from the Broad Street water pump.

Based on all these facts, Snow was able to convince the local civic leaders to remove the handle to the water pump a week after the outbreak started. While the cholera outbreak had probably subsided due to the exodus of people out of the neighborhood, what Snow accomplished was more than just a precautionary measure—it strengthened his position that cholera was a waterborne illness. Afterward, with the help of a local cleric, Reverend Henry Whitehead, Snow was able to uncover the source of the contamination—an infant that died from cholera had its soiled diapers rinsed into an old cesspit that leaked directly into the Broad Street pump's water supply. In various publications after the event, Snow shared a now-famous map of the Soho neighborhood with black bars indicating how many cholera deaths occurred at each residence or business in close proximity to the Broad Street water pump. In his December 1854 report to the Cholera Inquiry Committee, his data was depicted as a *Voronoi diagram* (see Figure 4.13) with a dotted enclosure indicating how many deaths were closer (in walking distance) to the Broad Street water pump than another local pump.

SNOW'S VORONOI DIAGRAM OF BROAD STREET PUMP DEATHS

Figure 4.13 This variation of Dr. John Snow's map of the Soho cholera outbreak has a red line indicating the reach of the Broad Street water pump by walking distance. Each cholera death is marked by a black bar. People outside of the dotted line would have been closer to a different water pump; however, due to the popularity of the Broad Street pump, its effects probably extended beyond this dotted line.

Source: http://johnsnow.matrix.msu.edu/work.php?id=15-78-55. Public domain.

Many people have debated whether Snow used the map to analyze the cholera epidemic or to convince the local board of governors to remove the water pump handle. As we learned in the previous chapter, data alone will rarely persuade a skeptical audience—narrative and visuals are often needed. However, what we can be certain of is that he used the map to help others see and understand how cholera was most likely transmitted through water. As Snow historian Steven Johnson noted, the map was a "marketing vehicle for his idea" that cholera was a waterborne disease (Borel 2013). Unfortunately, Dr. John Snow died from a stroke at the age of 45 in 1858 before he was able to complete his mission against cholera. He left the skeptical English medical community to continue its debate about the source of the deadly disease. However, when London's next cholera outbreak occurred in 1866, health officials issued the first known boil water advisory (BWA)—no small tribute to Snow's efforts (Wikipedia 2019).

Both Nightingale and Snow played an active role in the success of their insights. Not only were they able to identify meaningful, life-saving insights, but they were also able to communicate them in visually persuasive ways. As the storyteller, you will play an integral role in crafting and delivering your own data stories. The success of your narratives will depend on your ability to effectively perform the following tasks and responsibilities as the data storyteller:

- **Identify a key insight.** As the storyteller, you are responsible for directly or indirectly finding a meaningful data insight and deciding whether it needs to be prepared and shared as a data story.
- **Minimize or remove bias.** Everyone has inherent biases. It's important to be mindful of what yours are and strive to make your data communication as objective as possible.
- **Gain adequate context.** Prior to telling a data story, you should have ample contextual or background knowledge to ensure the insight is meaningful and will resonate with your audience.

- **Understand the audience.** Each insight will appeal to a particular audience. You will be instrumental in tailoring the content appropriately for the intended recipients.
- **Curate the information.** As the storyteller, you will apply your judgment to determine what data should be included or not included in the story. Too much information will overwhelm your audience, but too little may not catch their attention.
- **Assemble the story.** As you direct your data story, you will decide on the flow of the story and how the different elements come together. The organization or structure of the information can be just as crucial to the story's success as the underlying data itself.
- **Provide narration.** The storyteller acts as a guide through the information and helps the audience to understand and interpret the data. By adding your voice to the numbers, you unavoidably become a central part of the story.
- **Choose the visuals.** With various chart types and visualization options to choose from, your design decisions will shape how a key insight is perceived and understood by the audience. In this area, you wield significant influence as a single dataset can often be visualized in multiple ways and convey vastly different messages.
- **Add credibility.** The storyteller's reputation and expertise can lend credibility and authority to the numbers. If you are perceived as being untrustworthy or overly biased, you can undermine the validity of an otherwise sound data story.

On closer examination, it is hard to separate the storyteller from the story. The insights or ideas that someone shares through visual narratives represent discoveries that have enlightened that individual's mind. A data story can never be just an arbitrary collection of facts that is passively disseminated. Each data story is prepared and told by someone who cares about the numbers and sees a purpose in sharing the data with others. The presence of the data storyteller is felt not only in terms of their labors to create a compelling narrative and engaging visuals, but also in their conviction and advocacy to see the information is understood, embraced, and acted on.

Depending on the way data is communicated, the format can alter the data storyteller's involvement with the story and interaction with the audience. In some cases, the data is communicated *directly* to the audience. For example, Dr. John Snow presented his facts about the contaminated water to the board of governors to advocate the removal of the water pump handle. In these scenarios, the storyteller is present to guide the audience through the insights, explain what they mean, and respond directly to questions. Today, this form of *two-way* communication is common with most data presentations (see Figure 4.14). When you present directly to an audience, you have the opportunity to observe their response to the insights and assess their level of engagement. You also have the flexibility to speed up by skipping over content or to slow down so you can drill deeper into a specific data point as needed. In these direct scenarios, the data storyteller takes center stage in the delivery of the story content.

DIRECT OR INDIRECT COMMUNICATION DIFFERENCES

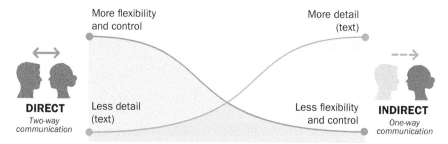

Figure 4.14 In direct communication scenarios, you have more control and flexibility as the storyteller. You can speak to the content so it doesn't need as much detail or text. However, in indirect scenarios, where you're not present to deliver the content as the storyteller, the opposite occurs. You can't be as flexible and must provide more annotations (text) to explain your insights.

When you're trying to reach a broader audience, however, it isn't always feasible for you to present your findings directly to everyone individually or in small groups. Instead, you must share your story using an *indirect, one-way* method such as a report, video, infographic, or article, which can be distributed more widely and consumed at your audience's convenience. Both Nightingale and Snow frequently relied on various print publications to propagate their ideas and messages to broader audiences. When you aren't able to personally guide the audience through your content, your verbal speaking points are replaced by text. With an indirect approach, you still have to anticipate the audience's needs and structure the content in a logical manner, but you must also provide ample commentary to ensure the audience can understand your insights. For example, annotations on the charts and diagrams take on greater importance when you're unable to directly explain them. Essentially, through text-based explanations, your influence as the data storyteller becomes embedded within the data story. While you may not be as overtly prominent in these indirect situations, your "backstage" guiding presence will be felt throughout the data story.

Beware of the Slideument

In 2006, *Presentation Zen* author Garr Reynolds coined the term *slideument*, which is a cross between a *slide deck* and a *document* (Reynolds 2006). This hybrid presentation is often used to address both direct and indirect communication needs: a slide deck to be delivered in person (direct) and a detailed report to be shared as a standalone reference or handout (indirect). It may seem efficient to create a single document that serves both of these needs, especially when you know you'll require a standalone document after the presentation is delivered.

While slideuments can be more visual, faster to create, and more approachable than standard reports, they should *never* be presented—only read. The intent of having more detailed text on slides in a slideument is to compensate for the *absence of the storyteller*. If a slideument is presented, the audience will struggle to read the text and listen to the storyteller at the same time. Rather than reinforcing your data narrative, the added detail will actually interfere with your verbal messages. If you anticipate needing a handout, it is often better to create two versions: a less-text-heavy presentation for presenting and a more-detailed slideument as a handout. Trying to use a single presentation for both use cases will only lead to a disappointing experience for you and your audience.

In the future, technology may assume the role of data storyteller in the form of intelligent agents that craft meaningful data stories from disparate data sources. In 1950, English mathematician Alan Turing developed the Turing test, which tests whether a computer exhibits intelligence that is indistinguishable from that of a human. While machines can mimic some of the required tasks involved with data storytelling, it will be some time before they can equal the natural storytelling ability of human beings.

Part of the delay is that many technology companies don't yet appear to understand what data storytelling really entails. For example, natural language generation (NLG) vendors tout the ability for their tools to translate data into text. Interestingly, they position data visualizations as being confusing or overwhelming, and they suggest people prefer automated text they can read. However, descriptive text that outlines in minutes what a well-designed chart can communicate in seconds doesn't represent the dawn of automated data storytelling. It's like advocating for WiFi-enabled fax machines because email isn't working. While advanced NLG technology will be a key element of future data storytelling agents, its focus will need to expand from simply *describing* data to *explaining* it—a much higher standard to achieve.

We are beginning to see glimpses of automated storytelling's potential. In November 2017 at Amazon's AWS re:Invent conference, technology firm AGT/HEED announced their partnership with the Ultimate Fighting Championship (UFC) league to leverage the Internet of Things (IoT) and artificial intelligence (AI) to provide more compelling fight coverage (Bradley 2018). By collecting real-time data from sensors in the fighters' gloves and octagon floor, video cameras, and audio microphones, AGT/HEED founder Mati Kochavi indicated the platform could generate 70 different insights from a single fight (see Figure 4.15). Its benefits extend beyond storytelling, of course—the Nevada State Athletic Commission approved an initial test of the glove sensors at UFC 219 to help address fighter safety and concussion protocol issues. The ability of this promising new technology to distill all of these disparate data points into a main insight and tell an engaging story will be the real test of its storytelling capabilities.

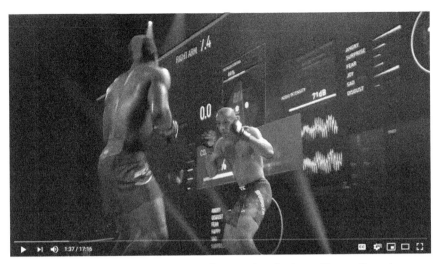

Figure 4.15 New AI-based storytelling technologies will transform how we view and consume sporting events. A partnership between AGT/HEED and UFC will pave the way for automated, real-time insights to be shared with MMA fans during and after contests.

Source: Reproduced with permission of HEED.

In 2016, the *Washington Post* developed an in-house automated storytelling technology called Heliograf. The media company designed the technology to target smaller audiences with automated news stories about local topics such as high school football or election results. Since its inception, Heliograf has been used to create approximately 850 short articles (Moses 2017). Based on narrative templates created by editors, Heliograf matches relevant data to corresponding phrases or keywords in the templates to develop and publish stories (Keohane 2017). Scot Gillespie, chief technology officer at the *Post*, stated, "Technology like Heliograf can be transformative for a newsroom, greatly expanding the breadth of coverage and allowing journalists to focus more on in-depth reporting" (WashPostPR 2017). While today the focus is on breadth, the technology may evolve to take on more in-depth content. For now, human beings are still the dominant storytellers, but we will see technology increasingly used to augment our storytelling abilities, helping us to both discover and tell better, richer data stories.

Know Your Audience before Telling Your Story

You've got to keep your finger on the pulse of what your audience is thinking and know what they'll accept from you.

—Dwayne Johnson, actor

One of the critical mistakes you can make as a data storyteller is to not know your audience. In fact, nothing can ruin a good data story faster than a disconnect between you and your audience. While we may not always recognize it, the audience plays an influential role in shaping a data story's focus and direction. To illustrate this point, let's pretend you've been asked to host a movie night for a group of Robin Hood fans you don't know. While there is a wide selection of Robin Hood movies to choose from (see Figure 4.16), it's difficult to pick the right one when you don't know your audience. Even though the movies all focus on the same tale of the famous English outlaw, each one tells the same story in a unique way that appeals to a specific audience. Without knowing more about the target audience, it's possible you could select something that misses the mark, such as showing Russell Crowe's 2010 PG-13 version to a group of six-year-olds.

ROBIN HOOD: SAME STORY, DIFFERENT AUDIENCES

Movie Title	Year	Actor	Rating	IMDB Genres		IMDB Score
Robin Hood	1922	Douglas Fairbanks	PG	Family	Romance	7.5
The Adventures of Robin Hood	1938	Errol Flynn	PG	Action	Romance	8.0
The Story of Robin Hood	1952	Richard Todd	G	Action	Family	6.9
Robin Hood	1973	Brian Bedford	G	Animation	Comedy	7.6
Robin and Marian	1976	Sean Connery	PG	Drama	Romance	6.6
Robin Hood: Prince of Thieves	1991	Kevin Costner	PG-13	Action	Drama	6.9
Robin Hood: Men in Tights	1993	Cary Elwes	PG-13	Comedy	Musical	6.7
Robin Hood	2010	Russell Crowe	PG-13	Action	Drama	6.7
Robin Hood	2018	Taron Egerton	PG-13	Action	Thriller	5.3

Figure 4.16   Even though each of these adventure movies focuses on the same general story of Robin Hood, they are targeted to different types of audiences. With your data story, you must determine the target audience and how the story should be tailored for them.

Source: IMDB.

Ideally, you would have an audience in mind before you begin your analysis. However, sometimes you may come across unexpected insights that may interest different people. First, you will want to align your data story to the right audience. Ideally, it will be shared with people who have the influence or power to effect change—individually or collectively. Second, you need to consider how your data story must be tailored for the intended audience. There are eight audience considerations that can influence how you approach your data story:

1. **Key goals and priorities.** If you understand what matters to your audience, you can ensure your data story is relevant and meaningful to them. No matter how interesting or unique your insights are, they must relate to things your audience cares about. For example, if your target audience is a group of executives who are focused on improving company sales, you will be hard-pressed to win their attention with topics unrelated to sales performance. It is important to make sure you are aligned with your audience's key objectives and strategic priorities so you don't waste anyone's time—yours or theirs.

2. **Beliefs and preferences.** Your audience will often have pre-existing beliefs, assumptions, and attitudes on different topics. Knowing upfront whether your audience will be accepting, resistant, or neutral toward your insights can influence how you prepare and tell your story. As Aristotle astutely said, "The fool tells me his reasons; the wise man persuades me with my own." In addition, you may need to consider what unique preferences they have for consuming the data. One audience may expect a PowerPoint presentation while another may prefer to read a detailed report. Some audiences may be accustomed to seeing data visualized a specific way (bar charts) and be resistant to unfamiliar approaches (scatterplots). A keen awareness of your audience's beliefs and preferences can help direct and streamline your data storytelling.

3. **Specific expectations.** When you share a data story, an audience may have a preconceived notion of what will be covered and have specific questions they would like to see answered. If you're not mindful of these expectations, the disconnect between you and your audience can become frustrating and lead to disappointment on both sides. Whenever possible, you must try to anticipate your audience's questions and weave thoughtful answers into your data story. If there's ever a mismatch between their expectations and

what your data story covers, you may want to reevaluate the focus of your data story.

4. **Opportune timing.** In Chapter 2, *kairos* was introduced as another form of persuasion from Aristotle's *Rhetoric* that emphasizes the importance of recognizing the right time and place to present an argument or idea. Even if you're presenting insightful data to the right audience, *the timing may be wrong*. For example, a shift in your audience's responsibilities or priorities can make your insight more or less timely. Depending on the circumstances, you may want to be more forward about sharing your data story if the interest is high or wait for a more opportune time when more pressing questions or concerns have been addressed.

5. **Topic familiarity.** Audiences will have different levels of domain knowledge and expertise. If your audience is less familiar with the subject matter of your data story than you are, you may need to spend time explaining key concepts and providing ample context before delving into your insights. For example, if your audience knows very little about mobile marketing—the focus of your analysis—you may need to provide some background information before revealing how it can be optimized. However, if your audience already has a deep knowledge of mobile marketing, you can dive directly into your insights. Their familiarity with the topic could also lead to deeper questions and the need for more detailed information on your insights.

6. **Data literacy.** Some audiences may not spend as much time interacting with data and may even be intimidated by the numbers. Whenever your audience is less data-savvy, you will want to reduce the amount of detail you cover and refrain from using unfamiliar jargon. They will be overwhelmed if you are not selective about the data you share with them. Rather than expecting your audience to understand statistical or analytics terminology, you need to be careful to translate the technical words and numbers into business terms they can follow. When you are presenting to a more data-literate audience, it does not mean you have permission to drown them in data either. Even data experts will appreciate a concise data story that is easy to follow. Extra

preparation may be required for more analytical audiences, as they may try to probe the edges of your insights.

7. **Seniority level.** For senior executives, time is a precious commodity. They often don't have the patience or bandwidth to sit through an entire data story without knowing it will be worth their time. They frequently expect an executive summary instead of a long report or presentation. However, one of the drawbacks of summarizing your analysis results is it can spoil the powerful narrative structure of your data story. Just imagine creating an executive summary for Shakespeare's *Romeo and Juliet*: "Both of the title characters kill themselves due to a miscommunication and unfortunate timing" would surely ruin the epic tale for most people. In Chapter 6, I'll discuss a strategy on how to address this executive summary challenge.

8. **Audience mix.** When you share a key insight, you may have a diverse audience with different backgrounds, interests, and agendas—making it somewhat difficult to balance their conflicting needs. For example, you may have both business and technical people in your intended audience. The strategic considerations that interest the business managers won't appeal as much to the technical folks, who in turn want to spend more time reviewing the technical details. When you encounter a diverse audience with competing needs, it may be helpful to establish upfront where, when, and how each group will receive the information they're after. Alternatively, you may decide it would be best to present a tailored version of the data story to each group separately.

Data visualization expert Edward Tufte once said, "If the statistics are boring, then you've got the wrong numbers." While this may be true in some situations, in others, you may simply have the *wrong audience* for your numbers. The critical question is: *How well do you know your audience?* The more you know about your audience, the more you'll be able to tailor your data story's content to their needs and interests. If you realize you don't really know your audience, you may want to hold off on sharing your story until you can learn more about them. Knowing your audience will not only influence how you tell your data story but also predicate its success.

The Strategic Use of Pre Meetings

Change can be difficult in business environments where politics and a lack of buy-in can suppress or kill good ideas. If your insights may be viewed as controversial or disruptive, you may need to use a more measured approach with how you communicate them to overcome resistance and gain support. In these situations, it can be an effective strategy to schedule pre meetings selectively with key individuals to review the findings before you present them in a group setting. This approach provides you with an opportunity to identify your potential allies and detractors. When you eventually present to the entire group, you will know beforehand which key decision makers support or oppose the insights.

In addition, during the process of meeting with these different individuals, you'll receive invaluable feedback that can inform how your data story can be strengthened and refined. For example, they may identify gaps in your analysis or recommend better solutions to the problems you've identified. They may know the priorities and preferences of key decision makers or who may be the most interested in the data. Pre meetings may require additional work, as you may need to adapt the content to each individual's viewpoint and specific interests. However, through the process of sharing your data story multiple times, you'll not only enrich the narrative but also improve how you tell it.

When It Makes Sense to Craft Data Stories and When It Doesn't

Storytelling is the essential human activity. The harder the situation, the more essential it is.

—Tim O'Brien, author

Data stories are powerful tools for sharing insights. However, not all insights need to be crafted into narratives. It takes time and effort to prepare and craft a data story—after you may have already spent hours analyzing the data to find your key insight. Rather than saying every insight requires "its story to be told," you can be selective based on the nature of each discovery. Clearly, the *value* of the insight is an important determinant in whether a particular finding merits being turned into a data story. For example, if a business insight could help your organization save a significant amount of money, it's most likely going to be worth your time to build out a data story for it. However, not even all high-value insights necessarily need to be made into full-fledged data stories. You must also consider how *easy or hard* the insight will be for the audience to understand and accept. Before you build out a data story for your insight, consider the following criteria that could influence your approach:

- **Agreeable versus unpleasant.** If your findings are favorable or acceptable to your audience, they won't need much convincing or persuading to accept them. However, as we saw in the previous chapter, people will primarily scrutinize data they don't like. For example, if the analysis of a new employee retention program showed it's ineffective, it's going to be harder for the people who developed and implemented the program to accept the poor results than for those who advocated for an entirely different approach.

- **Conventional versus disruptive.** When your insights fit within a conventional way of doing things, they will be familiar and comfortable to the audience. However, when your insights are disruptive or break with tradition, it is going to be harder for your audience to embrace or understand them. For example, it will be more daunting for your organization to embark on a completely new strategic direction than to simply refine or improve what it's currently doing.

- **Expected versus unexpected.** When your insight simply validates an expected result for your audience, it won't need to be explained as vigorously. However, when the results don't live up to the audience's expectations, more explanation will be required so they can understand what happened. While nobody likes bad news, even positive results that underachieve what was anticipated can be problematic. For example, if a product team was excited for the launch of a new feature, they will be surprised and disappointed when it only receives a mild or lukewarm response from customers. Without a data story to lean on, this team may struggle to grasp why the new capability wasn't better received.

- **Simple versus complex.** If an insight is fairly simple or straightforward to grasp, it may not need to be built into a data story. In fact, doing so may actually interfere with its ability to communicate in a direct manner. On the other hand, for a complicated, multifaceted issue, the audience may require more help and guidance from an expert to understand it. Using a data story, you can break down a complex insight into more manageable chunks so it is easier for the audience to follow and comprehend.

- **Safe versus risky.** When an insight highlights a change that is safe for the audience to make, you will see fewer concerns about embracing it. For example, if an insight aligns with the CEO's current viewpoint, her leadership team will be more willing to pursue it. However, if the insight instead conflicts with the CEO's position, her executives may be less enthusiastic to stake their careers on supporting it. The higher the risk—either from a personal or organizational perspective—the more people will need to be persuaded by a data story to accept the numbers.

- **Inexpensive versus costly.** Some insights can be relatively inexpensive to pursue and implement. In these situations, very little persuasion is required because most people will feel foolish to not act on these types of insights. Even if one of these insights doesn't pan out as expected, it won't have cost very much to test. However, in other cases, a high-value insight may also be costly to implement. For example, an analysis could reveal the potential for significant productivity gains, but only after a substantial investment in a new technology. Someone may consider this type of investment to be risky because the insight may not generate the anticipated return.

- **Intuitive versus counterintuitive.** Whenever your insight aligns with an audience's intuition, they're going to have a far easier time of accepting it. Conversely, human nature can be difficult to overcome when an insight doesn't align with common sense or someone's gut instinct. In these situations, you must summon the special powers of storytelling to somehow persuade an audience to consider information from a new perspective. Indeed, a data story may represent the only fighting chance that a counterintuitive insight has—sadly something I didn't discover until later in my career.

American mythologist Joseph Campbell said, "If you're going to have a story, have a big story, or none at all." The same philosophy applies to your insights in terms of data storytelling. If you have a big (valuable) insight to share, there's a good chance it's going to require a data story in order for it to be properly understood and accepted. In fact, between the insight's potential impact and what type of insight it is (hard vs. easy), there's a sweet spot called the *Story Zone* where data storytelling excels (see Figure 4.17). It spans an area where the insight is "medium-to-high" in value and falls into the "hard" category for the reasons listed above. While there's no guarantee that a data story can overcome all the factors of resistance, it represents the best chance you have at persuading your audience with numbers.

DATA STORYTELLING IS REQUIRED IN THE STORY ZONE

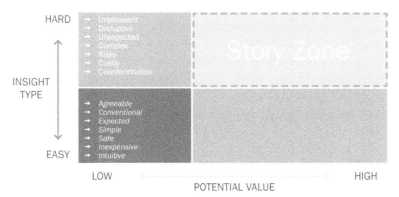

Figure 4.17 When an insight falls into the *Story Zone* (Hard/Med-High), it should be communicated as a data story. If it falls outside of the *Story Zone*, it is questionable if it should be told as a data story. It may not merit the extra time and effort (Hard/Low), or it may not necessarily need a data story to be understood and embraced (Easy/Med-High).

If you recall, in the personal experience I shared at the very beginning of this book I discovered an insight that challenged an entrenched practice of the ecommerce group for whom I was working. The survey data indicated customers didn't require or appreciate a specific shipping option that was provided to them. I would conservatively consider such an insight to be of at least medium value. It could have led to a re-evaluation of current practices and potentially the discovery of a better shipping option that the customers would truly appreciate. However, because the insight conflicted with the established beliefs of the department (and most importantly the department's leader), it was viewed as disruptive—potentially unexpected, risky, and counterintuitive. Regrettably, at the time, I didn't realize I should have invested more time in crafting a data story for the insight. Its short-lived fate was sealed before I even delivered it. Rather than making the same mistake as I did, you're now ready to turn your insights into engaging and persuasive data stories. In the next chapter, we'll begin by focusing on data—the fundamental building blocks of every data story.

References

Bostridge, M. 2015. Florence Nightingale: Saving lives with statistics. http://www.bbc.co.uk/timelines/z92hsbk (accessed 17 May 2019).

Borel, B. 2013. Happy birthday John Snow, father of modern epidemiology: A Q&A with Steven Johnson. *TEDBlog*, March 15. https://blog.ted.com/happy-birthday-john-snow-father-of-modern-epidemiology-a-qa-with-steven-johnson/.

Bradley, L. 2018. How real-time data, insights, emotion can enhance UFC storytelling. *SportTechie*, January 3. https://www.sporttechie.com/real-time-data-insights-emotion-enhance-ufc-storytelling/.

Keohane, J. 2017. What news-writing bots mean for the future of journalism. *Wired*, February 16. https://www.wired.com/2017/02/robots-wrote-this-story/.

McDonald, L. (ed.) 2012. *Florence Nightingale and Hospital Reform: Collected Works of Florence Nightingale*, Vol. 16. *Waterloo, Ontario, Canada*: Wilfrid Laurier University Press.

Moses, L. 2017. The *Washington Post*'s robot reporter has published 850 articles in the past year. *Digiday*, September 14. https://digiday.com/media/washington-posts-robot-reporter-published-500-articles-last-year.

Oxford Living Dictionaries. 2019. Curate. https://en.oxforddictionaries.com/definition/curate (accessed 17 May 17, 2019).

Planes, Trains, and Automobiles (1987). [Film]. John Hughes. Dir. USA: Paramount Pictures.

Reynolds, G. 2006. "Slideuments" and the catch-22 for conference speakers. Presentation Zen, April 5. https://www.presentationzen.com/presentationzen/2006/04/slideuments_and.html.

Simmons, A. 2009. *The Story Factor: Secrets of Influence from the Art of Storytelling*. New York: Basic Books.

Small, H. 1998. Florence Nightingale's statistical diagrams. Presentation to Research Conference organized by the Florence Nightingale Museum, St. Thomas's Hospital, March 18. http://www.florence-nightingale-avenging-angel.co.uk/GraphicsPaper/Graphics.htm.

Snow, J. 1855. *On the Mode of Communication of Cholera*, second edition. London: T. Richards. https://archive.org/stream/b28985266#page/40/mode/2up.

Tufte, E.R. 2001. *The Visual Display of Quantitative Information*. Cheshire, CT: Graphics Press.

WashPostPR. 2017. The Washington Post leverages automated storytelling to cover high school football. *WashPost PR Blog*, September 1. https://www.washingtonpost.com/pr/wp/2017/09/01/the-washington-post-leverages-heliograf-to-cover-high-school-football/.

Wikipedia. 2019. Boil-water advisory. https://en.wikipedia.org/wiki/Boil-water_advisory (accessed May 17, 2019).

——— 2019. Florence Nightingale. https://en.wikipedia.org/wiki/Narrative (accessed May 17, 2019).

——— 2019. Narrative. https://en.wikipedia.org/wiki/Narrative (accessed May 17, 2019).

Chapter 5

Data

The Foundation of Your Data Story

"Data! Data! Data!" he cried impatiently. "I can't make bricks without clay."
—Sherlock Holmes by Sir Arthur Conan Doyle, author

In 2015, a team of German researchers made an astounding discovery: eating chocolate could actually accelerate weight loss. The researchers ran a three-week clinical trial with a group of adults aged 19 to 67 who were assigned to one of three diet groups: a low-carbohydrate diet, a low-carb diet with a daily chocolate bar, and a control group. Head research director of the Institute of Diet and Health Dr. Johannes Bohannon found people who were on a low-carb diet lost weight 10% faster when they consumed dark chocolate on a daily basis. The team's research paper was published in the *International Archives of Medicine*, and the findings were mentioned in several media outlets such as the German newspaper *Bild*, the UK's *Daily Star*, the *Irish Examiner*, and many others (see Figure 5.1).

Figure 5.1 Multiple news publications featured the German researchers' findings on the health benefits of chocolate.

However, the research was actually part of an elaborate hoax for a documentary film on junk science. The producers of the film wanted to show how easy it was to turn bad science into headlines for fad diets. Dr. Johannes Bohannon is actually John Bohannon, a science journalist. He does have a PhD in molecular biology—just not for humans but, instead, for bacteria. The Institute of Diet and Health was just a made-up website. The clinical trial was scientific, but its results were dubious due to the limited sample size—only *15 people*. From the rigorously "peer-reviewed" science journal that accepted the article without edits for 600 Euros, to the countless media publications that touted the appealing research, no one questioned this small but crucial detail about the study. As Bohannon explains:

> Here's a dirty little science secret: If you measure a large number of things about a small number of people, you are almost guaranteed to get a "statistically significant" result. Our study included 18 different measurements—weight, cholesterol, sodium, blood protein levels, sleep quality, well-being, etc.—from 15 people. (One subject was dropped.) That study design is a recipe for false positives.
>
> Think of the measurements as lottery tickets. Each one has a small chance of paying off in the form of a "significant" result that we can spin a story around and sell to the media. The more tickets you buy, the more likely you are to win. We didn't know exactly

what would pan out—the headline could have been that chocolate improves sleep or lowers blood pressure—but we knew our chances of getting at least one "statistically significant" result were pretty good. (Bohannon 2015)

In this example, the researchers knew their results were going to be invalid. In fact, it was their exact intention to make a point about bad science. In their book on research design, authors Light, Singer, and Willett state rather bluntly, "You can't fix by analysis what you bungled by design" (Light, Singer, and Willett 1990). In this case, the very foundation of the chocolate diet study was shaky before any analysis or storytelling was even done. It illustrates how the data stories we seek to tell are only as strong as the data foundation on which they're built. If you are not careful with your analysis, weak or flawed data can unravel all of the hard work you put into building a compelling data story. When your data foundation crumbles and falls apart, all you're left with is a misleading narrative that won't help anyone—you or your audience.

The purpose of this chapter is *not* to teach you how to analyze data. An entire library wing could be devoted to explaining different analysis techniques and tools. For this chapter, I will assume you are capable of finding insights—independently or with assistance from a data specialist (or maybe an intelligent machine). Whether your insight comes from examining a simple data table or from building an advanced statistical model, it will face the same challenge: to be properly understood and accepted by others. The first part of this chapter will focus on ensuring you have a viable, meaningful insight before you even consider building a data story. The second part will ensure you—*the discoverer of the insight*—don't unknowingly interfere with its effective communication.

Examine the Building Blocks of Your Data Stories

It is not the beauty of a building you should look at; it's the construction of the foundation that will stand the test of time.

—David Allan Coe, songwriter

Data points are the building blocks of every data story. If you are building a new home, you want to be sure you're using high-quality concrete to pour its foundation. While a home builder can certainly choose to cut corners by using unsuitable or cheaper concrete, it is not a strategy for long-term success. Eventually, a price will be paid by the builder. The costs of warranty issues and loss of future business due to negative feedback from unhappy customers will catch up with the contractor. Similarly, as you are both the architect and master builder of your data stories, you need to ensure your insights are based on data that is both *relevant* and *trustworthy*. Just like inappropriate or defective materials can weaken a building's foundation, insights drawn from irrelevant or unreliable data can ruin what could have been a well-crafted data story.

Relevance

Are your insights based on the most relevant and appropriate data? The relevance of your data will ultimately depend on the types of questions you're trying to solve with it. To be relevant, your data must be applicable to the situation or problem you're attempting to analyze and understand. The more directly related the data is to the topic at hand, the higher the number of insights it can potentially yield. After answering an initial set of questions, the data might need to be broadened or deepened to answer follow-on questions. You need to assess whether your data, like a good building foundation, will be able to support the width and height of an entire data story.

For example, if you were sharing interesting real estate trends with a group of Phoenix-based investors, your insights will be more relevant, applicable, and impactful if they are based on data from the actual Phoenix, Arizona, market. If your findings are based on data from outside regions (Las Vegas, Nevada, or Austin, Texas) or nationwide statistics, a Phoenix-based audience may question whether the same trends apply to their local area. In addition, the freshness or timeliness of your data can also impact its relevance. Data can have a limited shelf life and become less and less useful over time. For example, three-year-old data on the Phoenix market isn't going to be as useful as data from the past 6–12-month period. While a historical perspective on Phoenix trends may provide good context, the investors will place more weight on recent results than what happened three or more years ago.

Frequently, it's not possible to acquire the most ideal data to answer every business question. The data may not exist because nobody thought to collect it. Or, it may exist, but you may not be able to access it because it's owned by another organization. Even when you possess the right data, it may have inherent reliability or completeness issues that prohibit its use. In these situations, you may need to work with less-than-ideal datasets. They may not be as relevant or appropriate, but they might be more accessible or reliable. If your audience understands the inherent data challenges, it may appreciate your willingness to explore other related datasets. Alternatively, the audience members may reject anything that isn't based on the data they envisioned. Understanding your audience and its tolerance for relevancy will be important before building your data story.

Trustworthiness

Are your insights based on data that is accurate and reliable? Trustworthy data is correct or valid, free from significant defects and gaps. The trustworthiness of your data begins with the proper collection, processing, and maintenance of the data at its source. However, the reliability of your numbers can also be influenced by how they are handled during the analysis process. Clean data can inadvertently lose its integrity and true meaning depending on how it is analyzed and interpreted. For example, if you were to average a set of averages, you would miscalculate the true statistical mean. If you transposed a figure as you copied it from one system to a spreadsheet, you could make erroneous calculations and incorrect conclusions. No data is ever going to be perfect—every dataset is going to have its imperfections. However, you should strive to ensure your data is as clean, complete, and reliable as possible—*before* and *after* you've interacted with it.

Several years ago, in the early days of online marketing, a product marketing manager made some minor adjustments to his product's main landing page so it would be better optimized for search engines. Shortly thereafter, he witnessed a massive spike in traffic to his product page. He immediately printed out the chart and ran around telling everyone in the company—including the vice president of marketing—of his successful search engine optimization (SEO) efforts. Unfortunately, in less than five minutes, an analyst found the traffic spike was actually generated by a website monitoring tool that had sent artificial traffic to the product landing page as part of a test. Because the surge in webpage traffic aligned with the story the marketer wanted to tell, he overlooked validating whether the story was actually true. Not only did this marketer embarrass himself, but he lost credibility within the organization.

While you can't always guarantee your data will be free of imperfections, every effort should be made to ensure your audience can trust your insights. Most people are not trying to intentionally deceive or manipulate others with data. Carelessness is a far more common problem, but it can be equally damaging to a data story. Going back to Aristotle's *ethos* appeal mentioned in Chapter 2, your competence and character as a data storyteller will directly contribute to whether your insights are believed and embraced by audiences. When you ensure the accuracy and reliability of your numbers, not only does your story gain credibility, but *you do as well*. This is important because you give your audience the confidence it needs to move forward with your insights.

As we know from Chapter 3, people can have a hard time accepting information that conflicts with their current beliefs or viewpoints. An analytical audience might even question insights that "sound too good to be true." The validity of your data will often be the first thing to be questioned by an audience, so it's critical you're prepared to defend it. In some cases, you may build supporting details preemptively into your story or have them ready in an appendix if questions arise. Ultimately, the storyteller–audience relationship is built on trust. Even when an audience may not agree with all your points, they can still respect your perspective and expertise, especially if you're trying to anticipate their data concerns.

Every Data Story Needs a Central Insight

The purpose of computing is insight, not numbers.
—Richard Hamming, mathematician

Before you can even consider creating a data story, you must have a meaningful insight to share. One of the essential attributes of a data story is a central or main insight. Without a main point, your data story will lack purpose, direction, and cohesion. A central insight is the unifying theme (*telos* appeal) that ties your various findings together and guides your audience to a focal point or climax for your data story. However, when you have an increasing amount of data at your disposal, insights can be elusive. The noise from irrelevant and peripheral data can interfere with your ability to pinpoint the important signals hidden within its core.

Rather than being overwhelmed and ending up lost in a mountain of data, you need to be able to ask the right questions of the numbers. French philosopher Voltaire highlighted the significance of questioning when he said, "Judge a man by his questions rather than his answers." As you approach the data, the quality of your questions will influence the value of the insights you're able to uncover. Data scientists Hilary Mason and D.J. Patil acknowledge this key skill in their book, *Data Driven: Creating a Data Culture*. The ability to ask the right questions "involves domain knowledge and expertise, coupled with a keen ability to see the problem, see the available data, and match up the two" (Patil and Mason 2015). Without adequate domain knowledge and context, it's difficult for anyone—including data scientists and analysts—to ask the right questions and identify meaningful insights.

While a question can launch you on a valiant data quest, it's not enough. In the ancient Greek tale of *Theseus and the Minotaur*, the young Greek hero volunteered to be locked in King Minos's labyrinth as a sacrificial tribute for the half-bull, half-man Minotaur. Theseus was determined to slay the Minotaur with his bare hands and end Athens' obligation to send a group of young tributes every nine years to be devoured by King Minos's monster. When his ship arrived in Crete, the king's daughter Ariadne fell in love with the handsome Athenian prince. Before Theseus entered the maze, the princess secretly passed him a ball of thread that could be tied to the entrance. Ariadne knew that even if Theseus defeated the Minotaur, he wouldn't be able to find his way out of the dark, confusing labyrinth without the thread to guide him back. While Theseus had a purpose (kill the Minotaur), he didn't have a complete plan (escape the labyrinth).

When you're analyzing data, it can often feel like an endless maze with multiple potential paths to follow. The right question can provide direction and purpose. Nevertheless, it should still be accompanied by a plan that can lead you safely in and out of the numbers. If you're not adequately prepared for how you're going to question the data, you can easily get lost in the process. Each question you ask the data should be tied to a specific audience that cares about the answer to the query. If you know your audience fairly well, you can apply a simple framework called 4D (four dimensions) that can serve as a guide as you navigate through the numbers. With a particular audience in mind (chief marketing officer, ecommerce team, investors, branch managers), you can use four interconnected dimensions—*problem, outcome, actions,* and *measures*—to keep your bearings in the data and sharpen the focus of your analysis (see Figure 5.2).

**THE 4D FRAMEWORK FOR FINDING
MEANINGFUL INSIGHTS**

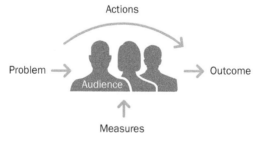

Figure 5.2 For each unique audience, the four dimensions of the 4D Framework can give you critical context and keep your analysis more focused.

Problem: A key challenge or issue your audience wants to address. Often, it is something they would like to make more efficient or effective than it currently is.

Outcome: A strategic goal or desired end result your audience wants to achieve. If a problem represents something occurring in your *current* state, an outcome signifies a preferred *future* state. The more explicit the outcome (a specific target), the more helpful it will be to your analysis.

Actions: The key activities and strategic initiatives your audience is putting into place to fix a problem or achieve a desired outcome. These actions attempt to close the gap between where an organization currently is and its desired future state.

Measures: The key metrics and other data used to highlight the problem, monitor the effectiveness of the initiatives, and define the achievement of the desired outcome.

Your everyday use of a GPS device illustrates how these four dimensions can help you maneuver strategically through the maze of data and find answers to your questions (see Figure 5.3). Your starting point usually involves exploring something that's broken—a *problem*—which often reflects your audience's present or current state. Frequently, there will be a destination in the form of a better *outcome* or future state in which the identified problem has been addressed. In order to reach this

THE 4D FRAMEWORK: GPS ANALOGY

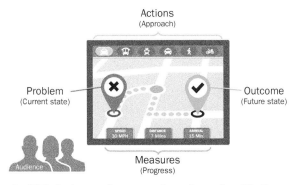

Figure 5.3 A GPS device analogy can show how the 4D Framework can be helpful in your analysis for a specific audience. To not get lost in the data, you should understand the audience's starting point (problem), their destination (outcome), their route and mode of transportation (actions), and their progress to the goal (measures).

endpoint, a path or approach has been chosen. Much like selecting the mode of transportation or the route on a GPS device, you'll focus on the different *actions* or strategic initiatives that the audience is currently executing to achieve the desired end result. In order to measure the progress to the goal or target, you'll have different *measures* or metrics that indicate how far the audience has come and how much further they have to go. For each analysis scenario, the more deeply you understand these four dimensions for a specific audience, the better positioned you will be to question the data the right way and identify useful insights.

Whether you're a data novice or an expert, you may question whether all four of the dimensions are really necessary. If time is not an issue for you, you can spend as much time as you wish foraging through the data for insights. However, while you might have an abundance of data, you probably don't have an equivalent abundance of time. Each dimension provides guidance that can keep you focused and reduce the time you spend looking for answers to your questions.

- *Why do you need to know the problem?* The better you grasp a problem and its consequences, the better prepared you will be to uncover its potential causes. If you're not able to clearly and confidently articulate what the problem is, your investigation will meander and struggle to isolate potential solutions. For example, if you were examining a business-to-business (B2B) lead-generation issue, you may look in the wrong places for answers if you don't understand the core problem. Before you dive into the numbers, you may want to discuss the problem with your audience to gain more context and direction. Key stakeholders usually don't mind sharing their thoughts on the challenges they are facing if you take time to meet with them. While your analysis may take you down unexpected paths, having a solid starting point and baseline understanding will be important to your success.

- *Why do you need to know the outcome?* Knowing the desired outcome or goal state helps you gauge what's been accomplished so far and what's left to accomplish. While you may understand the problem, without a desired end result or target, it's hard to know to what degree the problem must be fixed. Going back to the B2B leads example, there's a big difference between having to increase marketing leads by 25% compared to having to double them (100% increase). If the ideal outcome or target hasn't been properly defined, it may be important to establish what it is before you go too far into your analysis—even if you have to set or assume a reasonable target on behalf of your audience.

- *Why do you need to know the actions?* Frequently, your analysis will center around key actions or strategic initiatives because they represent the actual levers that are being pulled today to achieve the desired outcome. For example, the B2B marketing team may be focused on expanding its digital marketing efforts and improving the performance of its event marketing. Rather than examining all of their marketing efforts, you can begin exploring how these two areas are contributing to the overall lead generation goals. By evaluating the key activities and strategic priorities of your audience, you're focusing on areas where time and resources are being spent—and that are typically relevant and "top of mind" for your audience. Any discoveries you uncover in these areas will generate interest from the audience and are more likely to be acted on.

- *Why do you need to know the measures?* You need a good sense for what the critical measures of success are. Because not all of the data will be relevant or useful, you need to determine which metrics and dimensions will be instrumental to understanding the identified problem or achieving the desired outcome. In the B2B marketing example, the key measures might be inquiries, qualified leads, and cost per lead. Once you've isolated the necessary metrics and dimensions, it will then be important to thoroughly understand what they mean—*and don't mean*—before you begin analyzing and interpreting them. At many companies, it's not uncommon for key metrics to be misinterpreted. Depending on how a metric is collected, processed, and calculated, its meaning can vary dramatically.

  For example, a simple metric like "customers" can be defined differently across different functions within the same organization. One department might define customer as individuals who have made a purchase in the last 12 months. Another group might define a customer as anyone who has made a purchase in the last 10 years. Yet another team might factor out companies who were referred and serviced by a partner. Without clarity on a metric's definition, you are susceptible to misinterpreting what it actually means and to misusing it.

In many situations, you may begin with a good understanding of just one of the 4D dimensions. For example, you may have a specific key performance indicator (KPI) in mind (net promoter score, or NPS) or know what the problem is (low retention). However, if you only consider one or two of the dimensions, you will have an incomplete perspective, which will limit the quality and quantity of insights you're able to draw from the data. On the other hand, if you expand your knowledge to cover all four dimensions for an intended audience, you will have a more comprehensive, focused perspective that will enable you to ask better questions of the data. Based on adept questioning of your data, you'll be able to emerge from the data labyrinth with precious insights that could help change your team, department, or organization for the better. As William Edward Deming said, "If you do not know how to ask the right question, you discover nothing." The 4D framework can help you to ask better questions of your data and assist you in emerging safely from the data labyrinth with something in hand that warrants a story.

Do You Have an Actionable Insight?

Without knowledge, action is useless, and knowledge without action is futile.

—Abu Bakr, religious leader

Once you've found an insight that has shifted your understanding of something, you must determine whether it merits becoming the basis of a data story. As the climax of your story, your insight must provide a good payoff for the audience's focus and attention. Because it takes time and effort to craft an effective data story, you need to be sure you have something that is both meaningful and actionable. Consequently, every insight must pass the "so what?" test before it can be made into a data story. Digital marketing evangelist and author Avinash Kaushik recommends evaluating each insight in the following three ways, which form the foundation of his "so what?" test (Waisberg 2016):

1. Why should your audience care?
2. What should they do about it?
3. What's the potential business impact?

If you can't find a compelling reason why your insight will matter to the audience, it shouldn't be shared with them. If it's not clear what they should do about the insight, it's just nice-to-know information but nothing more. Finally, if the potential business impact is insignificant or minimal, it will be hard for it to generate attention when most people will have more important or urgent matters to address.

When you evaluate your insight with these three questions, you're determining whether or not you have an actionable insight that needs its story to be told. The term *actionable insight* has been used fairly loosely in the business world as an interesting finding or result. Ultimately, an insight that persuades people to act is going to be far more valuable than one that simply answers a question or piques curiosity. Actionable insights sit at the apex of the data pyramid, and they are the genesis of effective data storytelling that leads to change. To help in assessing the actionability of your insights, I've assigned a couple of criteria to each of Kaushik's "so what?" questions (expanding the three originals into six):

Why Should Your Audience Care?

1. **Valuable.** Depending on the perceived return of your insight, monetary value can be a motivating factor that pushes indecisive people off the fence to act. As human beings, we are generally conditioned to resist change and risk. However, if the perceived upside significantly outweighs any downside, your audience will be more confident in pursuing it. Not all insights will pan out as expected, but generally, the greater the reward with acceptable risk, the less hesitant your audience will be to act.
2. **Relevant.** An insight can be a strong signal for one audience and noise for another. The more relevant the insight is for the intended audience, the more likely the insight will receive proper

attention and drive people to act. The timeliness of an insight can also contribute to its relevance. Some insights may be time-sensitive and may become less and less relevant (and useful) as time passes. A relevant, timely insight for the right audience can help stimulate action (as per Aristotle's *kairos* appeal from Chapter 2).

What Should They Do about It?

3. **Practical.** While your insight may be bold and daring, it should still be perceived as feasible and realistic. In some cases, you may need to temper a great insight by breaking it down into something more manageable that your audience can handle. For example, if you discovered employees could significantly benefit from data literacy training, you may propose a pilot project to first test the idea with a local team before recommending a company-wide data literacy program. Even though your insight could have broader repercussions, it's important that your audience feels as though they have the power or ability to act on it. If your insight overwhelms the audience, it could stall and go nowhere.

4. **Specific.** Sometimes insights based on high-level metrics can uncover interesting anomalies but lack sufficient detail to drive immediate action. For example, knowing your revenue is up 35% this month may feel good, but it doesn't indicate how it was achieved and whether it can be replicated or amplified. Clarifying that the 35% revenue increase is directly attributed to a BOGO (Buy One, Get One Free) promotion is more specific and complete, raising interest in doing more of these types of promotions. If an insight doesn't adequately help to explain why something occurred, it's not yet actionable and may need deeper probing before it's ready for primetime. The more precise and conclusive your insight is, the clearer it will be to your audience how they can run with it.

What's the Potential Business Impact?

5. **Concrete.** The more concrete you can make your insight, the more likely it will drive action. For example, you would be

thrilled to discover a way to increase your company's productivity by 18%. However, this figure could be made even more concrete by sharing the estimated revenue it could generate: $800,000. If you can monetize the impact of your insight, it will draw more attention and motivate people to act on it.

6. **Contextualized.** In order for your insight to be actionable, it needs to be accompanied with an adequate amount of context so your audience can fully appreciate its significance or uniqueness. Frequently, a standard or benchmark is required so the audience can fully comprehend the meaning of an insight and be motivated to act on it. For example, without context, product sales of $3.4 million in a particular month will mean very little—it is just a fact, not an insight. It's only when you know what the sales were the previous year ($1.1 million) that the result gains more significance (209% growth!). Without some kind of yardstick, a context-less finding may only raise questions and objections rather than generate action.

The more an insight aligns with these six characteristics, the more actionable it will be. Some insights may crumble and never be able to meet this standard, and others may simply need some minor refinement to be made more actionable. However, if you rely on the 4D framework as a guide during the exploratory stage, you will be in a stronger position to end up with actionable insights. Its four audience-centered dimensions—*problem*, *outcome*, *actions*, and *measures*—keep your data discovery focused and steer you toward insights that will meet the six actionability criteria. When your insight aces the "so what" test, you have the makings for a great data story. With so much data and information competing for attention, actionable insights hold an advantage over less actionable information. When you have an actionable insight at the core of your data story, it will emit a strong signal that will be hard for the (right) audience to miss or ignore. While the increased actionability of an insight doesn't guarantee its adoption or application, it prepares the way by grabbing people's attention and challenging them to tap into the insight's value.

The Analysis Process: Exploration to Explanation

I'm a storyteller; that's what exploration really is all about. Going to places where others haven't been and returning to tell a story they haven't heard before.

—James Cameron, filmmaker and underwater explorer

Analysis is a two-step process that has an exploratory and an explanatory phase. In order to create a powerful data story, you must effectively transition from data discovery (when you're finding insights) to data communication (when you're explaining them to an audience) (see Figure 5.4). If you don't properly traverse these two phases, you may end up with something that resembles a data story but doesn't have the same effect. Yes, it may have numbers, charts, and annotations, but because it's poorly formed, it won't achieve the same results. To better appreciate why the transition from data exploration to explanation matters, I'd like to compare the process to my childhood hero, *Indiana Jones.*

THE TWO-STEP PROCESS FOR DEVELOPING A DATA STORY

Figure 5.4 The formation of a data story begins with using exploratory data visualizations to discover insights. Once a meaningful insight is uncovered, explanatory data visualizations are used to tell the story.

If you're familiar with the action-adventure films by George Lucas and Steven Spielberg, you'll know Indiana (Indy) Jones as a rough-and-tumble, bullwhip-toting archeologist in the 1930s. As Indy pursued rare antiquities around the world, he would often find trouble and battle a variety of evil henchmen along the way. It's easy to forget Indy was also a college professor who would share the tales and spoils of his archeological adventures with his students and fellow faculty. As shown in Figure 5.5, Indiana Jones embodies both sides of the analysis process as an adventurer/archeologist (exploratory) and teacher/communicator (explanatory).

THE TWO SIDES OF INDIANA JONES

Archaeologist
(Exploratory)

Professor
(Explanatory)

Figure 5.5   Indiana Jones embodies the two sides of the analysis process. As an archaeologist, he would discover valuable artifacts (exploratory). As a professor, he would educate students on his archeological findings (explanatory).

When you begin examining a dataset for meaningful insights, you're like a daring, inquisitive archaeologist. Whether you're analyzing a simple or complex dataset, data visualizations will often serve an integral role in helping you to uncover key patterns, trends, and anomalies in the data. At this stage, you're focused on speed and flexibility; you use data visualization as a tool to analyze the data. They don't have to be clean or pretty—just functional—as you navigate through the data in an iterative manner until you discover something valuable.

At this stage, you are the sole audience of these *exploratory* data visualizations. They only need to speak to you and no one else. Because you prepared the charts, you should have an intimate knowledge of the underlying data. While you may seek to confirm a hypothesis or hunch, you won't yet know what narrative will emerge from the data. Your initial ideas may be proven right, completely contradicted, or even pulled in an unexpected direction.

However, once you discover a meaningful insight, you now have a story to tell and must transition to the explanatory phase. You now become the professor of archeology and classroom lecturer. Now, you are no longer the primary audience, as you seek to share your key findings with others. There's also a very good chance your intended audience won't know the data to the same degree as you do. Simplicity, clarity, and cohesion become essential elements in your usage of *explanatory* data visualizations. Most notably, the data visualizations that helped you to discover an insight may need to be refined or even replaced to more effectively communicate what you discovered to a less-knowledgeable audience.

In Table 5.1, there are distinct differences between the two stages of the analysis process. If the transition between them isn't properly managed, you may end up with something less effective—in this analogy, *a data forgery*. While a data forgery can be mistaken for a data story, on closer inspection, you will find it is missing one or two of the essential attributes that form an effective data story. Just like Indiana Jones was adept at spotting fake relics (Holy Grail), you'll want to avoid the following flawed imposters because their weak narratives, questionable insights, and meaningless charts will end up hindering—not helping—your audience.

Table 5.1   Differences between the Two Stages of the Analysis Process

	Exploratory	Explanatory
Goal	Understand	Communicate
Audience	You	Other people
Data familiarity	Very familiar (you)	Less familiar (others)
Visualization focus	Flexibility and speed	Simplicity, clarity, and cohesion
Narrative	Unknown	Known
Outcome	Insight	Action

Data Forgery #1: The Data Cut

Well-meaning data experts frequently encounter this data forgery. Everything starts off the right way as they begin slicing and dicing the data to discover meaningful insights (see Figure 5.6). However, once a particular cut of the data yields an interesting insight, nothing is done to then package it up for meaningful consumption by other people. In this scenario, they mistakenly assume because the raw information speaks to them, it will speak equally well to their target audience.

DATA FORGERY #1: THE DATA CUT

Data   Insight   Audience

Explore

Figure 5.6   A data cut starts off right by exploring the data for insights; however, it fails to communicate the insight using an effective narrative and explanatory visuals.

Unfortunately, like an unedited director's cut, the *data cut* leans too heavily on the impact or persuasiveness of the raw facts. It ignores the importance of having a well-crafted narrative and explanatory visuals to help others better understand the insight's significance. Unfortunately, Ignaz Semmelweis, mentioned in Chapter 3, fell into this trap.

Warning Signs You Might Be Falling into the Data-Cut Trap:

- You feel the data speaks for itself because the evidence is so strong.
- You aren't sure how the audience will receive or interpret the results.
- You haven't spent much time tailoring your charts to your audience.

Data Forgery #2: The Data Cameo

Business users—not data experts—are more susceptible to this next data forgery. Interestingly, it is rich in narrative and may even showcase a few key data points. However, its origin is not data but instead a preconceived story—or perhaps, more accurately, an agenda (see Figure 5.7). Data is later added to support or strengthen the desired narrative. Only data points that uphold the narrative are "selected," while conflicting ones are ignored—either intentionally (selectivity, omission) or unintentionally (confirmation bias). This approach is common

DATA FORGERY #2: THE DATA CAMEO

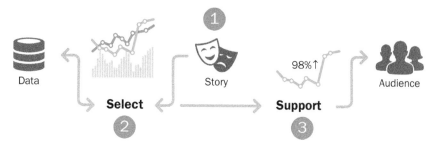

Figure 5.7 The data cameo starts with a predefined story—not data. Various data points are selected to bolster or substantiate the desired narrative. Without a solid data foundation, the data cameo can quickly unravel under closer scrutiny.

whenever someone feels they must justify a decision or show why a particular action or initiative was successful. Unfortunately, data only makes a "cameo" appearance in this narrative—more for show than as the foundation of the story that it should be. Because data isn't central to the overall story, a *data cameo* can quickly unravel under closer scrutiny.

Warning Signs You Might Be Falling into the Data-Cameo Trap:

- You already know the narrative you want to tell before examining any data.
- You are selecting data that supports a particular viewpoint.
- You aren't looking to disprove your preferred viewpoint.

Data Forgery #3: The Data Decoration

The last forgery has emerged as more individuals have gained access to data visualization tools. With more data than they know what to do with, people can display it in lots of different, interesting ways. However, this addictive combination of limitless data and graphical eye candy has led to the emergence of *data decorations*. This scenario occurs when individuals stumble through the exploratory phase without identifying a clear insight, and then jump ahead to visualizing data for others without crafting a cogent narrative (see Figure 5.8). By simply sharing the data charts and sidestepping the real analysis work, they hope someone consuming the data will somehow find something meaningful. However, rather than adding value, *data decorations* can often just add confusion and unwanted noise.

DATA FORGERY #3: THE DATA DECORATION

Figure 5.8 With data decoration, insufficient time is spent on actually analyzing the data for clear takeaways or insights before visualizing the data for consumption.

Warning Signs You Might Be Falling into the Data-Decoration Trap:

- You don't have a clear focus or emphasis for the visuals you're creating.
- You are more focused on the data visualization tool than the actual data.
- You want to visualize the data so other people with more domain expertise can make better sense of the numbers.

Each of these data forgeries excels in one key aspect of what is needed to form an effective data story but has flaws in the other two essential areas. For example, the *data cut* is strong on data but is weak in both narrative and visuals. The *data cameo* is rich in narrative but short on data. The *data decoration* offers appealing (if not particularly clear or meaningful) visuals but lacks a focused narrative. Only a true data story combines all three key aspects—data, narrative and visuals—effectively. It is imperative that you understand how a data story is properly formed because it will make a difference in the effectiveness of your data communications.

Analyzing and Communicating
Data Demands Discipline

It is a capital mistake to theorize before one has data. Insensibly one
begins to twist facts to suit theories, instead of theories to suit facts.
—Sherlock Holmes by Sir Arthur Conan Doyle, author

Even with a solid narrative and insightful visuals, a data story cannot
overcome a weak data foundation. As the master architect, builder, and
designer of your data story, you play an instrumental role in ensuring
its truthfulness, quality, and effectiveness. Because you are responsible
for pouring the data foundation and framing the narrative structure
of your data story, you need to be careful during the analysis process.
Because all of the data is being processed and interpreted by you before
it is shared with others, it can be exposed to cognitive biases and logical fallacies that distort or weaken the data foundation of your story.

In Chapter 3, we saw how the human mind processes information both unconsciously and consciously using two systems—System 1
and System 2. Both of these systems—especially System 1—influence
how your insights are received by other people. In your brain, these
same two systems will also shape how you process the data and how
you communicate your insights. System 1's imperfect, unconscious
heuristics help us to cope with the vast amounts of information that
we need to absorb on a regular basis. They help us to quickly focus
our attention and make sense of what's happening around us, but
System 1's cognitive biases can also lead us astray during the analysis
process. While modern psychology currently lists more than 180 cognitive biases, I will focus on three common, representative examples
that demonstrate how cognitive bias can distort your data stories in
various ways.

Confirmation Bias

Confirmation bias is the tendency to search for and accept only evidence that supports your existing beliefs or views. It also causes you
to ignore contrary information that refutes your existing opinions.

American businessman Warren Buffett noted, "What the human being is best at doing is interpreting all new information so that their prior conclusions remain intact." When you begin an analysis, you may have an opinion or hypothesis about the subject matter you're analyzing. If you're not aware of your biases, you may selectively analyze the data until you uncover an insight that confirms your opinion or hypothesis.

The scientific method was introduced to combat confirmation bias by having researchers attempt to *disprove*—not just confirm—their hypotheses. Unfortunately, even within the scientific community, competitive pressure to produce significant positive findings has led many scientists astray. In 2005, Stanford professor John Ioannidis boldly proclaimed most published research findings were false (Ioannidis 2005). For example, the biotechnology firm Amgen could only reproduce six (11%) of 53 "landmark" cancer studies, and another study could only reproduce 39% of 100 psychology research findings (Nuzzo 2015). If you succumb to your own confirmation bias, you may find exactly what you expect to see in the numbers—and miss what's really happening.

Survivorship Bias

Survivorship bias is the tendency to focus only on what succeeded or survived while ignoring what failed or didn't survive. One of the most storied examples of survivorship bias occurred during World War II. The United States military wanted to reduce the heavy losses to its bombers and flight crews. The military commanders were looking to add more armor to the bombers, but the added weight would also reduce their maneuverability and increase their fuel consumption. To find the optimal distribution of armor, they turned to a group of mathematicians for help. The military's analysis of the returned planes showed most of the damage occurred along the wings and fuselage. When the US military asked to know how much armor they should distribute across these locations, statistician Abraham Wald's reply shocked them—none. The bullet holes in these locations showed where bombers could be hit and still return safely. Wald hypothesized that the combat damage occurred uniformly across the planes, and the sections where the surviving planes weren't as damaged (engines) represented the vulnerable locations (see Figure 5.9).

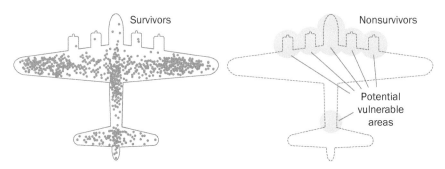

SURVIVORSHIP BIAS: WORLD WAR II BOMBER ANALYSIS

Figure 5.9   During World War II, statistician Abraham Wald noticed that the US military were making armor placement decisions based on data from the surviving bombers—not the planes that didn't return safely. The bullet holes on the surviving bombers indicated locations where the planes could receive damage and still fly home. Wald hypothesized the planes that didn't return received major damage in locations where the surviving ones had only minimal damage.

If your analysis suffers from survivorship bias, you will have an incomplete picture of what's happening. Your perception of what the success factors are may be distorted by the missing failures, or nonsurvivors. For example, if you were analyzing new store locations, your analysis would be skewed if it was only based on criteria from your best stores—not your worst-performing locations. Rather than exclusively focusing on what succeeded or survived, valuable insights may come from your failures and understanding what caused them to fail.

Curse of Knowledge

The Curse of Knowledge is the tendency to assume other people have the necessary context or knowledge to follow what you're communicating. Once you become familiar with a topic, it can be hard to imagine *not* knowing what you know. When you were learning to ride a bike, it was awkward and challenging. Then suddenly, one day you figured out how to ride . . . and immediately you were worthless at explaining how to ride to people who couldn't. Because you are "cursed" with a deeper understanding of the topic, it becomes more difficult to see the subject matter from the perspective of a novice. In short, if you are data literate, it may be hard to view the data you're sharing from the perspective of someone who is less data literate than you. In these scenarios, your knowledge interferes with your ability to communicate effectively.

At Stanford University in 1990, an experiment was conducted in which a group of individuals were assigned to two roles: a "tapper" or "listener." Each tapper was asked to tap out the rhythm of a well-known song such as "Happy Birthday to You" or "The Star Spangled Banner" for a listener who would be asked to identify the song. When they asked the tappers how often they thought the listeners could correctly guess the songs, they estimated 50% of the time. However, when they measured the listeners' actual success rate, they were correct only 2.5% of the time (Heath and Heath 2006). While the tappers had the advantage of hearing the melodies of the songs in their heads as they tapped, the vast majority of the time, all the listeners could perceive were random combinations of finger taps. Likewise, as you spend time analyzing a dataset, you'll often gain a deeper knowledge of the data than your audience will have. When you have uncovered an insight you want to share, the curse of knowledge can impede your ability to communicate it clearly and concisely to your audience. Knowing your audience, being self-aware of your own proficiency, and using stories to convey your data in a concrete manner can help you to counteract this cognitive bias.

Besides the cognitive biases that are introduced by System 1, your analysis can also suffer from logical fallacies that occur in System 2. While cognitive biases influence our *unconscious* patterns of thought, logical fallacies represent defects in our *conscious* reasoning. You may be blind to many of the heuristics and prejudices that shape your thinking, but you can learn to spot irrational reasoning in the form of flawed arguments. In modern psychology, you'll find more than 130 logical fallacies, but I've chosen three common ones that can erode the data foundation of your storytelling.

Correlation Fallacy

The correlation fallacy occurs when someone mistakenly interprets coinciding events as being part of a cause-and-effect relationship. Different variables are *correlated* if they fluctuate together in a similar or inverse manner. While correlation does not imply causation, *xkcd* cartoonist

Randall Munroe noted, "It does waggle its eyebrows suggestively and gesture furtively while mouthing 'look over there.'" Frequently, researchers and analysts will encounter these correlated relationships in their analyses. With further examination, they may eventually uncover the root cause of a problem or the key driver of an opportunity. For example, scientists found smoking was highly correlated with lung cancer before they were able to isolate the actual carcinogens in cigarettes.

Figure 5.10   This *xkcd* cartoon by Randall Munroe highlights the unique relationship between correlation and causation.
Source: https://xkcd.com/552/ Courtesy of xkcd.com.

However, it's important to remember that even though two variables may trend in a related manner, it doesn't imply one variable is directly causing the other. For example, while there may be a strong correlation between ice cream consumption and shark attacks, it would be irrational to believe ice cream causes shark attacks (or the inverse). Instead, a third *confounding variable*—the outdoor temperature—influences both of these variables. Moreover, the correlation between two variables may only be happenstance. Tyler Vigen's fun website and book, *Spurious Correlations* (2015), highlight several absurd correlations, including the strong correlation (99.26%) between Maine's divorce rate and the US per capita consumption of margarine (see Figure 5.11). Because our brains are programmed to assign causality and form narratives, it is easy for us to assume imaginary cause-and-effect relationships exist when the variables are merely correlated. While correlations can be enlightening, they can't be anything more than just associations until they can be studied and tested for causality.

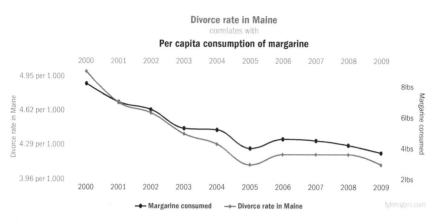

Figure 5.11 While the divorce rate in Maine is highly correlated with the per capita consumption of margarine (99.26%), nobody in their right mind would suggest there's a causal relationship between these two variables.

Source: https://tylervigen.com/spurious-correlations Courtesy of Tyler Vigen.

Texas Sharpshooter Fallacy

The Texas sharpshooter fallacy happens when someone assigns significance to a random set of coincidences. This fallacy draws its name from an interesting anecdote about a Texan cowboy who practiced his shooting skills on the side of a barn. Afterward, he painted targets around the tight clusters of bullet holes to imply he was a skilled marksman. Instead of bullet holes on the side of a barn, you may approach a large set of data and assign meaning (signal) to a small set of anomalies while ignoring the rest of the data as noise. However, the danger of painting targets around certain data points is that you might be assigning meaning to patterns that just occurred by chance. *You Are Not So Smart* author David McRaney noted that we "tend to ignore random chance when the results seem meaningful or when [we] want a random event to have a meaningful cause" (McRaney 2010).

A prime example of this fallacy occurred in 1992 when Swedish researchers studied the effects electrical power lines had on families in close proximity. They tested the subjects for 800 potential ailments over a 25-year period. The researchers found the incidence of childhood leukemia was four times higher in households living close to power lines. While this was undoubtedly alarming news for parents and local governments, the researchers had fallen victim to the Texas sharpshooter fallacy. By having more than 800 potential risk ratios or "targets," the researchers had a high probability that at least one illness would generate a statistically significant difference by chance alone. Since this landmark study, subsequent research into the effects of power lines has failed to confirm its findings (Smith 2016). There's a significant difference between having a hypothesis or theory (painting a target) *prior* to analyzing your data and forming one *after* analyzing the numbers. In the latter case, it becomes important to test your theory with fresh data to confirm whether your finding truly is signal or just the product of randomness.

Hasty Generalization Fallacy

The hasty generalization fallacy occurs when someone makes a broad claim that isn't justified by sufficient or unbiased data. We often look down on making generalizations, but we frequently rely on them to make sense of our complicated world. When it comes to analysis in particular, you will often generalize your findings so they can be more broadly applied to a set of similar circumstances. For example, you might discover a certain type of prospect responds well to product demos. For prospects with this specific profile, you may decide to feature your product demos more prominently on your website. While not every one of these prospects may be equally receptive to product demos, your data shows—in general—there's a higher probability they'll convert after seeing a demo. In this case, a generalization based on the prospect data can help improve your sales efforts.

Because we are prone to jumping to conclusions as human beings, we need to be careful with how quickly we form our generalizations. The "hasty" aspect of this fallacy is what really can get us into trouble. This logical fallacy occurs when you identify something interesting in an unrepresentative sample and then assume it applies to the larger population. For example, your conclusion about product demos could have come from talking to a few salespeople who said their prospects loved them. Making a *hasty* generalization based on ad hoc feedback from a few salespeople is different than coming to the same conclusion based on extensive analysis of the behaviors of thousands of sales prospects. The larger, more representative the sample is for your insight, the stronger your data foundation will be.

When data must be filtered through you—an intelligent but fallible human being—there's always the possibility that biased or flawed reasoning can twist and contort your data stories. While I've covered some key cognitive biases and logical fallacies, there are hundreds of others that can also lead you astray. Many people don't realize how much *discipline* is required in the analysis process. Theoretical physicist Richard Feynman said, "The first principle is that you must not fool yourself—and you are the easiest person to fool" (Feynman 1974). Your own weak or faulty reasoning can end up sabotaging your insights before they're shared with anyone else. If you want to build an effective data story, you need to be aware of the potential biases or prejudices that can (and will) affect your judgment. While you won't be able to disable them like features on your smartphone, you can be on guard for them during the analysis process. Data visualization expert and author of *The Truthful Art* Alberto Cairo acknowledged how challenging this can be:

> It's true that human beings can't be completely factual or objective. Our brain is a flawed meat machine chiseled by evolution, not a computer. We all have cognitive, cultural, and ideological biases, but that doesn't mean that we can't strive to be factual. Truth is unattainable, but trying to be truthful is a realistic and worthy goal. . . . There's a deep difference between those who surrender to their own biases, or willingly embrace them, and those who work hard to identify and curb them, even if they'll never completely succeed. (Cairo 2016)

When you don't monitor how your views and biases can impact your research, your data foundation will be susceptible to cracks and fissures. If you find yourself rushing your analysis, you may end up with a convenient but logically-flawed insight. However, if you're disciplined through both the exploratory and explanatory phases, you'll establish a sturdy foundation on which to build your data story. Analytical discipline can shape the trajectory of your data stories—whether they're embraced as gospel or dismissed as delusion. The more you can strengthen your insights by being objective and truthful, the more enduring and powerful your data stories will be.

When Too Much of a Good Thing Is Bad

A wealth of information creates a poverty of attention.
            —Herbert A. Simon, economist and political scientist

Imagine you've performed an in-depth analysis, and you've uncovered an incredible insight. You're now excited to share your findings with an influential group of stakeholders. Let's assume you've been careful to be objective and watch for potential biases or logical fallacies that could potentially taint your analysis. As you prepare to share your data with others, you're still prone to one more common misstep—*information overload*. In your excitement to share your analysis journey and what you've uncovered, you fill your report, presentation, infographic, or dashboard with so much information your audience can't possibly comprehend it all. Instead of delivering a clear, strong signal to your audience, you mistakenly smother it in minutiae and shroud it in noise. Rather than engaging and enlightening your audience, you leave them confused, frustrated, or maybe even a little numb.

When you find yourself in a situation in which you have a wealth of information to share, you need to recognize how human memory works. Like a computer, the human mind has a large hard drive for storage but limited memory capacity for processing unfamiliar information. Input or stimuli from our various senses is held temporarily in our unconscious *sensory memory* for less than a second until it is either discarded or chosen for further processing (see Figure 5.12). When something catches our attention, our conscious *working memory* acts like a central processing unit (CPU) where it examines the information and encodes it for storage in our *long-term memory* as schemas. However, the information only has a short window of opportunity in the working memory—often less than a minute—to make a meaningful connection, or it will be forgotten.

HUMAN MEMORY PROCESSING

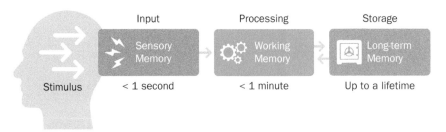

Figure 5.12 When stimulus (audio, imagery, touch, etc.) is received by the brain, it spends less than a second in the sensory memory. If something catches our attention, it is processed for less than a minute in the working memory. If it is deemed to be important, it will be stored in the long-term memory as a schema.

Because the working memory acts as a gatekeeper for new information, you need to understand how it can become overloaded. In 1956, Princeton psychologist George Miller asserted people can hold only seven pieces of information (plus or minus two) at a time in their working memories (Miller 1956). More recent research indicates the "magic" number may be only four (University of New South Wales 2012). In order to process incoming information, we frequently group individual pieces into more manageable chunks. For example, we will process a mobile number (+18881234567) as four chunks (+1 888 123 4567) instead of 12 separate characters. As you assemble the various elements of your data story, you'll want to be mindful of the importance of "chunking" your information in a manageable fashion. In the next chapter, you'll see how narrative can add structure to your data and make it easier to digest for your audience.

Educators and instructional designers face a similar challenge as data storytellers in terms of finding the right balance of information that imparts key insights and concepts to an audience but doesn't overwhelm the audience members either. In the late 1980s, educational psychologist John Sweller examined the working memory's limited capacity and explored the reasons why people found it difficult to understand and retain new information. Sweller developed the *Cognitive Load Theory (CLT),* in which he identified three types of mental activities that occur in the working memory that impact learning efficiency (Sweller 1988):

1. **Intrinsic load:** This type of cognitive load represents the inherent difficulty or complexity of the topic at hand. The intrinsic load will depend on the subject matter being shared—and the complexity of the topic can't necessarily be changed by the person delivering the information. For example, it is easier to teach someone how to fold a paper airplane than how to fly a jet airliner. Some topics are naturally going to be harder to teach and learn than others.

2. **Extraneous load:** This type of load is effort associated with the non-relevant instructional elements that aren't essential to the learning task. Because there's a finite capacity for the working memory to process new information, any time spent on processing nonessential items such as an unintuitive layout, decorative pictures, distracting animations, and so on, means less time can be devoted to comprehending the core information. For example, step-by-step written instructions

for how to fold a paper airplane would introduce more extraneous cognitive load than a simple how-to diagram (see Figure 5.13).

3. **Germane load:** This load type reflects the actual effort spent on processing and organizing the information into schemas for long-term memory. Learning any new idea or concept is going to take effort. Germane load represents the desirable type of load that helps people to gain new skills and knowledge. For example, if you want to teach someone how to fold a paper plane, the best approach will be a guided, hands-on exercise using paper. For the learners, the mental effort involved with following clear instructions and making the correct folds will be beneficial germane load.

When you're attempting to share data that can be both complex and cumbersome for an audience, CLT techniques for *managing* intrinsic load, *minimizing* extraneous load, and *maximizing* germane load are incredibly helpful for data storytellers. While you can't necessarily simplify the complexity of the subject matter you've analyzed, you can *manage* the impact of its intrinsic load. One useful tactic is to break up your findings into more manageable segments or chunks that your audience can more easily absorb and follow. Rather than dumping too much data on your audience too quickly, you can reveal the data gradually in stages so they can build schemas as they become familiar with your information.

HOW TO FOLD A PAPER PLANE (TEXT)

1. Fold a piece of 8.5x11″ paper in half lengthwise to create a crease down its center. Then fold the top two corners to the center crease.

2. Take the top two corners and fold them again into the center crease.

3. Fold the two sides inward to the center crease so they are touching.

4. Create the first wing by creating a fold along the length of the paper about 1–1.5″ from the spine. The fold should make the wing perpendicular to the body of the plane.

5. Repeat the above step to create the other wing for your paper plane.

HOW TO FOLD A PAPER PLANE (VISUAL)

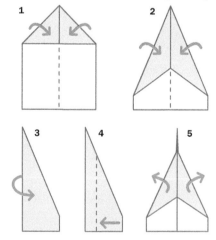

Figure 5.13 For most audiences, the text-based instructions on the left are going to generate more extraneous cognitive load than the diagram on the right.

If your findings are complex, you'll want to start with simple concepts and build up to more complex points. The level of your audience's expertise on your topic will also impact the intrinsic load. A novice audience is going to experience more intrinsic load than an expert audience that is already proficient with the subject matter. The beginning point and ramp time will be different for each audience type.

An essential goal in effective data storytelling is to minimize the extraneous load that is placed on an audience. The data forgery—the *data cut*—is an example of how extraneous cognitive load can derail a data communication. When you share unedited, raw findings, your audience is forced to work harder to understand and appreciate them. Any mental effort the audience members waste on extraneous items reduces their capacity to focus on your core message. To avoid inadvertently taxing the working memories of your audience, you want to minimize the extraneous load in the following ways:

- Use effective chart types to convey your information.
- Remove irrelevant data or redundant charts.
- Don't combine multiple data points into a single chart, thinking that reducing the number of charts will simplify things.
- Avoid dense text in slides, charts, and infographics.
- Sort, group, or label your data for easier consumption.
- Organize or lay out your content in a manner that is easy to follow.
- Remove nonessential chart elements such as unnecessary 3D effects, dark gridlines, and nonstrategic use of color.
- Share your data in a consistent manner (naming conventions, colors, symbols).
- Signal to the audience where they should focus their attention.

Unlike intrinsic load, you control how much extraneous load your audience will experience. It's in your best interest to streamline your content and avoid placing any extra processing burden on your audience, especially if it doesn't help them to better understand your insights. In Chapters 7 and 8 on visuals, you'll learn various visualization techniques that will help you to minimize this particular form of cognitive load.

Fortunately, storytelling is naturally conducive to maximizing germane load. In the next chapter, you learn how the story structure can help engage the audience and package the information in a way that is easier for the working memory to process. When appropriate, you may consider incorporating analogies into your data stories to make complex concepts more approachable and comprehensible for your audience. In addition, rather than relying only on high-level, aggregated results, you may want to include specific, concrete examples that can help bring your overall findings to life for your audience. For example, you might have uncovered a customer service issue that is affecting thousands of customers and costing your company millions of dollars. However, it might be even more impactful to share a specific example of how the issue is impacting one of your most valuable customers. The more relatable your data is, the easier it will be for your audience to process and apply it.

When you share too much information, your data story can crumble under the sheer weight of your data. As you shift from exploratory to explanatory phases in the analysis process, you're often going to have more data than you actually need to tell a single story. American writer Henry David Thoreau said, "It's not what you look at that matters, it's what you see." While you may have analyzed or looked at a lot of data, it's really only the insights that matter—what you saw that stood out.

Researchers Nadav Klein and Ed O'Brien discovered we tend to overestimate how much information someone needs to see before making a decision (Klein and O'Brien 2018). Based on several experiments, they found subjects overestimated by a factor of *double to quadruple* how much information is necessary to support decision making. For example, in one study, they divided a group of more than 200 subjects into predictors and experiencers. They asked the predictors to estimate how many pieces of artwork someone would need to see before he or she could determine whether they liked the art style or not. The predictors estimated they would need to see 16 to 17 pieces on average, but the experiencers only needed to review three to four pieces on average before making up their minds.

In another study, they asked more than 100 MBA students to write a number of essays to highlight their past management experience for a hypothetical job application. More than 100 professional hiring managers were asked to review the essays and stop when they felt they had a good sense of the individual's abilities as a manager. The students prepared an average of four essays while the recruiters only read two on average. These expectation gaps indicate that your data stories may need far less information than you think they do—*maybe even less than half the evidence your intuition (System 1) is telling you to include.*

When you evaluate the data foundation for your story, it's important to separate the essential from the extraneous. Your goal shouldn't be to show how much work you did or how smart you were in your data exploration. Your goal should be to tell a memorable story based on your key findings. Even before you begin formulating your story, you can begin narrowing down the analysis results and filtering out less useful data by asking the following questions:

- What data is irrelevant?
- What data is redundant?
- What data is confusing or ambiguous?
- What data is weak or questionable?
- What data is not aligned with your central insight?

Even before you build your data story, you can deprioritize data that is unnecessary and isolate key data points that may be useful to your narrative. As *New York Times* graphics editor Amanda Cox stated, "Data isn't like your kids, you don't have to pretend to love them equally." Some of your data points are going to be more important to your story than others. As you reduce the competing noise, you'll find the signal of your story will strengthen. As the English author Henry Green noted, "The more you leave out, the more you highlight what you leave in." In fact, as you assemble your key points into a story, you'll find the narrative structure will further help you in isolating which data points to focus on. In the next chapter, you may discover some of your interesting findings may not fit your narrative—and that's okay. They may merit their own data story and need to be temporarily set aside. All you need is a few reliable, sturdy building blocks of data that fit together for you to have the foundation of a credible and powerful data story. With a solid data foundation in place, you're ready to begin crafting a compelling narrative.

References

Bohannon, J. 2015. I fooled millions into thinking chocolate helps weight loss. Here's how. *Gizmodo*, April 27. https://io9.gizmodo.com/i-fooled-millions-into-thinking-chocolate-helps-weight-1707251800.

Cairo, A. 2016. *The Truthful Art: Data, Charts, and Maps for Communication*. Thousand Oaks, CA: New Riders Publishing.

Feynman, R. 1974. Cargo cult science. Speech presented at Caltech's 1974 commencement address in Pasadena, CA (June 14).

Heath, C., and Heath, D. 2006. The curse of knowledge. *Harvard Business Review*, December. https://hbr.org/2006/12/the-curse-of-knowledge.

Ioannidis, J.P.A. 2005. Why most published research findings are false. *PLoS Medicine* 2 (8): e124. https://doi.org/10.1371/journal.pmed.0020124.

Klein, N., and O'Brien, E. 2018. People use less information than they think to make up their minds. *Proceedings of the National Academy of Sciences* 115 (52): 13222–13227.

Light, R.J., Singer, J.D., and Willett, J.B. 1990. *By Design: Planning Research on Higher Education*. Cambridge, MA: Harvard University Press.

McRaney, D. 2010. The Texas sharpshooter fallacy. *You Are Not So Smart*, September 11. https://youarenotsosmart.com/2010/09/11/the-texas-sharpshooter-fallacy/.

Miller, G.A. 1956. The magical number seven, plus or minus two: Some limits on our capacity for processing information. *Psychological Review* 63: 81–97.

Nuzzo, R. 2015. How scientists fool themselves—and how they can stop. *Nature* 526 (7572): 182–185. https://www.nature.com/news/how-scientists-fool-themselves-and-how-they-can-stop-1.18517.

Patil, D., and Mason, H. 2015. *Data Driven: Creating a Data Culture*. Sebastopol, CA: O'Reilly Media.

Smith, G. 2016. *Standard Deviations: Flawed Assumptions, Tortured Data and Other Ways to Lie with Statistics*. London: Duckworth Overlook.

Sweller, J. 1988. Cognitive load during problem solving: Effects on learning. *Cognitive Science* 12: 257–285.

University of New South Wales. 2012. Four is the "magic" number. *Science News*, November 28. https://www.sciencedaily.com/releases/2012/11/121128093930.htm.

Waisberg, D. 2016. Data stories with Avinash Kaushik and Daniel Waisberg. November 28. https://www.youtube.com/watch?v=PcKrtCo4Zmo.

Chapter 6

Narrative

The Structure of Your Data Story

A lost coin is found by means of a candle; the deepest truth is found by means of a simple story.

—Anthony De Mello, author

Emily, a rising star at a large technology company, was tasked with piloting a promising initiative for a new product. One of her first tasks as the product manager was to gather feedback from existing customers on the new technology's potential. While her intuition told her the new product would be well received by customers, she wanted to gather evidence to confirm her theory. After surveying more than 100 of her company's top customers and receiving highly positive feedback, she was confident the new technology would fill a critical gap in his company's product portfolio. After working with a small team of developers to build a working prototype, Emily shared the concept with various internal product teams to gauge their interest and support. Similar to the external feedback she gathered, the internal response to the idea was equally positive.

Armed with impressive survey findings, powerful customer quotes, internal support, and a working demo, Emily crafted a compelling data presentation that featured several insightful data visualizations. Over the years, she had also established great rapport with many of the decision makers who would be approving her project, including a few key female executives whom she viewed as career mentors. When it came time to present the slides to the product leadership team, Emily felt as though securing funding for the project would just be a formality. However, despite the overwhelming evidence in support of the new product, it wasn't selected as one of five initiatives to receive funding that year. Emily's project team was subsequently disbanded, and she was assigned to focus on other product needs.

Puzzled and frustrated by what happened, Emily endeavored to determine what went wrong with her team's pitch. After some probing, she found she had made two critical mistakes. First, she thought she provided all the information the audience would use to evaluate and prioritize her project. However, Emily discovered too late that there was actually some hidden resistance to her project. While the other product teams openly showed support for her team's idea, it turned out another team coveted the new technology and thought they should be the ones to introduce it. Unbeknownst to Emily, a false rumor was circulated that its M&A team was close to acquiring another firm with similar technology, which unexpectedly dropped her project off the executives' priority list. Emily's promising project became the victim of office politics as she allowed another team to shape the narrative.

The second mistake Emily made was being seduced by her own data. She was so confident in the strength of her insights and visuals that she didn't accompany them with an airtight narrative. If Emily had known she was up against some resistance, a stronger narrative could have allayed her audience's concerns, corrected any misinformation, and driven home the importance of moving forward with the new solution. Years later, Emily still shakes her head at what could have been. Her company didn't end up buying or building the technology, and it still represents a clear gap in the company's product strategy. As this example shows, even with a great data foundation and supporting visuals, your insights still need a well-formed narrative to drive action and change.

Defining a Narrative Model for Data Stories

> Storytelling is ultimately a creative act of pattern recognition. Through characters, plot and setting, a writer creates places where previously invisible truths become visible. Or the storyteller posits a series of dots that the reader can connect.
>
> —Douglas Coupland, novelist

After you've conducted an analysis and found a valuable insight, the next challenge is to determine how you're going to present your findings in a meaningful way to your intended audience. Using a narrative structure to organize your information not only makes it easier for an audience to consume your content, but it also helps you prioritize what is essential to your message—and sometimes, more importantly, *what isn't*. While piecing together a series of facts into a meaningful story may not be the same as crafting a fictional story, the time-tested dramatic structure can be adapted and applied to data storytelling. In the journey to find a narrative approach for data storytelling, I encountered three common narrative models:

1. **Aristotle's Tragedy Structure.** The Greek philosopher Aristotle was one of the first to examine the basic structure and rules of drama in his book *Poetics*. For Aristotle, the plot—the organization of a sequence of incidents or events—was the "soul" of a story. He saw it as the most essential aspect of a Greek tragedy, ahead of characters or any other narrative elements. Aristotle implied stories have a simple structure—*a beginning, middle, and end*—that are connected through a series of cause-and-effect events (see Figure 6.1). Many people have interpreted his structure to represent three acts—a setup, an obstacle/confrontation, and a resolution. However, he actually only identified two key parts in a traditional

ARISTOTLE'S TRAGEDY STRUCTURE

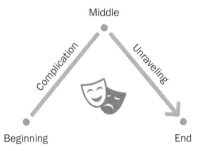

Figure 6.1 Aristotle's model is fairly straightforward, but it has had a significant influence on how people view narrative structure.

Greek tragedy—a complication and unraveling—that represent the plot turns being like a knot that is tied and then untied. Even though his views were expressed more than two millennia ago, Aristotle's simple narrative model continues to have a significant influence on how stories are crafted today.

2. **Freytag's Pyramid.** The German playwright and novelist Gustav Freytag (1816–1895) studied Greek and Shakespearian drama to understand how they were structured. Building on Aristotle's simple model, Freytag developed a more robust narrative framework to better understand the arc or progression of a story (see Figure 6.2). In his book, *Technique of the Drama* (1895), he lays out a "pyramid-based" dramatic structure with five key stages:

   a. *Exposition (introduction):* The beginning of the story when the setting is established and main characters are introduced. It provides the audience with ample background information to understand what's going to happen.

   b. *Rising action:* The series of events that build up to the climax of the story.

   c. *Climax:* The most intense or important point within the story. It is often an event in which the fortune of the protagonist turns for the better or worse in the story.

   d. *Falling action:* The rest of the events that unravel after the main conflict has occurred, but before the final outcome is decided.

   e. *Dénouement (conclusion):* The conclusion of the story where all of the conflicts are resolved and outstanding details are explained. *Dénouer* is actually the French verb for "to undo or untie" (a knot).

FREYTAG'S PYRAMID

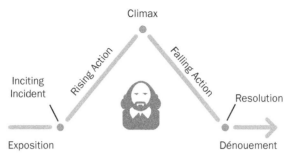

Figure 6.2 Freytag's model builds on Aristotle's model, adding more elements that provide more guidance around the narrative structure.

Similar to Aristotle's model, Freytag's model has been adapted and modified since it was first introduced. One key addition is the *inciting incident,* which is a major point in the plot where it transitions from the introduction to the beginning of the action or conflict. Today, Freytag's five-stage model is used to analyze all kinds of stories found in books, plays, and films. Researchers have even used it to analyze TV advertisements. They found 30-second Super Bowl ads that closely matched Freytag's dramatic structure were rated significantly higher than other ads that didn't (Rosen 2014).

Harry Potter and Freytag's Pyramid

If you are familiar with J.K. Rowlings' first book, *Harry Potter and the Sorcerer's Stone* (1997), Freytag's Pyramid can be used to illuminate its narrative structure. Starting with the *exposition,* you meet a mistreated 11-year-old orphan, Harry Potter, who lives in a cupboard under the stairs in the house of his uncaring aunt and uncle. The *inciting incident* occurs when Harry unexpectedly uses magic to free and communicate with a snake at a local zoo. The *rising action* ensues when Harry is brought to the Hogwarts School of Witchcraft and Wizardry and fears someone is plotting to kill him. Eventually, in the *climax,* Harry confronts the villain Voldemort, who murdered his parents. In the *falling* action, Harry learns Headmaster Dumbledore was able to foil Voldemort's plans

(continued)

(continued)
to steal the Sorcerer's Stone. In the *dénouement*, Harry's Gryffindor house is awarded the Hogwarts House Cup. Triumphantly, Harry and his new friends leave the school to enjoy their summer break. You will find Freytag's Pyramid can be applied to most popular films and books.

CAMPBELL'S HERO'S JOURNEY

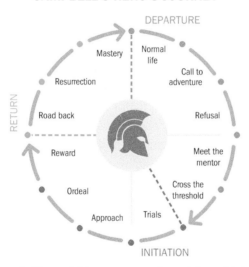

Figure 6.3 Campbell's model is more complex with multiple stages and has a cyclical pattern rather than a triangle or pyramid format.

3. **Campbell's Hero's Journey.** The last model was popularized by American mythologist Joseph Campbell in 1949. After studying various myths and fables from different cultures and genres, Campbell found they followed a universal narrative archetype that he called the *Hero's Journey* or *monomyth* ("one story"). The structure centers around a hero being called on an adventure, overcoming challenges, and then returning as a champion. Campbell divided his archetype into 17 different stages that can be grouped into three main sections: departure, initiation, and return (see Figure 6.3). Subsequent authors have simplified Campbell's 17 stages down to 8–12 stages. Compared with the previous two models, Campbell placed more emphasis on the central character

of the story. His model is also represented as a cyclical pattern rather than a triangle or pyramid. When George Lucas was finalizing his script for *Star Wars: A New Hope*, he leaned heavily on Campbell's writings (Seastrom 2015). If you examine the *Star Wars* plot, you can see how the protagonist Luke Skywalker passes through each stage in Campbell's hero journey.

As I evaluated each of the narrative models in terms of data storytelling, I felt like Goldilocks in the fairy tale *Goldilocks and the Three Bears*. I found Aristotle's beginning-middle-end structure to be too simple, as it didn't provide enough direction on how to construct a story. Without more definition around the narrative structure, you could say multiple things—a report or a textbook—have a beginning, middle, and end, but that clearly doesn't make them stories. At the other end of the spectrum, I found Campbell's Hero's Journey with its multiple stages to be too complicated for assembling data stories. While it might be helpful for screenwriters and novelists, it's too complex to be useful for data storytellers. Like Goldilocks, I found the middle option—Freytag's Pyramid—to be "just right" in terms of detail and ease of use.

Using Freytag's Pyramid as a foundation, I developed a four-stage narrative structure called the Data Storytelling Arc (see Figure 6.4).

DATA STORYTELLING ARC

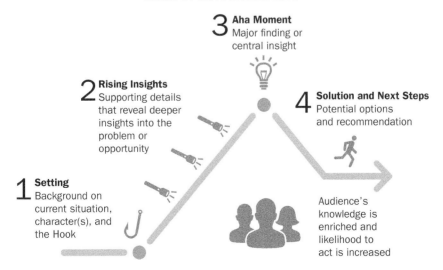

3 Aha Moment
Major finding or central insight

2 Rising Insights
Supporting details that reveal deeper insights into the problem or opportunity

4 Solution and Next Steps
Potential options and recommendation

1 Setting
Background on current situation, character(s), and the Hook

Audience's knowledge is enriched and likelihood to act is increased

Figure 6.4 The Data Storytelling Arc uses Freytag's Pyramid as a foundation for how to tell stories with data in four steps.

In a traditional literary story, the exposition would introduce the setting details (location, timeframe, situation) and main characters (appearance, personality, background). At the beginning of a data story, it's important to establish key details such as the area of focus and time period. While you may not have actual characters in your data story, you may have a segment of people such as customers, employees, investors, and so on that you will focus on. The *Setting* of your data story should provide the audience with "just enough" background information so they can easily grasp the data you share with them. Many analysts make the mistake of beginning their data story with an in-depth summary of their entire analysis process. While this approach provides a significant amount of context, the extra detail can easily overwhelm your audience and should be relegated to an appendix. Most audiences will not care about the steps or process you used to find your insights—they're more curious about what you discovered.

A key part of the Setting phase is the *Hook*, which is a data story's equivalent of the inciting incident. While the rest of the information in the Setting provides crucial background information, the Hook is a notable observation that acts as a turning point in the story and begins to reveal a problem or opportunity (sort of a "hmm moment"). The combination of the contextual information and the Hook creates a powerful juxtaposition. Your audience should understand what's normal or expected so they can appreciate something that's extraordinary. For example, a significant spike or dip in the daily results for a key metric can serve as the opening teaser of your data story.

After the Hook has introduced something notable or unusual to the audience, the next stage is the *Rising Insights* phase, in which the subject of your analysis is explored at a deeper level. Rather than offering up a loose collection of random facts, the goal is to peel back the layers of the problem or opportunity in a directed, focused manner. You want to include only the information that is necessary to advance the desired narrative because less relevant or tangential findings will weaken your data story.

Eventually, you will reach a climax, or the *Aha Moment,* of your data story—this is when you share the main finding or central insight. It provides a clear insight, not just an interesting observation as the Hook does. How much time you spend in the Rising Insights stage will depend on your Aha Moment and how much build-up it requires. Some central insights may be fairly straightforward to explain, but others may need multiple supporting details for the audience to fully understand or accept.

But just because you've shared your Aha Moment with your audience, that doesn't mean your data story is complete. Just like a literary story doesn't end directly after its climax, your data story must continue forward and share how the audience should leverage the new insight. In order to drive action and change, the last *Solution and Next Steps* stage is essential to effective data storytelling. If you don't guide your audience through the different options they have, they may not know what to do after being enlightened by your findings. If you're not proactive with suggesting a potential solution or discussing next steps, the opportunity to drive change may be lost.

To demonstrate how analysis results can be assembled into a data story with this narrative model, let's turn to a simple ecommerce example. Rather than using real charts, I'll use pseudo charts to not get caught up in the visualization details (see Figure 6.5). In the Setting stage, you can see how the total online sales follow a cyclical pattern each quarter. This year's sales (blue) have been trending above the previous year's results in every period until recently. For some reason, the current quarter's results took an unexpected downward turn. This anomaly is the Hook for this particular data story.

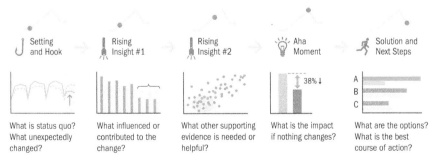

Figure 6.5 The ecommerce data story shows how insights in each of the four stages combine to form a meaningful data story. Depending on the length or complexity of your story, you may have several rising insights or none at all.

The first Rising Insight highlights how the dark gray product categories are outperforming the results of the previous year. However, the three orange product categories are underperforming last year's results. In the second Rising Insight, the different individual products or SKUs in these three product categories are plotted out, and the lower, undesirable quadrant (low product views and orders) contains a cluster of products from the same brand. Whatever change that occurred impacted a specific brand of goods that is being sold on the ecommerce site.

Unless the brand issue can be resolved, the ecommerce team will miss its quarterly sales target by 38% (Aha Moment). Because the team's bonuses are tied to reaching the sales target, you suddenly have everyone's interest and attention. Your audience is ready for the final stage (Solution and Next Steps), when you explain three different options for solving the identified brand problem. By highlighting the merits of the first option, which offers the most brand-related revenue for the least amount of cost, you show how the organization can address the issue and move forward. Through this simplified example, you've seen how all of the stages of the narrative model work together to form a compelling data story.

How Does the Data Storytelling Arc Compare with Other Communication Models?

While I've primarily focused on fiction-based models for narrative structure, you may have come across other communication models for structuring business information. When I was preparing a data storytelling workshop for a business client, the employees were already accustomed to forming their business presentations in a manner that conformed to one of these models. After some research and comparison, I found that the *Data Storytelling Arc* is compatible with a variety of business communication models. Each of the models I found had three stages, similar to Aristotle's model. As shown in Figure 6.6, you can tailor your data story to work within these structures if needed.

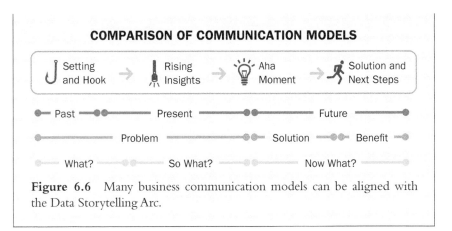

Figure 6.6 Many business communication models can be aligned with the Data Storytelling Arc.

Fleshing Out Your Narrative with Story Points

Plot is what happens in your story. Every story needs structure, just as everybody needs a skeleton. It is how you "flesh out and clothe" your structure that makes each story unique.

—Caroline Lawrence, author

Now that we have a basic narrative structure to follow, we can begin assembling the data points to fill out your data story. In literature and film, writers string together various plot points to advance their stories. These plot points are the twists, turns, and other developments in a story that move the characters through the narrative arc. For example, a plot point might be a memorable scene in which the hero is first trained by a mentor, meets a love interest, or witnesses a villain defeating an ally.

Similarly, your data story will be crafted from a series of key data points, which I will refer to as *story points*. From your Hook to the Aha Moment to your recommendations, the story points will shape and inform the various scenes of your data story. How many story points you have will depend on the depth or breadth of your data story. Generally, only a small portion of data points from your analysis will become actual story points. Most of your story points will come from the key findings or insights that caught your attention during the exploratory analysis phase. Other story points may simply provide context or supporting details to help form a coherent narrative, especially as Rising Insights.

In 2015, former Tableau evangelist Ben Jones identified seven different data story types; I found these useful in defining the various types of story points (Jones 2015). Modifying and expanding on Jones's seven variants, I settled on nine common types of story points (see Figure 6.7).

NINE COMMON TYPES OF STORY POINTS

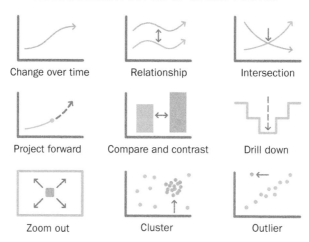

Figure 6.7 Your key insights will most likely align with one of these nine common types of story points.

While there may be other types of story points, this initial set should cover the most common forms:

1. **Change over time** focuses on how a metric shifts over time. For example, you might highlight how there's a downward or upward trend in a key metric (gradual or sharp). Even no change in a trended line may be a story point when something was expected to happen. For example, your company's investment in safety training doesn't reduce the workplace injury rate.

2. **Relationship** highlights how two things are related to each other in some way. You may show how there is a positive or negative correlation between two metrics that may or may not imply causation. For example, you could show how higher customer satisfaction scores may be contributing to a higher customer renewal rate.

3. **Intersection** reveals the moment when one metric surpasses or falls below another metric (or the same thing happens between

two plotted values). When one metric crosses or intersects with another, it could be a positive or negative sign depending on the situation. For example, you may be highlighting when your start-up's revenues surpassed costs (finally profitable), or when revenues fell below costs, indicating you still have operational issues to address.

4. **Project forward** shows what is predicted to occur in the future. Whereas the rest of the story points are primarily focused on what happened, this story point forecasts what may occur at some point. For example, you could highlight the forecasted growth of a city's population over the next five years.

5. **Compare and contrast** exposes the similarities or differences between two or more items. For example, you may contrast the overall equipment effectiveness rates of two factories—one that has been recently updated and the other that needs upgrading. This story point is probably the most popular type and is frequently featured in most data stories. Facilitating simple comparisons will be a key focus of the next chapter.

6. **Drill down** moves from a higher-level or aggregated view of a metric to a more detailed view. Essentially, you break down an overall number by different dimensions of varying levels of granularity. For example, you may start with sales results at a national level and then drill into the regional or individual store-level results.

7. **Zoom out** moves in the opposite direction of the *drill down* story point, expanding from a more granular view to a more aggregated view. For example, you may start with an individual store's sales results and then position its results alongside cohorts in the same region or in terms of national store averages.

8. **Cluster** reveals a concentrated grouping or distribution of results within a dataset. A large concentration in one area may indicate an opportunity or problem. For example, you may show how your hospital's costliest segment of patients is comprised of smokers.

9. **Outlier** uncovers an anomaly that differs dramatically from other data points. An aberration or deviation from the norm can highlight an opportunity or problem, depending on the context. For example, you may display how, in terms of repeat purchases, a specific product significantly outperforms all others in a product line.

As you evaluate your own story points, you'll find the story point types can overlap, but in most cases, a dominant type will emerge. One thing to keep in mind is you might have one or more story points in a single data visualization—there doesn't need to be a one-to-one relationship between story points and visualizations. That's why some data visualizations are capable of telling a more robust story than others—because they contain more than one story point such as Minard's Napoleon map in Chapter 4.

As you look to craft your data story, you need to be mindful of your narrative's flow and whether your story points form a cohesive story. Being familiar with the various types of story points can give you another perspective on how your data story should be formed. For example, if you were to examine the story point types used in the ecommerce data story above, you'll see how different types of story points are utilized to form the data story (see Figure 6.8).

THE ECOMMERCE EXAMPLE AND ITS STORY POINTS

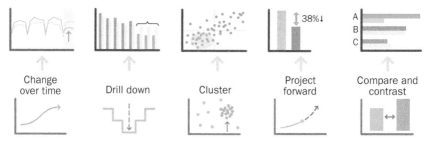

Figure 6.8 The ecommerce data story used various types of story points to convey its message. While you may use only a few of the types on a regular basis, it is helpful to know the full breadth of options you have.

Now that you better understand the concepts of a narrative structure and story points, you're ready to learn how storyboarding can help organize your story points into an effective storyline.

Storyboarding Your Data Story

The storyboard's primary value is that it forces you to have a reason for, and a consistent approach to, everything you do.

—David Becker, eLearning consultant

In the early 1930s, the Walt Disney Studio introduced the use of storyboards to plan the sequence of scenes for its animated films. Today, the technique has been adopted for other situations—such as live-action films, presentations, training courses, and so on. When you're planning the structure of your data story, storyboarding can help you organize the flow of your story points and determine what is essential to your data story. Whether you use sticky notes, a notepad, or a whiteboard, storyboarding helps you to determine which findings need to be a part of your story and how best to sequence them. It also helps you identify potential gaps where you may need to gather more supporting data. In a team scenario, where multiple individuals might be providing different story points, the storyboard provides a unifying vision to tie together all of the contributions into a cohesive data story.

Too often, the tendency is for people to dive in and "just start creating." When you jump into visualizing your data story too quickly without storyboarding, you pass up an essential opportunity to step back and consider what the overall narrative structure should look like. The process of storyboarding helps you craft a tighter, more impactful narrative, but it can also be a big time-saver. Instead of wasting an inordinate amount of time generating content that may or may not be included in your data story, you can pinpoint beforehand what exactly is needed. While simpler data stories may not require much storyboarding, you can't afford to skip this important method of pre-visualizing your narrative when it is complex with multiple story points.

Before getting into the four-step process for storyboarding, I want to emphasize its primary purpose is to *build a story*—not to determine which data visualizations you're going to create. Until you've established the flow of your data story, focusing on the data visualizations will only be a distraction. While you may have some rough ideas about how you'll visualize your information, it's better to suspend any in-depth visualization work until you have your narrative structure in place. Depending on how your story points come together, you may find an interesting data chart from your exploratory analysis is no longer essential to your story. With this perspective in mind, let's begin with the first step in the storyboarding process.

Step 1: Identify Your Aha Moment

The first step is to identify the main insight or takeaway of your analysis (see Figure 6.9). It will become the climax and focal point of your data story—the Aha Moment. Before you settle on a particular insight, you want to perform the "so what?" test that was covered in the previous chapter. Why should your audience care about this insight? What's significant about it? What are its implications? An Aha Moment isn't just an interesting data point. It would be incomplete without an explanation of what the numbers mean for your audience. For example, you may have found 45% of your company's construction projects are currently delayed by 60–90 days. As relevant and interesting as this data point may be to your internal stakeholders, unless you can confidently answer the "so what" question, it's deficient. When you explain this level of delay will incur an extra $5 million in idle labor and equipment costs that weren't budgeted for—now you have an Aha Moment.

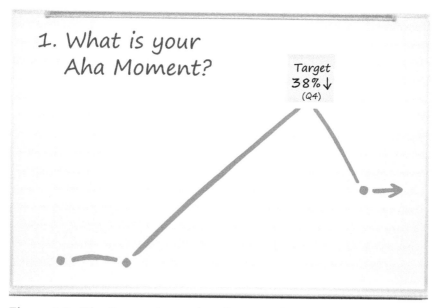

Figure 6.9 The first step in storyboarding your data story is to identify your Aha Moment.

Whenever you can attach a monetary value to your major finding, you make it significantly more concrete for your audience. Most decision makers think in terms of money—revenues, profits, costs, investments, and so on. Therefore, you want to quantify what the insight will mean to their profit and loss (P&L) statement, equity, budget, or bank account. In addition, it might be advantageous to turn a monthly figure into an annual figure to emphasize its potential value. For example, an incremental revenue source of $100,000 per month might garner more attention if it were positioned as an additional $1.2 million in *annual* revenues. You want to be careful you don't sell your insight short by inadvertently reducing its perceived value. On the other hand, you also don't want to artificially inflate its value by choosing an arbitrary or unrealistic timeframe.

Lastly, to ensure your Aha Moment is memorable, you want to articulate it as succinctly as possible—preferably in a single sentence. The sentence will be a combination of what the insight is and its meaning or impact. For the ecommerce data story I shared in the previous section, the Aha Moment could be conveyed as follows:

> *Due to poor sales of Brand X, we're going to miss our quarterly sales target by 38%, which puts our entire team's performance bonuses in jeopardy.*

If you're unable to explain your Aha Moment in a single sentence or two, you may not have found your central insight yet, or you haven't fully determined why your audience should care about it. When you can distill down your insight to a concise statement that is clear and persuasive, you're better positioned to see your data story succeed.

The reason you start with the Aha Moment is to verify you have something that even merits a data story. In addition, when you start with the end in mind, you know where you need to take your audience. Ultimately, you want your audience to draw the same conclusions from your analysis as you did, and having a clear destination will help you to design the right path. Every proceeding story point can be weighed and measured in its ability to advance the story toward the climax or Aha Moment.

Step 2: Find Your Beginning (the Hook and Setting)

After you've determined where you need to take your audience, you must then determine where your data story begins (see Figure 6.10) and establish the Hook (first) and Setting (second). Until you identify your Hook, you won't know what you need to cover in your Setting to properly frame it. In attempting to tell their data story, many analysts mistakenly retrace the steps of their analysis efforts. In painstaking detail, they explain everything they looked at before they eventually found something noteworthy. This approach, which I call the *Analysis Journey*, may stem from an unconscious desire to establish the accuracy of the data or to show how clever or thorough they were in their analysis. However, it doesn't resonate with most audiences who just want to "eat the cake"—not hear about its ingredients or the recipe steps. They want insights—not an overview of the analysis process.

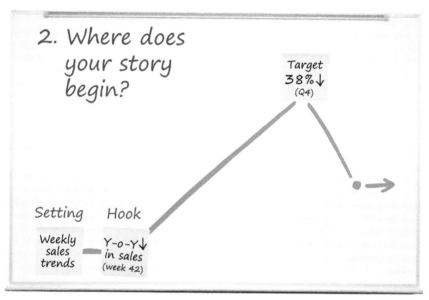

Figure 6.10 The next step is to identify your Hook and the Setting that is needed.

Rather than spending time on nonessential information, you must quickly catch your audience's attention with a key observation that entices them to learn more. In storyboarding, the reason you start by identifying the Aha Moment and not the Hook is to ensure you have the most important part of the data story covered—the central insight. Even with a compelling hook, your narrative can meander and lead to nowhere without a clear destination (Aha Moment). In some cases, a potential Hook for your data story may have originated from your audience. For example, a leader may have spotted an anomaly or trend in a report and questioned what it meant. A data point that piqued someone's curiosity can be used as the entry point to your data story in the following way:

> Recently, you noticed our fourth-quarter sales numbers are trending below last year's results by 28%. I'd like to show you how this trend could have a significant impact on . . .

However, in other cases, your analysis may not have been prompted by an audience member's questions about a data point. In these scenarios, you will need to comb through your findings and reflect on what initially caught your attention during the analysis phase. If your analysis were a detective case, the Hook would be the first substantial clue you uncovered. Going back to the B2C retailer example in Chapter 1, the unexpected double peak (what made the data science team go "hmm") would be a great Hook to tee up the team's international reseller discovery (Aha Moment).

In many cases, you may have observed a shift or change in a metric that indicated a potential problem or opportunity. *Resonate* author Nancy Duarte found that many successful presenters, such as Abraham Lincoln and Martin Luther King Jr., created conflict by juxtaposing "what is" with "what could be" (Duarte 2010). The comparison creates dramatic tension, which helps engage the audience in a topic. Similarly, you can draw your audience into your data story by contrasting "what is" with "what was" after a significant change occurred. For example, a company may be accustomed to retaining 85% of its customers. However, a few weeks ago, the retention rate dipped to 68% (a 20% decrease). This type of juxtaposition provides both context and the Hook. It not only establishes what the expected norm is (85%), but turns the variance (20% decrease) into a compelling mystery that can be used to grab the audience's attention.

Finally, once you have your Hook, you'll want to evaluate how much background information your audience will require to adequately comprehend and appreciate the Hook's significance—this forms your Setting. If your audience lacks sufficient context to grasp your Hook, its impact can be severely reduced or even negated. On the other hand, if you provide too much background information in your Setting, your well-intended context can become noise. You want to select *just enough* context so they can orient themselves to the story points you're going to share. For example, in order to appreciate a recent decrease in quarterly sales, the audience will need to be familiar with quarterly sales performance over the past four-to-eight quarters. The purpose of the Setting section is to get everyone in the audience on the same page. However, if your Setting is not concise and to the point, it may cause your audience to lose interest before your Hook can even catch their attention.

Step 3: Select Your Rising Insights

Now, you're ready to build out your narrative from the Hook to the Aha Moment (see Figure 6.11). Each data story will be different, so there isn't a single pattern or a required number of story points for the Rising Insights section. Depending on the depth or breadth of the findings from your analysis, you may have multiple Rising Insights or none at all. However, while it is possible to go directly from the Hook to the Aha Moment, most data stories will require some level of supporting data or story points to ensure your audience fully grasps your main insight.

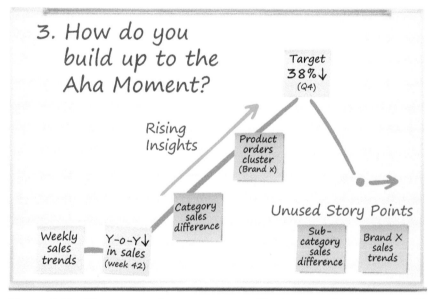

Figure 6.11   The next step is to connect your Hook to your Aha Moment with relevant story points that become the Rising Insights of your data story.

Initially, you'll want to document all of the story points from your analysis that could potentially go into your data story. Next, you'll want to be selective about which story points become Rising Insights. Anything that doesn't fit on the path between your Hook and Aha Moment may not make sense for your data story. The following questions can help you determine which story points to use as Rising Insights:

- *Which supporting data points develop the plot or provide crucial context?* Some data points will be critical to understanding the Aha Moment either because they provide deeper insights or add necessary context.
- *Can you preemptively address audience questions with your findings?* As you look to build your story, you may want to include information that addresses key questions that you anticipate your audience having. In some cases, your audience may be resistant to certain findings, and you may be able to address their concerns strategically with the right story points.
- *What findings were unexpected or surprising?* While you don't want to include irrelevant information, you'll want to highlight facts that were extraordinary or unusual that may surprise your audience and spur their interest.
- *What findings can be removed without hurting the narrative?* As a final check on what you decide to include, you'll want to confirm if any story points can be removed without impacting the story. You might find some of your findings are redundant, carry less weight, or end up being tangential to your main idea. As with most communications, less is more with data storytelling. As was highlighted at the end of the previous chapter, you may not need as many story points to convey your message as you think you do. Running your story by a colleague may help you identify information that is superfluous to your narrative.

As you storyboard your Rising Insights and sequence them in the order in which you'll share them, you want to ensure your story points form a smooth narrative flow. Sequence your points in a logical manner that mirrors the path your audience's curiosity would naturally follow. Through the storyboarding process, you may uncover a gap or rough transition in your Rising Insights. You may need to perform more analysis to close a gap or smooth a transition in your narrative. Until you've laid out your story points in a storyboard, it may be difficult to anticipate narrative gaps or awkward transitions beforehand. However, this sort of attention to detail is the difference between just sharing your findings and crafting a data story that is both coherent and engaging.

Step 4: Empower Your Audience to Act

After you've built out your story to its climax—the Aha Moment—your story still isn't finished. If you provide the decision makers in your audience only with an insightful takeaway and nothing more, they may not know what they should do with the new information. Most decision makers will want to weigh options and then make an informed decision. However, because they may lack the necessary analytical skills, time, or resources to investigate all the potential solutions, your central insight may end up going nowhere. It's important to strike while the proverbial iron is hot (*kairos* appeal), or the initial interest generated by your Aha Moment may wane and then be pushed aside as more pressing matters grab your audience's attention.

In order to drive change and action, at this point, you need to cover the *Solution and Next Steps* (see Figure 6.12). A *complete* data story provides guidance on how your audience can move forward with your idea or insight. For example, in the ecommerce data story, a cost-benefit analysis of each alternative solution could empower the audience to consider the different options and come to a faster decision on next steps. Along with an analysis of the various alternatives, your audience may also welcome a recommendation on the best solution or path forward. If you've done a thorough job of analyzing the data and crafting a story, your audience will value your judgment. While they may not fully agree with your assessment, they will at least be interested in your perspective after you invested significant time and effort in preparing the data story.

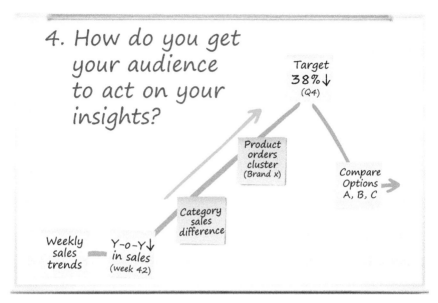

Figure 6.12   If you're looking to drive action and change, you need to help the audience understand what it can do with your insights by helping them identify a Solution and Next Steps.

Even when you've examined various options and provided a strong recommendation, your audience may still delay making a decision. In these situations, the perceived cost of *not making a decision* is viewed as being lower than that of *making an immediate decision*. Another critical piece of your data story may be to create a sense of urgency around solving the problem you've identified or seizing the opportunity before a window closes. Frequently, if you can quantify the cost of *not making a decision* from a daily or weekly perspective, it can help motivate your audience to act on the insights you've shared with them. For example, after sharing a recommendation on how the ecommerce team could improve product sales, you could emphasize how delaying the proposed changes costs the company $2 million each week in lost potential revenue. Once you attach monetary figures to the cost of delaying a decision, your audience will better appreciate why a decision must be made in a timely fashion. Ultimately, the better you understand your audience, the more you'll be able to tailor the Solution and Next Steps section to your audience's decision-making style and preferences.

Finally, if you are presenting your data story directly to your audience, you need to leave sufficient time for questions and discussion. It can be a critical step in gaining buy-in and alignment from a group of stakeholders with diverse opinions. At one presentation I attended, a manager laid out an impressive data story to a group of executives. Just as he was finishing his presentation, I noticed the executives had already started closing their laptops to head to their next meeting. A wave of panic swept over the manager's face as he realized he hadn't given his audience an opportunity to discuss the insights and agree on a course of action. A few weeks later, he was able to reschedule another meeting so they could discuss and decide on next steps, but he lost some momentum in the process. If you've crafted a compelling data story, anticipate that it will generate a healthy amount of questions and discussion. Ensure you leave adequate time at the end of your data story (or during) for two-way communication to occur—it may end up being essential to persuading your audience to act on your insights.

What If You Don't Have All the Answers?

In some situations, you may have discovered a great Aha Moment, but you may find yourself struggling to develop meaningful recommendations. This can be due to not having the required authority, expertise, or domain knowledge to propose legitimate solutions. You definitely don't want to undermine your credibility by suggesting impractical or untenable options just so your narrative conforms with the Data Storytelling Arc. In some scenarios, it may be more expedient to share the story up to the Aha Moment and then leverage the collective know-how and resources of the audience to determine the best course of action. The narrative structure can set the stage for collaborative problem solving and ensure the group clearly understands the nature of the situation, its level of urgency, and desired outcomes. While you may not always have all of the answers at your disposal, you can still spearhead the search for solutions and enlist the help of a capable, invested audience.

When They Want Just the Facts

I was a kind of hyper-intense person in my twenties and very impatient.
—Bill Gates, Microsoft founder and philanthropist

When I've shared the Data Storytelling Arc at presentations and workshops, I'm often asked how data storytellers should handle impatient executives who "just want the facts." These time-challenged individuals are unlikely to wait patiently for you to build up to your Aha Moment. You may have no more than 10–15 minutes (sometimes less) to get your main point across before they lose interest and shift their attention to another pressing topic. In these situations, the generally accepted practice is to provide an executive summary in which you review the most important information at the outset. However, as I noted in Chapter 4, this approach negates many of the benefits you would gain from having a narrative structure. Just imagine creating an executive summary for the popular Star Wars movie *The Empire Strikes Back.* Hearing "Darth Vader is Luke Skywalker's father" at the outset would surely ruin the cinematic experience for most people. The same effect can occur when you give an audience "the facts" up front without a story.

With this type of audience, you can't just launch into your data story. Even when you know they'll care about your findings, they're not conditioned to receive information in a story format. To accommodate an impatient executive, you'll need to create a *data trailer* for your data story (see Figure 6.13). Similar to movie trailers that are designed to promote a film and draw in an audience, your data trailer is designed to *pique the interest* of your audience and *gain their permission* to tell the entire story. While a movie trailer tries not to ruin the story by giving away any spoilers, the data trailer includes a brief Setting and Hook with a major spoiler—the Aha Moment. In situations where an impatient boss or executive must be convinced of the payoff for listening to a data story, you reveal why your insight is worth 20 minutes of attention. After hearing the data trailer, the executive has the option to say "tell me more" or indicate they're not interested in learning more. A data trailer isn't an alternative to having a complete data story—it's simply a tool for gaining an executive's buy-in and inviting them to explore the rest of your data story.

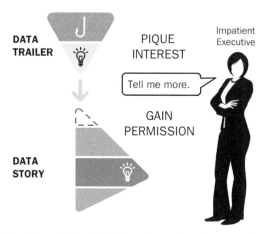

Figure 6.13 The Data Trailer is designed to pique interest from the impatient executive and gain her permission to tell your data story. If you gain permission, you've already set up your data story, so you can dive immediately into the Rising Insights.

Data storytelling is still a relatively new approach for data communication. Up until now, most executives have been exposed to mind-numbing data dumps on a repeated basis over the years. Their insistence for "just the facts" may just be a coping mechanism to avoid being overloaded and inundated with too much noise. If you see a potential opening, I'd encourage you to test a simple data story on this type of executive—even if it means starting with the modified data trailer approach. Despite their hardened exterior, everyone loves a good story—it's in their DNA. Once they've experienced what effective data communication feels like, don't be surprised when they advocate for data stories to be shared throughout your organization.

Uncovering the Heroes in Your Data Story

I think the best stories always end up being about the people rather than the event, which is to say character-driven.

—Stephen King, author

Characters are an essential element of stories. What would *Pride and Prejudice* be like without Elizabeth Bennet, or the *Harry Potter* series without Lord Voldemort? While the plot of the story is important, it's the characters—the protagonist and antagonist—who breathe life into the tale and make it truly interesting. As we turn to our raw data, it can seem cold, distant, and impersonal. Some analytical individuals may prefer to keep the data somewhat detached and neutral. However, in order to make your insights more engaging and relatable, you should consider *humanizing* the data for your audience by revealing the faces behind the numbers. While you may be enamored with a particular insight you've discovered, your audience will relate better to people than to an abstract data point. In Chapter 2, we saw how the story of the seven-year-old Malian girl, Rokia, was much more compelling than an assortment of statistics on the suffering of children across Africa. The more you can bring out the characters or heroes hidden within your data, the more your story will resonate with your audience.

Fortunately, most data is either directly or indirectly related to people—your customers, prospects, employees, partners, patients, citizens, and so on. Some of your most useful and enlightening data will be based on the behaviors, attitudes, and attributes of people. Even when your data appears to be generated by processes or machines—not humans—it can usually still be tied back to humans. Rather than looking at transactional data (process-generated) as the outputs of a business system, you can envision it as the purchasing behaviors of individual consumers or organizational buyers. Rather than seeing the sensor data (machine-generated) from connected cars as vehicle information, you can view it as reflecting the usage patterns of drivers. Most likely the heroes of your data story are standing in front of you; you just need to adjust your frame of reference to see them.

Confusion about Who Is the "Hero" of a Data Story

From time to time, I've heard people say the "audience is the hero of a data story." I believe this viewpoint can lead to confusion and misdirect the focus of your data story. Its original

(continued)

(*continued*)

intent was probably to emphasize making the story as relatable as possible to the audience. I believe this objective can be achieved without necessarily casting the audience as the lead role in your data story.

To be honest, most people don't want to be the focus of attention—they don't want a light shined on their accomplishments or (especially) their failures. Imagine how uncomfortable it would be to sit through a film or play depicting your life story. Between the painful inaccuracies and equally painful truths, you'd want to flee for the exit. However, audiences do like characters to whom they can relate and care about. Salespeople care about prospects. Doctors care about patients. Hiring managers care about job candidates. You get the idea. Depending on your audience, you choose the hero who matters to them in the data.

While your audience most likely won't be the main characters in your data story, I believe they can still be heroes in a different but critical way. Ultimately, you're going to need them to act heroically in enacting your solutions and recommendations. Your data story can prepare the audience to be real heroes as they embrace and apply your insights to drive value within an organization.

In my career in marketing analytics, I found it highly effective to highlight people—not just numbers—in my data stories. I found marketing audiences enjoyed getting deeper insights into their customers and prospects, so featuring them as characters in my presentations was an effective way of gaining their interest, attention, and buy-in. The following five-step process (see Figure 6.14) reveals how you can add heroes to your next data story:

HOW TO ADD A HERO TO YOUR DATA STORY

1 Determine where your insights intersect with people

2 Build a data-driven profile of your hero

3 Give your hero an identity

4 Give your hero a voice

5 Show your hero's journey

Figure 6.14 This five-step process will help you develop a hero for your data story.

1. **Determine where your insights intersect with people.** In some cases, it may be easy to identify the group of people your analysis touches. In these cases, the challenge is how broad or narrow your focus should be. For example, you could emphasize customers in general or a more targeted segment of customers that fits a certain profile (online, female, or repeat). In other cases where your data is a little more abstract, you may need to evaluate how your data relates to the people your audience cares about. Each audience is going to be interested in different key groups. If you can link your insights to people who matter to your audience, you're going to win their attention with your story.

2. **Build a data-driven persona of your hero.** In marketing and user experience design, it's common to develop personas to help the marketers and designers appreciate the goals, attributes, and behaviors of their customers or users. Each persona is typically portrayed as an individual but is representative of a particular segment of people. Synthesizing all the quantitative data you have on your intended segment, you can flesh out key traits for your hero and build a persona. Depending on what's relevant or important to your data story, you can profile different aspects—such as their gender, ethnicity, location, income level, interests, and so on. Sometimes,

you may include details that may not be essential to your story but are helpful in establishing an interesting and memorable character.

3. **Give your hero an identity.** Whether or not you're a fan of stock photography, a useful tactic in creating your hero is to show a representative picture of who they are. As human beings, we are naturally engaged by pictures of other people. Researchers at the Georgia Institute of Technology and Yahoo Labs discovered Instagram pictures with human faces were 38% more likely to generate "likes" than those without. They were also 32% more likely to be commented on (Georgia Tech 2014). In another study, researchers found including a patient's photo with imaging exam results made radiologists more empathetic and thorough in their analysis of the results. They found the radiologists were more likely to view the patients as human beings and not just as anonymous subjects (Radiological Society of North America 2008). A carefully chosen stock photo can be helpful in drawing in your audience—just like a cheesy picture can lose them. Using different images of the same model can be helpful in displaying different emotions (frustration, happiness) or situations/activities (work, recreation). Images will make your hero a visible, integral part of your data story.

4. **Give your hero a voice.** As you build your hero's persona, you should consider leaning on qualitative (non-numerical) data, not just quantitative (numerical) data. If you're able to access survey, interview, social, or product-review data, you have what you need to give your hero a voice. For example, if your analysis was about how customers were unhappy with a new policy change, one of the best ways to demonstrate their discontent would be to share feedback from actual customers. A few insightful remarks from customers may be the extra leverage you need to sell your audience on making a change.

5. **Show your hero's journey.** While your audience may be familiar with *whom* the hero represents, they may not be acquainted with that group's journey. Rather than just relying on data points to highlight the outcomes of a bad or good experience, you could show your audience what the hero actually encounters. By putting your audience in the hero's shoes, they will experience the pain or gain for themselves. For example, you may use screenshots to illustrate how an online application process is broken and confusing. You may diagram the back-and-forth nature of an inefficient process for submitting

time off. By helping the audience to experience something from a different perspective, you can open your audience's eyes to issues that wouldn't have been as apparent or urgent if they only saw the numbers and charts. In addition, you can reveal what a happy ending looks like for the hero, which is tied to your recommendations.

Inserting relatable and recognizable characters into your data story will help humanize your narrative and enable your audience to see your insights from a people-centered perspective. While it may not always be possible or easy with every dataset, any opportunity to show how your insights impact human beings should be pursued, especially when your audience cares about those individuals. By putting a human face on your numbers, you make the data much more approachable and engaging for your audience.

How Conflict Amplifies the Impact of Your Data Narrative

Conflict is to story what sound is to music.
                    —Robert McKee, screenwriting expert and author

In narrative, conflict is the challenge or problem the story's main characters must overcome to achieve their goal. Conflict is often viewed as an essential ingredient in forming a *compelling* story. How interesting would Oliver Twist be if he wasn't a poor, runaway orphan? In the *Lord of the Rings*, what if Frodo felt no burden or corrupting influence in his role as the Ring-bearer? Without struggles or obstacles, you are left with a boring, uninspiring tale.

Fortunately, data stories often have conflict at their core, as they are primarily centered on solving problems or seizing untapped opportunities. The source of conflict can be *internal*—your company, department, or team isn't measuring up to its past performance, expectations, or a specific goal or target. The source could be *external*—your group is underperforming when benchmarked against a peer group, a competitor, or the overall industry. Even though conflict will be an inherent part of your story, like a writer or director, you still need to decide how you're going to employ it strategically within your data narrative.

Simply having a problem or unexploited opportunity that provides conflict doesn't guarantee it will engage your audience. How you package and deliver the conflict will determine how impactful it is. Playwright William Archer once stated, "Drama is anticipation mingled with uncertainty." If conflict is used effectively in your data narrative, it can generate similar dramatic effects in your audience such as *intrigue*, *tension*, and *suspense*. For example, rather than just providing a basic summary of a problem, you could approach it from different perspectives or angles to tease out its unique features:

- How long has it been an issue?
- How frequently does it occur?
- How widespread is the problem?
- Who is impacted by the problem?
- What are its contributing factors?
- How difficult is it to address?
- What are the consequences if it isn't fixed?

With each additional revelation, the problem will gain deeper meaning and significance for your audience. While it may not be possible to explore all of the viewpoints, some specific insights may especially resonate with your audience and *intrigue* them to learn more. As your audience gains a deeper appreciation of the problem, it may feel growing *tension* as it waits to find out how the problem can be resolved. The tension evokes an emotional response in your audience members, drawing them into your narrative as their anxiety and stress levels increase. While chronic stress is harmful, small doses of acute stress can be beneficial and sharpen your audience's attention.

Conflict can generate *suspense* as the audience becomes more curious about the problem and how it will be overcome. Researchers at the Georgia Institute of Technology found that when people experience high-suspense moments, they focus less on peripheral information to focus more intently on the story (Georgia Tech 2015). In their study, they showed subjects different scenes from suspenseful movies such as *Alien* and *Misery*. As the participants watched the scenes, a flashing checkerboard pattern was shown around the edges of the screen. As the researchers monitored the participants' brain activity on MRI machines, they observed their visual focus would narrow as the suspense intensified and broaden when the suspense faded. Essentially, we get "tunnel vision" as suspense channels our attention to the most critical visual information.

When you prepare to add tension and suspense to your data narrative, you can turn to the *Unifying Theory of 2+2* as a guiding principle. In a 2012 TED Talk, Pixar writer-director Andrew Stanton described this storytelling theory in the following way:

> We're born problem solvers. We're compelled to deduce and to deduct because that's what we do in real life. It's this well-organized absence of information that draws us in. . . . Make the audience put things together. Don't give them four, give them two plus two. The elements you provide and the order you place them in is crucial to whether you succeed or fail at engaging the audience. (Stanton 2012)

Rather than just simply serving up answers ("four") to a passive audience, you can activate your audience's curiosity and problem-solving skills by having them participate in a closer examination of the numbers ("What is two plus two?"). If an audience can reach the same conclusion on their own ("The sum is four"), they will be more engaged by the narrative and will experience a mild form of germane cognitive load. In the previous chapter, we learned this form of cognitive load can help your message to be more memorable—it's not a bad thing. Here are some ways in which you can strategically employ the *Unifying Theory of 2+2* in your data narrative:

1. **What happened next?** In this scenario, you show the past results to provide some background context and then ask the audience to predict what they think happened next. For example, you could show the campaign results for May and then ask them what they expect the results to be in June. This approach also provides you with deeper insights into your audience's preconceived beliefs and expectations. In addition, it introduces tension and suspense because the audience usually doesn't want to be wrong and will be anxious to learn what actually occurred.

2. **Fill in the blanks.** With this technique, you partially reveal some of the results and ask the audience to fill in some data points that are strategically hidden by you. For example, you might reveal the sales performance for three regions and ask the audience to estimate what happened in the remaining region. Alternatively, you

could reveal the great sales results for a region but withhold its poor employee satisfaction scores. While this approach relies on speculation, it does bring the audience's beliefs and assumptions into clear view for everyone involved—both you and the audience. When your audience is shocked or surprised by the actual results, their attention and interest in your narrative will deepen.

3. **Do you see what I see?** In this strategy, using a data chart that lacks any highlighting or annotations, you ask the audience to tell you what's unusual or what stands out. After you have given them some time to evaluate the chart, you switch to a different version of the data chart that highlights key insights. A number of different outcomes can occur with this method. First, the audience may pinpoint the insights you found and feel clever that they were able to make the same observations. Second, they may notice something you didn't and contribute something new to the discussion. Third, they may not find anything meaningful in the chart and then will be surprised as you connect the dots for them. The audience will feel tension about finding something in the data and suspense over learning what you discovered.

Novelist William Landay noted, "Good stories are driven by conflict, tension, and high stakes." In certain situations, and with an audience you know well, these techniques can make your data story more compelling. However, you'll want to be careful to use them tactfully and judiciously. As you invite the audience to participate in the evaluation of the data, you need to be amply prepared for unexpected feedback and sidetracking observations. In addition, the goal isn't to embarrass anyone in your audience when they guess wrong or frustrate people with a slower interactive approach when they're anxious and ready to learn more. If they are employed wisely by the data storyteller, conflict and tension can be helpful at keeping your audience engaged and focused on your message.

Make Your Ideas More Digestible with Analogies

Analogies, it is true, decide nothing, but they can make one feel more at home.

—Sigmund Freud, neurologist and founder of psychoanalysis

Whenever your data narrative deals with a new or complex subject, there's another narrative tool that can be helpful—*analogies*. An analogy is a comparison of a *complex* or *unfamiliar* subject matter to another that is *simpler* or *more familiar*. As an example, in Chapter 5, when I introduced the concept of working memory, I compared the human brain to a computer, based on its input, processing, and memory components. Because most people have a high-level understanding of how computers work, they can more easily grasp the different functions of the brain when they are compared to the components of a computer. Analogies can serve as useful shortcuts that can significantly reduce the time it takes an audience to learn new or abstract concepts. As American attorney Dudley Field Malone recognized, "One good analogy is worth three hours of discussion."

In data storytelling, analogies can also be used to communicate key concepts or insights in a manner that is easier and faster for an audience to follow and absorb. They can be used at any stage in your data story if they can help sharpen or quicken the audience's understanding of your insights. Instead of having to invest significant time explaining new information to others, you can expedite the *knowledge transfer* process by tying off key ideas with relatable analogies. For example, you could compare the current challenges in a manufacturer's supply chain to a triathlon. When a triathlete struggles at one of her transitions (T1: swim-to-bike), the problems can cascade throughout the race like they do with supply chain issues. Just like smooth, efficient transitions at each stage are important to elite triathletes, they can be equally important to a manufacturer and its supply chain.

Analogies can also be used to reinforce the central theme or message of your data narrative, making it significantly more memorable and repeatable. When you're presenting your data story, they can also create opportunities to use visual imagery and add emotional power to your narrative. Even the mental imagery of a well-chosen analogy can make your data story more potent. For example, your findings could be about a new competitor that has recently emerged in your industry and is taking away key customers. Alternatively, your insights could be about a broken internal process that is inhibiting your sales growth. Either of these examples can be positioned as a villain that must be confronted and defeated. Creating an antagonist from your findings can be a great way of drawing attention to a new threat or problem.

Cultural anthropologist Mary Catherine Bateson said, "The human species thinks in metaphors and learns through stories." Good analogies can complement your insights by facilitating learning and injecting more narrative into your data story. However, if you're not careful, bad analogies can just as easily confuse your audience and weaken your overall story. In order to verify whether you have a solid analogy, you'll want to consider the following attributes:

1. **Is it relatable?** Depending on how well you know your audience, you should have a good sense for the relevance of your analogy. For example, if you knew a key stakeholder was a car-racing enthusiast, an analogy based on Formula 1 racing could really resonate with him, whereas it might fall flat on an audience that isn't as familiar with this type of sports event.

2. **Is it sound?** The soundness or "fit" of an analogy is based on how many parallel attributes the two subjects share. The more similarities they share, the more sound the analogy can potentially be. However, a critical mismatch or logical breakdown can weaken an otherwise sound analogy and undermine its overall usefulness.

3. **Is it clear?** If you're not careful, some analogies can end up being more complex than the abstract ideas they're designed to explain. You want a somewhat familiar analogy that is both clear and simple. If it places too much of a burden on the audience to comprehend the similarities, it will add extraneous load and potentially fail entirely.

4. **Is it concise?** The faster the analogy is to communicate, the more powerful it will be. If it takes a long time to develop and explain, the payoff may not be worth it because people may lose interest along the way.

5. **Is it interesting?** The more thought-provoking your analogy is, the more people will remember it. Dry, overused examples will be easily forgotten. However, something that is a *personal, topical,* or *unexpected* will make your audience more curious. For example,

if you had just had your first child, a "new parent" analogy would take on a personal tone that most audiences would find hard to ignore. On a different note, if you compared your current pricing policy to an out-of-control carnival ride, your audience will be intrigued to see how you could draw such an unusual comparison.

Analogies represent yet another powerful way of connecting with your audience through narrative and of making your ideas more engaging and approachable. An analogy can be used to clarify a minor aspect of your findings or to help underscore a major theme within your data story. Be mindful that not every subject can be easily tied to an analogy. For example, in the popular animated TV show *The Simpsons*, Homer Simpson once told his son, Bart, that women were like refrigerators: "They're about six feet tall, 300 pounds. They make ice, and . . . um . . . Oh, wait a minute. Actually, a woman is more like a beer" (O'Brien and Archer 1992). While most analogies don't fall apart this epically, each analogy will have inherent limits. How far you push a comparison can determine whether it supports your story or buckles under pressure.

As the writer and director of your own data story, you control how your insights unfold to the audience. While most people have placed a heavy emphasis on the visualization aspects of data storytelling, narrative plays an integral role in crafting effective data stories. If you wish to become a data storyteller, you must master the fundamentals of narrative and not just analysis or data visualization. How you develop the plot of your data story is equally important as which charts you choose to communicate your insights.

From this chapter, you've learned how narrative builds a sturdy structure on your data foundation, preparing the way for the visual elements to now be added. While data stories may not always embody all of the characteristics of traditional stories, the more "story-like" or "narrative-centered" they are, the more engaging and compelling they become. The next two chapters will examine the last remaining pillar of data storytelling—visuals—that brings your storyline to life.

References

Duarte, N. 2010. *Resonate: Present Visual Stories That Transform Audiences.* Hoboken, NJ: John Wiley & Sons.

Freytag, G. 1895. *Freytag's Technique of the Drama: An Exposition of Dramatic Composition and Art* (trans. E. J. MacEwan). Chicago: S.C. Griggs & Company.

Georgia Institute of Technology. 2015. Why Alfred Hitchcock grabs your attention. *EurekAlert!*, July 27. https://www.eurekalert.org/pub_releases/2015-07/giot-wah072415.php.

————— 2014. Face it: Instagram pictures with faces are more popular. Georgia Tech News Center, March 20. https://www.news.gatech.edu/2014/03/20/face-it-instagram-pictures-faces-are-more-popular.

Jones, B. 2015. Tapestry 2015: Seven data story types. DataRemixed, March 4. http://dataremixed.com/2015/03/tapestry-2015-seven-data-story-types/.

O'Brien, C., and Archer, W. 1992. New Kid on the Block (67). *The Simpsons.* Los Angeles, CA: 20th Century Fox Television.

Radiological Society of North America 2008. Patient photos spur radiologist empathy and eye for detail. *Science Daily*, December 14. https://www.sciencedaily.com/releases/2008/12/081202080809.htm.

Rosen, J. 2014. Super Bowl ads: Stories beat sex and humor, Johns Hopkins researcher finds. Hub, January 31. https://hub.jhu.edu/2014/01/31/super-bowl-ads/.

Rowling, J.K. 1999. *Harry Potter and the Sorcerer's Stone.* New York: Scholastic.

Seastron, L. 2015. Mythic discovery within the inner reaches of outer space: Joseph Campbell meets George Lucas—Part I. Starwars.com, October 22. https://www.starwars.com/news/mythic-discovery-within-the-inner-reaches-of-outer-space-joseph-campbell-meets-george-lucas-part-i.

Stanton, A. (2012). The clues to a great story. Talk delivered at TED2012 in Long Beach, CA (February 28, 2012).

Chapter 7

Visuals (Part 1)

Setting the Scenes of Your Data Story

The greatest value of a picture is when it forces us to notice what we never expected to see.

—John W. Tukey, mathematician

In 1989, in a remote part of the Democratic Republic of the Congo (formerly Zaire), a 41-year-old Swedish physician faced a life-or-death situation. He had recently established a field laboratory to gather research on a rare paralytic disease called *konzo* when an angry, machete-waving mob approached his camp. His translator suggested they try to escape, but the doctor knew fleeing would have only placed their lives in more danger. Instead, he decided to confront the agitated villagers face-to-face. With limited resources and a substantial language barrier, the doctor's communication skills would be essential to his survival.

After quickly rummaging through his knapsack, the Swedish physician pulled out a series of photographs of individuals who had

195

been crippled by the same disease in Mozambique and Tanzania. He remembered seeing several children exhibiting the same telltale effects of konzo when he had arrived at the local village. With the help of the nervous translator, he told the upset locals he thought he knew the cause of the debilitating disease shown in the pictures—the same one that was affecting their children. The doctor then explained he would like to gather blood samples from the local people to help verify his research. As the villagers mumbled to themselves, one of the more aggressive, machete-wielding men started screaming again to incite the crowd.

With his life hanging in the balance, the physician held his breath as an older woman stepped forward from the group. She turned toward the other villagers and reminded them of how konzo had impacted their village and in particular their children. She noted her own grand-child had been cruelly crippled by the disease. She also observed how outside vaccines were able to protect their village from several other illnesses. After rolling up her sleeve, she offered her arm to the doctor and admonished others to support his research by donating blood. Many of the villagers came forward after the wise old woman spoke, and the mob quietly dispersed (Rosling, Rosling, and Roennlund 2018). Through a combination of relevant images and impassioned narrative, a tense situation in a remote African village was pacified and turned in a positive direction.

The power of visual storytelling can have a similar effect in more familiar settings such as a boardroom, classroom, or town hall. You may not have an angry mob staring you down, but you might have a concerned, agitated group of employees, partners, or investors that may be equally intimidating. While your visuals will be mostly data charts, likewise they can help you engage and enlighten your audience in ways that words or numbers alone can't. This quick-thinking doctor went on to become one of the greatest proponents for using data visualizations to drive positive change around the world. Over the next two chapters, you're going to learn how you can develop similar skills in visual sto-rytelling.

If you've watched any TED Talks related to data visualization, you may already know this Swedish doctor. He was the late, great data sto-ryteller, Hans Rosling (1948–2017). Before Rosling was the Professor of International Health at Sweden's Karolinska Institute and a popular TED Talk speaker, he spent two decades studying hunger and disease in Africa. Along this unique journey, Rosling mastered the use of statistics and visualizations to form compelling stories. He displayed these skills in several TED Talks that debunked misconceptions about the developing world and public health. His 2006 TED Talk, "The Best Stats You've Ever Seen," has been viewed over 13 million times. The TED.com's speaker profile for Rosling describes his uncanny ability to turn seemingly dull data into powerful stories:

> A presentation that tracks global health and poverty trends should be, in a word: boring. But in Rosling's hands, data sings. Trends come to life. And the big picture—usually hazy at best—snaps into sharp focus. (TED 2019)

Figure 7.1   Hans Rosling (1948–2017)
Source: Jörgen Hildebrandt. Based on material from Gapminder.org.

Whether it was photographs of konzo victims or bubble charts of country-level fertility rates, Rosling understood the persuasive power that visuals have over us. To convey Hans's health and poverty insights in more meaningful ways, his son Ola led a team of developers in creating a data visualization tool, Trendalyzer, to turn global public data into powerful animated graphics. Hans also didn't just limit himself to just animated bubble charts either; he used various physical objects—Ikea boxes, pebbles, toilet paper, and so on—to explain his key points. Rosling recognized humans are visual creatures who need to *see* the numbers, not just hear or read them. Rather than expecting his audiences to rise to his level of knowledge and expertise, he brought his concepts and insights down to the masses through the skillful use of visuals. While Rosling was a rare talent, much of his success came from his astute understanding of how people process visual information. Becoming more familiar with the inner workings of human perception will help you discern *why* certain visual approaches work and others don't.

Human Perception and Our Innate Pattern-seeking Abilities

Heightened perception is the goal: becoming more aware of how you see, not just what you see.

—Michael Kimmelman, author

As human beings, we are highly dependent on our vision to interpret and understand the world around us. As highlighted in Chapter 2, more than 50% of the brain cortex is dedicated to the task of processing visual information. With this much brainpower devoted to vision, it shouldn't surprise us that a 2014 MIT study found we can process an image in 13 milliseconds (Trafton 2014). The rapid processing of visual information enables our brains to quickly direct where our eyes should look next. MIT professor Mary Potter stated, "What vision does is find concepts. That's what the brain is doing all day long—trying to understand what we're looking at." Therefore, when it comes to evaluating datasets, it can be challenging for us to fully appreciate what the numbers and statistics mean without the aid of data visualizations.

Modern data charts were first introduced by the Scottish engineer William Playfair in 1786. The important role they played in analysis wasn't recognized until the latter part of the twentieth century. In the early 1970s, English statistician Frank Anscombe grew increasingly concerned that statisticians focused too much on summary statistics and disregarded the importance of graphing data in their analyses. He lamented how he and his peers had been falsely indoctrinated that "numerical calculations are exact, but graphs are rough" (Anscombe 1973). While the statistical packages at this time didn't offer the same rich visualization options as we have today, they could be programmed to plot the data points and generate basic graphs.

In 1973, Anscombe published a landmark paper to illustrate the importance of visualizing data instead of just relying on statistical calculations. He created a table with four unique datasets that had almost identical values for their basic summary statistics (mean, variance, correlation, R-squared). Anscombe graphed each dataset to demonstrate how vastly different they were from each other when they could be visually inspected with a data chart (see Figure 7.2). In the four graphs that became known as Anscombe's Quartet, the English statistician was able to show how visualizing data is an essential step in the analysis process—one that has become critical to both analyzing data and communicating it effectively.

ANSCOMBE'S QUARTET

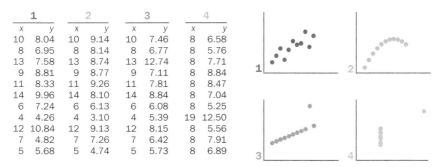

1		2		3		4	
x	y	x	y	x	y	x	y
10	8.04	10	9.14	10	7.46	8	6.58
8	6.95	8	8.14	8	6.77	8	5.76
13	7.58	13	8.74	13	12.74	8	7.71
9	8.81	9	8.77	9	7.11	8	8.84
11	8.33	11	9.26	11	7.81	8	8.47
14	9.96	14	8.10	14	8.84	8	7.04
6	7.24	6	6.13	6	6.08	8	5.25
4	4.26	4	3.10	4	5.39	19	12.50
12	10.84	12	9.13	12	8.15	8	5.56
7	4.82	7	7.26	7	6.42	8	7.91
5	5.68	5	4.74	5	5.73	8	6.89

Figure 7.2 Even though the summary statistics are similar for the four datasets, Frank Anscombe revealed they display very different patterns when they are graphed. These differences would not be nearly as discernable without the help of data visualization.

When you examine data charts like Anscombe's Quartet, you are relying on the same pattern-seeking abilities that helped our ancestors to survive their natural environments. The subconscious part of our thinking known as System 1 (mentioned in Chapter 3) is constantly processing visual stimuli based on various innate rules or heuristics. Before any focused attention is required, System 1 gains an initial impression based on various "preattentive" attributes such as color, shape, and intensity. Data visualization experts such as Colin Ware and Stephen Few have highlighted the significance of these preattentive attributes to information design. Ware noted, "When data is presented in certain ways, the patterns can be readily perceived. If we can understand how perception works, our knowledge can be translated into rules for displaying information" (Ware 2013).

Each of the following examples uses a single preattentive attribute to draw attention to particular object within a set of objects (see Figure 7.3).

COMMON PREATTENTIVE ATTRIBUTES

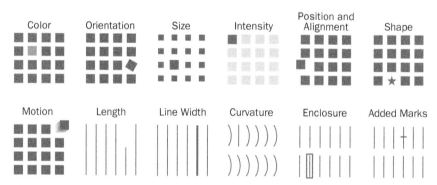

Figure 7.3 Preattentive attributes help people discern similarities and differences in data visualizations. These attributes can be essential in communicating your insights effectively.

As you'll discover later in this chapter, the ability to highlight or hide certain elements within your data charts will be essential to effective data storytelling. By encoding your key insights strategically with specific visual cues, you make it effortless for your audience to see and follow your main points. The preattentive attributes can inform the design of your data charts by drawing your audience's attention to key similarities or differences. For example, two colors could be used in a bar chart to distinguish between Canada (red) and the rest of the countries (gray). Conversely, a knowledge of these preattentive attributes can also help you avoid misusing them in ways that could inadvertently mislead or confuse your audience. Essentially, by carefully paying attention to preattentive attributes in the design of your visuals, you'll be able to both strengthen the signal and reduce the noise.

In addition to the concept of preattentive attributes, the principles of Gestalt Theory have also enhanced our understanding of human perception related to visual design and perceptual grouping. In the 1920s, Gestalt psychologists in Germany studied how people make sense of discrete visual elements by subconsciously organizing them into groups or patterns (System 1 in action again). The German word *gestalt* means "shape or form." One of its founders, psychologist Kurt Koffka, described the Gestalt Theory as "the whole is something else than the sum of its parts," which means the unified whole takes on a different meaning than the individual parts. Because data charts and tables typically feature multiple data elements, Gestalt principles can help us prepare and anticipate how the data in its entirety will be perceived by an audience. While there are many different Gestalt principles, the following ones are relevant and helpful to data storytelling (see Figure 7.4):

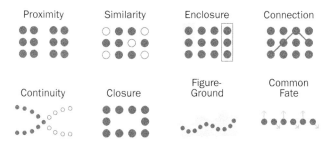

COMMON GESTALT PRINCIPLES

Figure 7.4 These Gestalt principles illustrate how human perception groups information together in different ways.

1. **Principle of proximity.** We perceive data elements that are near to each other as being a related group.
2. **Principle of similarity.** When items are alike in their properties, we group them together. The similarity could be based on different attributes such as size, shape, color, and so on.

3. **Principle of enclosure.** If a number of elements is surrounded by something such as a line or object, the elements will be perceived as being a group.
4. **Principle of connection.** We see elements that are connected by lines as being related to each other.
5. **Principle of continuity.** When we look at points, we will perceive them as smooth curves or continuous lines rather than sharp, broken lines.
6. **Principle of closure.** When we see gaps in lines or formations, we will organize them into complete shapes rather than seeing the parts as separate components.
7. **Principle of figure-ground.** We see objects that appear to be in the foreground as being separate from those in the background.
8. **Principle of common fate.** If objects move together in the same direction and speed, they are perceived as being a group (mainly applicable to animated graphics).

In the following diagram (see Figure 7.5), you can see how preattentive attributes and Gestalt principles play an active role in how people detect patterns and groupings. Even though each set has the same number of objects, their arrangement changes how we see the groupings of the objects. In your visual storytelling, preattentive attributes will be fundamental to how you isolate or highlight the *importance* of certain data points. Gestalt principles indicate *groupings,* so you can use them strategically to indicate which items are related and which aren't.

WHICH IS THE DOMINANT VISUAL ATTRIBUTE IN EACH SCENARIO?

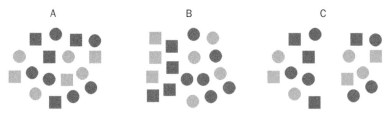

Figure 7.5 In the first two configurations, the principle of similarity influences how we perceive the groupings. However, the grouping is different for each—color (A) and shape (B). In the last configuration (C), the principle of proximity defines how we perceive its groupings.

As you design your visuals, you need to be mindful of how your audience will perceive information inside and outside of your charts. For example, placing a text label next to a line creates an association. A relationship can be implied by placing two charts close together or coloring them similarly. You need to be deliberate with your visual storytelling, or you'll inadvertently convey something that wasn't intended and confuse the audience in the process. Now that you're aware of these key perception concepts, you'll see their influence throughout the rest of the examples in this book.

Underlying all of these Gestalt principles is the Law of Prägnanz, which suggests people will interpret ambiguous or complex visual information in the simplest way possible. The German word *prägnanz* means pithiness or conciseness. In some ways, the Law of Prägnanz is similar to the Occam's Razor principle: the simplest solution or explanation is likely to be the correct one. Visuals that are simple, complete, and recognizable will be more easily embraced by an audience than those that are complex, incomplete, or unfamiliar. Even when your data visualizations are complex, your overarching goal in visual storytelling should be to streamline the interpretation of your charts. As the data storyteller, you must bear the burden of comprehension—not your audience. Your goal is to make it as easy as possible for your audience to understand your visuals and follow your overall story. When you arrange and design your charts to work *with* rather than *against* human perception, you're on the path to becoming a more effective data storyteller.

Facilitating Meaningful Comparisons with Visuals

> We are always looking at the things around us in relation to others.
> —Dan Ariely, behavioral economist and author

Context is essential to the soundness of any analysis and its recommendations. It helps clarify the setting, circumstances, or environment of the subject matter you're examining. Without proper context, you can easily be led astray by a narrow slice of data and jump to the wrong conclusions. Additionally, it's also hard for your audience to make decisions if the information you share lacks a relevant frame of reference. You'll often find missing context at the root of most audience questions. When both you and your audience have ample context, everyone will be more confident in the conclusions that are drawn from the data.

Context also goes hand-in-hand with a common task in analysis—making comparisons. When you're equipped with ample background information on a topic, you're able to explore the data more fully and examine various factors for important differences and similarities. For example, without any additional context, knowing a company has 1,000 employees is meaningless. However, when you learn the firm had only 500 employees six months ago, you gain an insight into how fast it has grown. When you discover other competitors with similar revenues have 10 times the number of employees, you uncover how productive the company is. In this case, the figure for total employees only becomes interesting when *context is added and comparisons can be made.*

The goal of most analyses is to break down a whole into its separate components for closer examination. When you lack a frame of reference, making sense of the data can be more difficult. However, when you can line up a set of related items next to each other, you have the context you need to uncover insights.

Data visualization is a powerful way to *show* context. Data charts can reveal crucial deviations or affinities in the data that can lead to insights. For example, data charts are used in many common types of comparisons (see Figure 7.6).

FIVE COMMON TYPES OF COMPARISONS

TIME	PEOPLE	PLACES	PROCESSES	THINGS
→ Hours	→ Individuals	→ Postal codes	→ Sales funnel	→ Raw materials
→ Days	→ Demographics	→ Cities	→ Checkout	→ Products
→ Weeks	→ Roles/Positions	→ States/Provinces	→ Hiring and onboarding	→ Features
→ Months	→ Teams	→ Countries	→ Manufacturing	→ Assets
→ Quarters	→ Departments	→ Store locations	→ Loan approval	→ Sentiment
→ Years	→ Customer segments	→ Regions/Zones	→ Treatment procedures	→ Organizations

Figure 7.6 We use all kinds of comparisons in our data communications. They often fall into one of these five types of comparisons. Depending on the scenario, we may compare individual elements (employees, products) or groups of elements (teams, product categories).

Even when comparison isn't the primary focus of your analysis, you're often examining the differences and similarities among individual data elements or among related datasets. For example, if you're analyzing a time series, you may compare individual data points to gain perspective (e.g., an outlier that is far removed from the general trend). Alternatively, you may gain insights by comparing a trend found in one line chart with those found in other line charts. Data visualization expert Edward Tufte highlighted the importance of comparisons to analysis when he said,

> The fundamental task in data analysis is to make smart comparisons—we're always trying to answer the question "Compared with what?" [. . .] It always comes down to making and showing smart comparisons. (Tufte 2016)

In his book *Predictably Irrational*, behavioral economist Dan Ariely found comparisons are a key factor in decision making, and that "we not only tend to compare things with one another but also tend to focus on comparing things that are easily comparable—and avoid comparing things that cannot be compared easily" (Ariely 2009). Regardless of the breadth or depth of your analysis, communicating your findings depends on one simple thing—*your ability to facilitate meaningful comparisons for your audience*. If you examine the story points of your data stories, you'll find most of them are based on comparisons or contrasts. They represent the key scenes in your data story—many of them will be Rising Insights—that will capture your audience's attention, engage their curiosity, and enlighten their minds.

When you provide the audience with a graphical comparison, you invite them to join you for a brief moment on your analysis journey. It's an opportunity for the audience to obtain an insight for themselves by making the same comparison on their own. As the Italian astronomer Galileo Galilei is accredited with saying, "You cannot teach a man anything; you can only help him to find it within himself." To help the audience see what you saw, it's imperative that the visuals are designed to make comparisons clear and easy to follow. Edward Tufte stated, "The whole purpose of an analytical display is to assist the viewer's cognitive task in looking at evidence" (Tufte 2016). Thus, the harder it is to see and understand your key points, the less likely your audience will appreciate what you have to share.

Whenever you create a data visualization, it will work for at least one person—*you*. However, there's no guarantee it will communicate equally well for others. If the cognitive load is too burdensome, your audience may mentally check out and leave with nothing—*no insights and no inspiration to do anything*. Frequently, poor visual communication occurs when data charts from the exploratory analysis are used— *without modification*—for explanatory purposes. A raw comparison is going to be more difficult to digest and interpret than one that has been designed to highlight a specific difference or similarity. The ability to *pivot* from exploratory to explanatory in the analysis process is what separates effective data storytellers from everyone else who is attempting to share data. To help you navigate this crucial transition and construct effective visual scenes for your story points, this chapter and the next will focus on seven essential principles for better visual storytelling (see Figure 7.7).

Figure 7.7 The seven key principles of visual storytelling are divided into two major sections or parts: the Setup and the Polish.

As I dive into each of these visual storytelling principles, my objective is to provide you with visualization tactics that will strengthen your comparisons and better communicate your key points. Visual storytelling often fails when too heavy a mental burden is placed on an audience to follow and interpret data. These seven principles will help steer you away from ineffective visual storytelling practices that require your audience to do tiring mind math, tricky memory games, and awkward cross-referencing.

While other data visualization books may cover aspects of these principles in more depth, I will focus exclusively on explanatory scenarios related to data storytelling. Across the different principles, you'll see the guiding influence of human perception models such as pre-attentive attributes and Gestalt theory. Understanding the principles behind how the brain processes visual information helps you better appreciate what can impede or amplify the effectiveness of your data charts. Ultimately, by focusing on these principles in your visual storytelling, you can achieve what German cartographer Alexander von Humboldt advocated, "Address the eye without fatiguing the mind."

> **Note:** All of the chart examples in this section were created in Microsoft Excel with some occasional help from Microsoft PowerPoint. While I could have used more advanced data visualization tools, I think it's important to show what you can achieve with a tool like Excel, which is widely available and familiar to most people. Even though Excel is fairly flexible, it isn't always easy to create non-standard charts. Sometimes, brute force was required to create certain visuals. At the companion website for this book, you can download an Excel file that contains all of the examples from Part 1 and 2.

Principle #1: Visualize the Right Data

Excellence in statistical graphics consists of complex ideas communicated with clarity, precision, and efficiency.

—Edward Tufte, statistician and author

As one of the three key pillars of data storytelling, data forms the foundation of every data story. If you don't have sound data, it is difficult to find meaningful insights. When you uncover an insight, you may assume you already have the right data for your data story. As a result, you end up repurposing the original chart you created in your exploratory analysis without questioning if a different view of the data might paint an even more vivid picture for the audience. For example, we often work with total values (counts or sums), but there may be a more meaningful way of expressing the same insight using different data (see Figure 7.8). Sometimes, a simple adjustment to the underlying data can make a good chart a great one.

FIVE DATA VARIATIONS TO CONSIDER

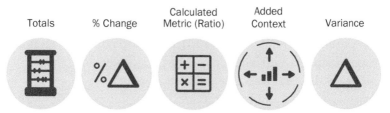

Figure 7.8 Sometimes, adjusting the underlying data may better convey your key insight to the audience.

In Figure 7.9, you can see how both the monthly revenue and number of customers are growing for this company. Generally, when these types of metrics move upward over time, it's viewed as a positive sign of a growing business. However, in this dual *y*-axis bar chart, it's difficult to see that the monthly revenue isn't expanding as rapidly as the customer base because each metric has a different scale. Even though this company is acquiring more customers, the new customers aren't spending as much money with the organization, which could be a concerning trend over time.

To show the differences between the growth rates of each metric, you could change the data to *percent change* rather than using total amounts (see Figure 7.10). With percent change, you can have metrics with different base units share a common axis, making it easier to

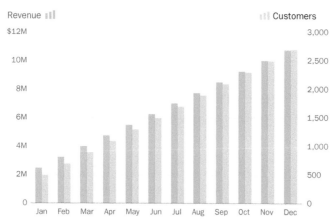

Figure 7.9 In this dual *y*-axis chart, both revenue and the number of customers have grown throughout the year. However, revenue isn't growing as fast as the customer base is expanding.

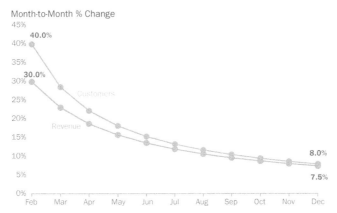

Figure 7.10 By displaying the percent change of the customers and revenue metrics, both measures can share the same *y*-axis for easier comparison.

compare changes between the metrics. However, in this case, using percent change also somewhat hides the impact to the business.

An alternative approach is to create a *calculated metric or ratio,* such as revenue per customer, to tell the story more dramatically. In Figure 7.11, you can see revenue per customer has decreased significantly during the year, even though the monthly revenue has risen steadily. Instead of relying on just totals, showing the percent change or creating a calculated metric may be a better option for communicating your key points.

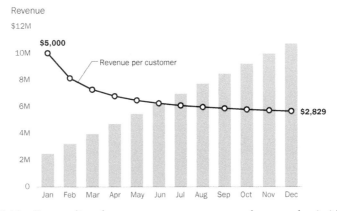

Figure 7.11 By trending the revenue per customer on the second axis, it's easy to see the company is acquiring more customers that spend less with their organization.

Having the *right* data can mean having adequate contextual data in your visualization to better appreciate your main point. IBM data scientist Jeff Jonas said, "Context is looking at the things around something to better understand the thing" (Jonas 2012). Often when we think of context for data, we think of the data's source (internal or external systems), how it was collected (observation, reporting), and what external factors may be influencing it (seasonal events, policy changes). However, data itself is also a form of context. For example, the audience gains a new perspective when they can compare the revenue per customer trends between the two years (see Figure 7.12). Even though the 2018 data in both charts is the same, the presence of the contextual data alters how the results are interpreted. For the audience, it can help them to quickly recognize when a particular result is positive, negative, or neutral.

Figure 7.12 In these two contrasting scenarios, the added context of having the previous year's result (2017) changes the message in each chart. Even though the 2018 data is exactly the same in both charts, the presence of the contextual data impacts what it communicates. (Note: The revenue bars could have been removed from these examples, but I chose to leave them in for context.)

Finally, it can be easy to run with the data chart that helped you uncover the insight you want to convey. Because you're intimately familiar with the raw data behind the visual, the insight will be obvious to you. However, it may not be as obvious to your audience, and you may want to experiment with different visual variants of the same data to find one that will work best for explaining the insight to others. For example, rather than having the audience perform difficult comparisons that may require some mental math, it may be beneficial to do the calculations for them by focusing on the *deviation* or *variance* between each pair of values. In Figure 7.13, the left chart shows the number of safety incidents at five plants across two years. If the change from year-to-year is important to your story, it may be better to show the right chart—which provides a distilled view of the change in safety incidents between years—so the audience can easily see the differences at a glance.

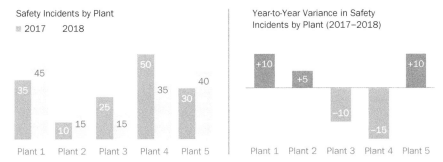

VARIANCE: DO THE MATH FOR YOUR AUDIENCE

Figure 7.13 The left chart requires the audience to compare the differences between the two years for each plant. The right chart does the math for the audience and focuses on the deviation between the two years by plant.

In some cases, shifting from comparing the total values to variances or deviations can also make your points more salient and impactful. For example, in Figure 7.14, you can see in the left chart the running total revenues for FY2017 and FY2018. While the left chart clearly shows that the FY2018 sales underperformed those of the previous year, the magnitude of the difference between years is somewhat muted. However, the right chart that trends the running variance provides a more vivid depiction of the growing shortfall in revenue and is more likely to catch an audience's attention. Simple enhancements to the underlying data can have a significant impact on how your charts communicate. Rather than just reusing the charts from your exploratory analysis, you may need to step back and consider whether you need to modify them with new metrics, different calculations, or more contextual data.

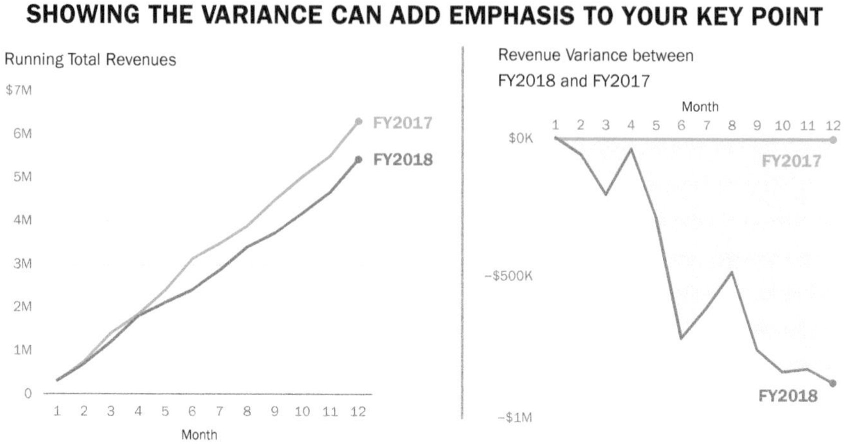

SHOWING THE VARIANCE CAN ADD EMPHASIS TO YOUR KEY POINT

Figure 7.14 The left chart reveals FY2018 is underperforming the previous year. However, the right chart, with its focus on revenue variance, highlights more emphatically how far FY2018 has deviated from the previous year's sales results.

Principle #2: Choose the Right Visualizations

The important criterion for a graph is not simply how fast we can see a result; rather it is whether through the use of the graph we can see something that would have been harder to see otherwise or that could not have been seen at all.

—William Cleveland, statistician and author

After you have the right data, you're ready to choose a data visualization to display your insights. However, with hundreds of variations to select from, it can be challenging to decide which one to use. In most cases, it's helpful to first consider the different categories of data visualizations and determine which one fits your particular use case. After you've identified the right chart type, you can then decide which specific chart best communicates your insight. In the following seven categories, you'll recognize some of the most common charts that business professionals encounter or find useful (see Figure 7.15):

MAJOR CHART TYPE CATEGORIES FOR BUSINESS PROFESSIONALS

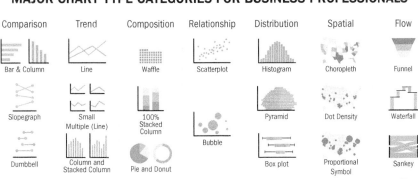

Figure 7.15 If you can isolate the right category of charts for your particular use case, you can then select which chart will be most suitable for your insights.

1. **Comparison:** These charts are used to display similarities and differences between discrete values for items or categories of items. For example, you could use a bar chart to display salespeople by revenue to see the top and bottom performers.

2. **Trend:** These charts plot the behavior or performance of something over time. For example, you could use a line chart to show the monthly fluctuations in the inventory levels over the past 12 months.

3. **Composition:** These charts are used to show the relative sizes of the parts of a whole. For example, you could use a pie chart to show how your budget was divided up into various expenditure areas.

4. **Relationship:** These charts display the relationship between variables in order to identify outliers, correlations, and clusters. For example, you could use a scatter plot to see the relationship between customer contract size and satisfaction score.

5. **Distribution:** These charts are used to show the frequency in which values are distributed across a range and reveal their central tendency and shape. For example, you could use a histogram to see the dispersion of hospital patients by age ranges.

6. **Spatial:** These charts overlay data on geographic and other spatial maps to reveal behaviors, patterns, and outliers. For example, you

could use a dot density map to see concentrations of a key customer segment within a major city.

7. **Flow:** These charts are used to depict the flow from one set of values to another through various nodes, connections, or stages. For example, you could use a Sankey diagram to display the flow of traffic from your website homepage to other pages or sections.

While this list of chart types and data visualizations isn't exhaustive, it should provide you with a good starting point in assessing what charts you'll need to convey your key points. Rather than just running with the exploratory charts you've already built, you need to step back and ask yourself two basic questions:

- Does each use case align with an appropriate chart type?
- If the use case matches its chart category, are you using the most effective data visualization option within that category to communicate your points?

After evaluating your use cases and current charts, you may find you need to switch to a different chart type or select a visualization that is more optimal for your particular use case. As you evaluate whether you have the best chart for your needs, you'll find some charts appear to support accurate comparisons more readily than others do. You may wonder why this is the case.

For the first two hundred years after data charts were introduced, nobody could really explain why some charts worked better than others. Intuition and rules of thumb guided most chart design until 1984, when AT&T Bell Labs statisticians William S. Cleveland and Robert McGill published the first scientific examination of human graphical perception (Cleveland and McGill 1984). Based on theory and experimentation, Cleveland and McGill developed a list of 10 elementary perceptual tasks commonly found in chart designs. A *perceptual task* is the mental-visual effort we employ to decode or extract quantitative information from a graphic. The researchers tested each of the graphical methods to see how accurately test subjects could detect differences in the data. They discovered some graphical forms led to more accurate judgments than others when the underlying data was the same. Figure 7.16 summarizes their key findings.

CLEVELAND AND MCGILL'S GRAPHICAL PERCEPTION MODEL

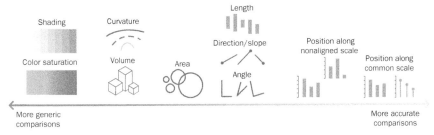

Figure 7.16 Cleveland and McGill found data visualizations that align more with the perceptual tasks on the right side of the comparison axis supported more detailed, accurate comparisons, while those that aligned more with the perceptual tasks on the left facilitated more high-level, generic comparisons.

Depending on the nature of your comparison, the graphical method you use should factor into how you visualize your insights. For example, if you want your audience to make precise comparisons between a set of values, then a bar or column chart will be a better choice than a heatmap. However, if you want to compare high-level patterns rather than specific data points, a chart that employs shading or color saturation may be a better choice. Sometimes, this may be the preferred approach when a more accurate graphical method could cause the audience to miss the overall relationship by focusing too much on specific data points. In addition, you'll find many charts require more than one perceptual task to be interpreted. For example, with a stacked column chart (see Figure 7.17), your audience can perceive the value closest to the horizontal axis by its position on the vertical scale. However, the rest of the values can only be compared by the lengths of their bars, as they aren't aligned to a common baseline.

Data visualization expert Alberto Cairo recognized Cleveland and McGill's perceptual task ranking as "an invaluable tool for grounding decisions in fact and reason, rather than aesthetic taste alone" (Cairo 2013). While no framework is perfect or applicable to all situations, Cleveland and McGill's model does offer helpful guidance to data storytellers whose primary objective is to facilitate meaningful comparisons. Using this framework, you can step back from the various data visualization options and more objectively evaluate how they will communicate your data. For example, if you examine the graphical

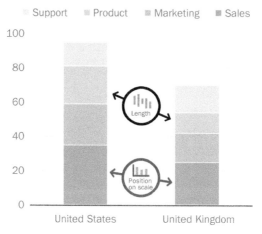

PERCEPTUAL TASKS CAN DIFFER IN THE SAME CHART

Figure 7.17   Only the bottom values in this stacked column can be compared by position with a common scale. The rest of the values must be compared by perceiving their length, which is harder for making precise comparisons.

methods that comprise a pie chart, you'll discover they require a combination of the *angle* and *area* perceptual tasks, which reside in the middle of the perceptual task ranking. On closer examination, you notice that both pie and donut charts are also encoded with *position* along their circumferences (circular scales) because they resemble something we observe on a regular basis—a clock or watch face. For this reason, when there are only a couple of slices, it's easy for us to deduce 25%, 50%, or 75% at a glance.

However, similar to the challenge we face with stacked bar or column charts, it becomes harder to judge the position of multiple slices when they don't align with a common baseline—in this case, the 12 o'clock position. If lengths are already moderately tough to compare, arc lengths are even more difficult. In most cases, the slices in a pie or donut chart must be labeled, especially if the slices are similarly sized. In contrast, if you visualize the same data in a bar chart (not stacked), you can quickly tell which values are larger or smaller without labeling even if they are very similar in size (see Figure 7.18). In most cases, you're going to label data visualizations, but this comparison illustrates how dependent some types of charts are on text to communicate. For some data visualizations, labeling becomes a necessity, while for others, it's just an amenity.

PIE CHART VERSUS BAR CHART

Figure 7.18   If you want to show the proportion of sales coming from different industry verticals, you may visualize the data in a pie chart, but without labels for the actual values, the size differences are difficult to determine. On the other hand, a bar chart offers more precise comparisons even without labeling.

Familiarity versus Novelty

As you decide which data charts to use in your data story, you also need to factor the intended audience into your decisions. For most basic comparisons, bar and column charts will be mainstays in your data visualization toolbox. Not only are they widely used and familiar to audiences, but they also align with the most effective perceptual task from Cleveland and McGill's model—position along a common scale. However, if you notice your audience is growing weary of bar chart after bar chart, there are other nonbar options that can communicate your data in a similar manner. For example, rather than using yet another bar chart, you could leverage a *dot plot* or *lollipop* instead (see Figure 7.19).

BAR CHART ALTERNATIVES: LOLLIPOP AND DOT PLOT CHARTS

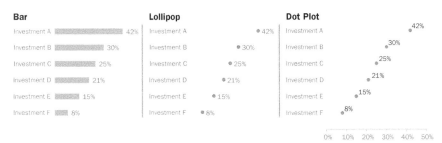

Figure 7.19   Lollipop and dot plot charts are two alternatives to the bar chart. They both support comparisons by position on a common scale but are more difficult to create in Microsoft Excel (not impossible, just harder).

In certain scenarios, when you have a large number of high values, a lollipop chart may be a better visual option than a bar chart. With a bar chart, the density of the chart will increase due to the length and thickness of the bars. However, because the stems of the lollipops are only thin lines, they can convey the same values with much less ink. But before you abandon bar and column charts for lollipop charts, they do have an inherent drawback: each value is found at the center of the lollipop's circle, which is less precise than the straight edge of a bar. Both of these bar chart alternatives are aligned to the same position-based perceptual task that makes bar charts useful for accurate comparisons. However, until they are included as default chart options in more data visualization tools, they won't be nearly as popular as the ubiquitous bar chart.

In addition to the dot plot and lollipop charts, there are other non-standard chart variations that can be useful for making comparisons. The *slopegraph* is a comparison chart that has recently grown in popularity and offers a viable alternative to paired column or bar charts (see Figure 7.20). It displays the relative differences or changes between a paired set of dimensional values across two categories using a series of connected lines. While the category scales on each side of the paired values can be different (revenues and expenses), slopegraphs work especially well for changes over time where the scales are the same

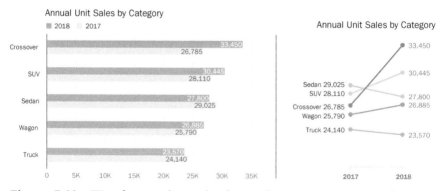

Figure 7.20   We often use bar and column charts to compare data for two different categories or time periods. Instead, a slopegraph can be used to represent the differences or changes between the paired values.

(units sold in 2017 and 2018). Although the scale may be less obvious in slopegraphs, it is a form of position along a common scale combined with the slope graphical method. Slopegraphs can be used to highlight significant rates of change or key rank/order switches across the two categories.

Another useful chart for comparisons is the *dumbbell chart*, which is a variation of the dot plot that focuses on the differences between two (or more) values. With dumbbell charts, we use the *length* perceptual task to interpret the variances. Instead of having to judge the differences between two bar lengths, dumbbell charts can simplify the audience's cognitive load by converting the variance into its own line (see Figure 7.21). Another variant of the dumbbell is the *tadpole chart*, which can clarify the movement direction for time-based comparisons.

VARIANCE ALTERNATIVES: DUMBBELL AND TADPOLE CHART

Figure 7.21 The dumbbell chart on the left shows the difference in unit sales for each automotive category. The tadpole chart on the right shows the same data but emphasizes the more recent year (2018).

Whichever chart types you choose to display your story points, you want to make your information as easy as possible for your audience to follow (Law of Prägnanz). Clarity—not simplicity—is the goal. Depending on how inquisitive, data literate, and patient your audience is, you may be able to go with a less familiar or more complex data chart that isn't necessarily simple, as long as it's clear. However, you must factor in which perceptive tasks it touches, and whether the data will be intrinsically easy or hard to perceive. Cleveland and McGill's model can help you navigate the vast array of chart options and guide you to the right data visualizations for your next data story.

Principle #3: Calibrate the Visuals to Your Message

> Information graphics should be aesthetically pleasing, but many designers think about aesthetics before they think about structure, about the information itself, about the story the graphic should tell.
> —Alberto Cairo, data journalism professor and author

After you've determined you have the right data visualization, you need to calibrate your chart to the message you want to convey. Sometimes, you'll see people attempt to tell data stories, but their visuals don't match their words or message. Even a small misalignment can interfere with the power of your data story. For example, I attended a breakfast event sponsored by a well-known market research firm. At one point during the event, a research analyst shared data on how people's device preferences for accessing digital content had been shifting from desktops to smartphones and tablets over the last three years. On a separate slide for each year, the analyst showed the relative shares of internet access by the three major device types (see Figure 7.22).

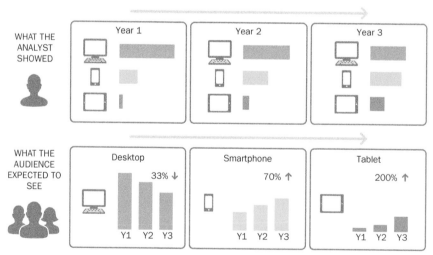

Figure 7.22 The analyst chose to focus on only the yearly changes for the different device types. However, the audience expected to also see the changes by device type across the three-year time period to fully appreciate his message.

When he finally presented the most recent year's data, I found myself wanting to look back across the three-year period to see how each device type's share had evolved over time. Unfortunately, all the audience could do to assess the overall changes was to go by memory of the previous slides. Even though the research analyst made the point that digital consumption was increasingly shifting away from desktops to mobile devices, he failed to show us the overall trends by device types that could have reinforced his message. Interestingly, the data for both views would have been exactly the same. However, the orientation or structure of the content limited the comparisons the audience could make. Consequently, the analyst missed an opportunity to tie his visuals more tightly to his key insights and strengthen his story.

As you configure the data visualizations for your data story, you need to have a clear understanding of the main point of each visual. Based on the message you're trying to convey with each chart, you need to anticipate how your audience will consume the information and come away with the insight you intended. If there are comparisons that are essential to setting up your message, they must be clear and obvious to the audience. You can't afford to have the structure or orientation of a data visualization interfere with the comprehension of key insights. In other words, your audience shouldn't have to wrestle with how the information is displayed to grasp important points.

When you look to assess whether your message and visuals are properly calibrated, there are three key areas you can focus on:

1. **Keep comparisons in close proximity.** Whenever possible, you want to place data elements that are being compared in close proximity to each other. It is much easier to compare two data points that are side by side rather than at opposite ends of a graph. For example, if you were presenting purchase data for various products across three different customer segments (see Figure 7.23), it would be harder for product managers to compare how their individual products performed across all the segments. However, if you rearranged the grouped bar chart to have products broken down by customer segment instead, it becomes much easier for individual product managers to evaluate how their products performed for the various

MAKE IT EASY FOR YOUR AUDIENCE TO MAKE COMPARISONS

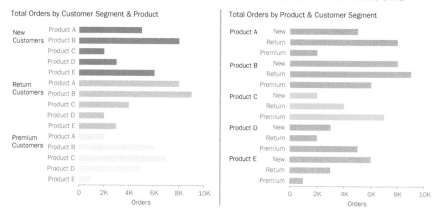

Figure 7.23 In the left bar chart, it's easier to compare the products within a segment. In the right version, it's easier to compare segments for a specific product. The data is the same; only the structure is different. Depending on your message, one version may align more closely to it. Note: For the chart on the right, I had to switch from monochromatic to a five-color scheme because the blue gradients didn't provide enough contrast between the categorical values.

customer segments. Both views or orientations of the data are accurate. However, depending on the message you're trying to convey, you'll want to align the chart's structure so the desired comparisons are close together and easy to make for your audience.

In some cases, you may want to accommodate diverse comparisons in the same visual, which is a common practice for exploratory visuals. With explanatory visuals, however, you can't be as ambitious. You must determine which comparison is central to your story. All other comparison options can offer additional context, but they should be secondary to your story. Ultimately, if your data chart doesn't make your main comparison easy to perceive and extract, you must recalibrate it to your message—or choose a better chart. For example, the back-to-back bar chart below shows the annual average wages of males and females within a department (see Figure 7.24). It would be good for displaying the overall pattern by each gender (curvature) or assessing different years for a specific gender (position) but not for comparing the values between genders in a particular year (length).

ALIGN THE PERCEPTUAL TASKS TO THE INSIGHT YOU'RE COMMUNICATING

Figure 7.24 With this back-to-back bar chart, you can compare the overall patterns (curvature) of the average salaries for both genders. It also supports comparisons between years for a specific gender (position). However, it's not very useful for comparisons between the two genders (length).

2. **Provide a common baseline for comparisons.** For stacked bar and column charts, the easiest values to compare are the ones that align with a shared baseline. When you know in advance which data series you want your audience to focus on, you should ensure it has a common baseline. The comparisons will be more accurate and less tedious for your audience. For example, instead of using a stacked bar chart (in which the stacked values are harder to compare), you may consider using a panel bar chart that offers each data series its own baseline for easier comparisons (see Figure 7.25). When you're presenting data in a 100% stacked bar or column chart, it is easy for the audience to compare the segments at either end of the chart. However, the values in the middle can be difficult to compare when there's again no shared baseline. For the Likert scale data that is used to measure attitudes and opinions in surveys, a diverging stacked bar chart can alleviate some of these comparison challenges. In the example (see Figure 7.26), the most extreme ends of the Likert scale are positioned in the middle, next to the

STACKED BAR CHART VERSUS PANEL BAR CHARTS

Figure 7.25   In the stacked bar chart, it is difficult to compare the stacked values that are not aligned with the baseline along the *y*-axis. To streamline the evaluation of quarterly results, a panel bar chart would give each quarter its own baseline for easier comparisons. Note: I included the axis line in this example, but it isn't always necessary, as people will perceive the baseline based on the left alignment of the bars.

100% STACKED BAR CHART VERSUS DIVERGING BAR CHART

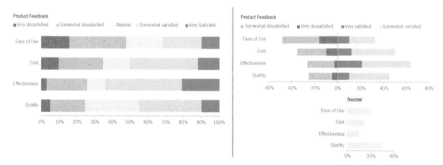

Figure 7.26   In the 100% stacked bar chart, it is easy to compare the values on the ends, but the values in the middle don't have a common baseline. The diverging bar chart can alleviate some of these problems if the neutral values (gray) are removed. While it's not as easy to compare the "somewhat" segments, this configuration enables you to see the overall dissatisfaction and satisfaction levels back-to-back with the extreme values closest to the middle axis.

axis, for easier comparison. The neutral values have been graphed separately, so it is straightforward to see the comparative levels of dissatisfaction and satisfaction across the different feedback categories. Depending on your message or insights, adjusting the alignment of your data can help make key values simpler to compare.

3. **Ensure charts are consistent for comparisons.** When you ask an audience to compare multiple charts at the same time, it's important to structure your visuals so they're consistent. Even subtle or insignificant inconsistencies can needlessly fatigue your audience when you want them to effortlessly consume your data and follow your key points. When there are small deviations or differences in *how* the data is displayed, the audience is left to wonder if you're doing it intentionally or accidentally. Everything from axis scales to colors and labeling should be consistent across the charts that are being compared. For example, if you were to ask your audience to compare the stock price of two companies (see Figure 7.27), the formatting and structure of the data shouldn't interfere with the overall insights you're trying to convey.

Figure 7.27   On the left, subtle differences between the two line charts can interfere with making comparisons. On the right, the visuals are consistent so the audience can focus on interpreting the data differences, not the extraneous design disparities. Note: Intentionally using a unique color for each company's 2019 results would have been acceptable to differentiate them.

As you design the visuals that form the scenes of your data story, you will sometimes need to make tradeoffs in how you present your data. Depending on what data elements you want to emphasize, you may need to change the structure of your chart so it better aligns with your messaging. Paying attention to the subtle graphical details—such as proximity, alignment, and consistency—will enhance the effectiveness of your visual communications, introducing harmony instead of dissonance between your data visualizations and key messages.

End of Part I: The Scenes Are Set

In this first chapter (Part I) on visual storytelling, the first three principles focused on assembling the rough visual scenes to form your data story. You start by confirming you have the right data to visualize each story point. Your choice of what data to visualize can mute or amplify the points you're trying to make. The next step is to select a data visualization that will communicate your insight clearly and effectively. While you may be able to visualize the same dataset a number of ways, you want to choose one that matches the types of comparisons you're trying to facilitate (accurate or generic). The last step is to ensure each chart is aligned with what you want to communicate to the audience. Even though you have the right chart, its configuration or orientation may cause your audience to work harder than you want them to.

After you've applied these first three principles, you're now ready to move on to the next stage of polishing. In the film industry, a movie director follows a similar process after he or she captures the raw footage for a film. While good cinematography is critically important, it alone doesn't guarantee a film's success. In the postproduction phase, the various editors play an integral role in transforming the raw video, audio, and special effects into an epic adventure that will engage and entertain an audience. In the next chapter on visuals (Part II), you'll learn how to polish and refine the charts you've chosen so your key insights and messages come through clearly and convincingly for your audience.

References

Anscombe, F.J. 1973. Graphs in statistical analysis. *The American Statistician* 27 (1): 17–21.

Ariely, D. 2009. *Predictably Irrational: The Hidden Forces That Shape Our Decisions*. New York: HarperCollins.

Cairo, A. 2013. *The Functional Art: An Introduction to Information Graphics and Visualization*. Berkeley, CA: New Riders.

Cleveland, W.S., and McGill, R. 1984. Graphical perception: Theory, experimentation, and application to the development of graphical methods. *Journal of the American Statistical Association* 79: 531–554.

Jonas, J. 2012. Why data matters: Context reveals answers. YouTube, March 14. https://www.youtube.com/watch?v=ipxRA7ira4c.

Rosling, H., Rosling, O., and Roennlund, A.G. 2018. *Factfulness: Ten Reasons We're Wrong about the World—and Why Things Are Better than You Think*. New York: Flatiron Books.

TED. 2019. TED Speaker: Hans Rosling. https://www.ted.com/speakers/hans_rosling (accessed 22 May 2019).

Trafton, A. 2014. In the blink of an eye. *MIT News*, January 16. http://news.mit.edu/2014/in-the-blink-of-an-eye-0116.

Ware, C. 2013. *Information Visualization: Perception for Design*. Waltham, MA: Elsevier.

Tufte, E. 2016. Keynote Session: Dr. Edward Tufte—The future of data analysis. Presentation at Microsoft Machine Learning & Data Science Summit 2016 in Atlanta, GA (September 28, 2016).

Chapter 8

Visuals (Part 2)
Polishing the Scenes of Your Data Story

This is my favorite part about analytics: Taking boring, flat data and bringing it to life through visualization.

— John W. Tukey, mathematician

For an upcoming data storytelling workshop at a Fortune 500 company, I was preparing some "makeover" examples to show how charts they had produced in the past could be enhanced and made more effective. This workshop was for a group of PhD scientists who supported the company's sales and marketing teams with in-depth technical expertise and research analysis. They worked heavily with data, so I knew data literacy wouldn't be an issue with this group. However, as I was examining one of the charts I was considering for a makeover example, I discovered it had a common flaw that occurs more regularly than I would expect.

In Figure 8.1, you can see a "before" version of the pie chart as well as the redesigned "after" version I hoped to produce—if I hadn't discovered the defect. Before you read ahead, can you spot what's wrong with both of these pie charts?

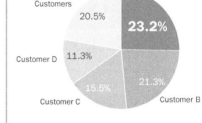

BOTH OF THESE CHARTS SHARE THE SAME FLAW

BEFORE
Annual Revenue by Top Customers

AFTER
Customer A generated almost a quarter (23.2%) of our revenue last year

Figure 8.1 The original pie chart on the left suffers from many design issues. The redesigned pie chart on the right addresses many of the original chart's issues. However, a key flaw still undermines both charts.

When you look closer at the pie charts in question, you'll discover the slices don't add up to 100%—only 91.8%! The parts of a composition chart must always sum to the whole (100%). After I delivered the workshop (in which I highlighted this critical mistake), I was approached by an embarrassed manager who admitted she was the one who had created the misleading pie chart. In a rush to get the data out, she accidentally forgot to include the aggregated "Other" value in the pie chart—a simple but significant mistake. Either due to carelessness or a lack of data literacy, this type of mistake happens more frequently than it should.

This example highlights how important is to have the right setup—data, chart type, and chart configuration—before proceeding to the next stage of polishing and refining your visuals. If your chart is fundamentally broken or misaligned with your message, no amount of polish can save it. Once you have the visual fundamentals discussed in Chapter 7 in place to support your key insights and messages, the next four visual storytelling principles can provide the final "post-production" touches that clarify and strengthen the signals that will emanate from your data story (see Figure 8.2).

**SEVEN ESSENTIAL PRINCIPLES
FOR BETTER VISUAL
STORYTELLING**

PART 1—THE SETUP

1 🗄 RIGHT DATA

2 📊 RIGHT VISUALIZATIONS

3 🎚 RIGHT CONFIGURATION

PART 2—THE POLISH

4 〰 REMOVE NOISE

5 ◉ FOCUS ATTENTION

6 🚪 MAKE APPROACHABLE

7 🛡 INSTILL TRUST

Figure 8.2   After you've set up your visuals correctly, you now need to focus on refining them so they tell a clear and convincing story.

Principle #4: Remove Unnecessary Noise

The signal is the truth. The noise is what distracts us from the truth.
—Nate Silver, statistician and author

During the exploratory analysis phase, most of the data you have access to won't be relevant or useful to answering your questions. The noise in the data can get in the way of finding a signal; it can mask what you're seeking or even lead you astray. However, if you're successful in cutting through the noise to find a valuable signal, your battle with it isn't over yet. As you transition from the *exploratory* to *explanatory* phase, you need to be careful of two things: first, that you don't *bring unnecessary noise* from your analysis into your story; and second, that you don't inadvertently *create noise* as you seek to visualize your story points. Following the advice of the famous abstract painter Hans Hofmann, you need to simplify your visuals by eliminating "the unnecessary so that the necessary may speak."

The first step to reducing the noise in your visuals is to evaluate the data that's being visualized. If you can simplify and declutter your information, you'll be able to reduce how much noise interferes with your signal. In Chapter 5, you learned about the different types of cognitive load. By streamlining how the data is represented in your visuals, you're essentially managing how much mental effort it takes your audience to interpret them. The variability and volume of data produces *intrinsic noise* that can interfere with your story. To minimize this latent form of noise, we can look to lessons learned in the field of data journalism. In her informative book *The Wall Street Journal Guide to Information Graphics* (2010), author Dona Wong lays out various rules of thumb that can be helpful to all data storytellers—not just data journalists. From her best practices in data journalism, we can glean three key ways to strengthen the signal-to-noise ratio of our visuals and reduce the intrinsic noise:

1. **Remove surplus data.** When you're analyzing data, you are unlikely to limit how much data you examine. You'll continue exploring more and more data until an insight emerges. However, as you cast an increasingly wider net in the exploration process, you'll be left with potentially more categories, data series, time periods, and granular data than you need to form your data story. A good step after you've visualized your data is to determine which data elements are required to make your point. Basically, if any of the visualized information isn't directly tied to your message or doesn't provide essential context, it can be removed. For example, rather than including multiple data series in a line chart, you may scale it back to include specific ones for comparison purposes (see Figure 8.3). You may prioritize certain elements by their familiarity, relevance, uniqueness, importance, or utility for benchmarking. Wong recommends keeping "the maximum number of lines to three or possibly four if the lines are not intersecting at many points" (Wong 2010).

2. **Aggregate less important data.** In your analysis results, you'll often have a "long tail" of small, insignificant values. The Pareto Principle, or 80/20 rule, underlines the supposition that the majority of consequences or outputs come from a small minority of causes or inputs (80% of sales come from 20% of customers).

SIMPLIFY A "SPAGHETTI CHART" TO REDUCE THE NOISE

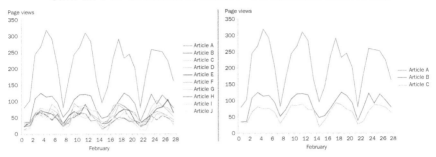

Figure 8.3   To simplify and declutter the confusing spaghetti chart (left) that shows the traffic levels of different web pages, only three lines are plotted. With this removal approach, the line chart on the right has less noise but still provides context for comparison purposes.

This means that outside of the information that directly contributes to your story, there will be a large portion of the data that is less relevant and potentially just noise. When you're using a composition chart such as a pie chart, donut chart, or stacked bar, you may want to aggregate the smaller segments into a combined group. For example, Wong suggests a pie chart should have no more than five slices and recommends combining smaller and less significant segments into a fifth slice labeled as "other" (see Figure 8.4).

COMBINE LESS IMPORTANT VALUES INTO "OTHER" GROUPING

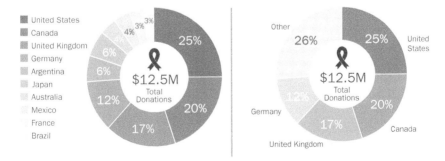

Figure 8.4   In order to simplify the donut chart on the left, the lesser slices are combined into an "Other" slice in the version on the right.

3. **Separate overlapping data.** For certain charts in which
   you can have busy, overlapping data such as line charts, slopegraphs, or scatterplots, you may want to reduce the noise by
   visualizing different aspects separately with a technique called
   faceting (also known as panel charts or small multiples). In the
   previous chapter, I used a panel bar chart to break apart a
   stacked bar chart (Figure 7.25), but faceting can be used with
   all kinds of charts. For example, line charts with multiple lines
   can be hard to decipher and are often referred to as spaghetti
   charts. However, when you create facets or panels for different cuts of the data, the individual charts make it easier to
   see patterns and make comparisons (see Figure 8.5). Another
   instance in which you'll see overlapping data is with a dual
   y-axis chart. Unless there's a meaningful relationship between
   the two metrics being visualized, it is better to display the data
   in separate charts.

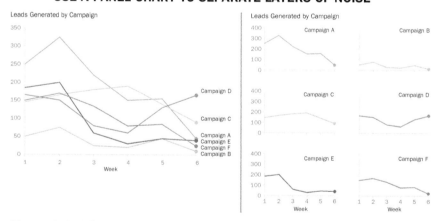

Figure 8.5   The separation of the busy line chart on the left into facets or panel
line charts makes it easier for people to make comparisons.

In addition to managing how the data is visualized to reduce noise,
you can also decrease the visual interference by minimizing the extraneous cognitive load. In these cases, the nonrelevant information
and design elements surrounding the data can cause *extraneous noise*.

Poor design or display decisions by the data storyteller can inadvertently interfere with the communication of the intended signal. This form of noise can occur at both a macro and micro level.

From a *macro* perspective, the story points of your data story will form a series of visual scenes. Each story point will be the focal point of its own scene. A single scene will include the necessary visual(s) and text to explain a specific story point. Depending on how you're delivering your data story, the scenes can take different forms (see Figure 8.6). The most common form of a scene is a presentation slide or a static image. However, scenes can be delivered sequentially in a video or laid out as sections in a report or infographic. Scenes can also be part of an interactive experience in which an audience uses scrolling, tabbing, clicking, or other methods to move between the different story points.

DIFFERENT METHODS OF DELIVERING THE SCENES OF A DATA STORY

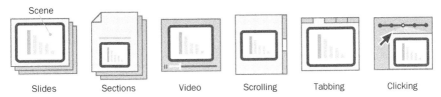

Figure 8.6   There are several different ways of delivering the scenes of a data story.

Within this context of visual scenes, extraneous noise occurs at a macro level when more than one story point is featured in a single scene. Basically, this means you need to limit your scene to feature only one visual. You can have multiple charts in the same scene as long as they're tied to a single story point. For example, you could have side-by-side charts that show the differing performance of two sales teams. Even though you have two separate charts, together they support your point that Team A is vastly outperforming Team B. However, if the two charts actually supported different story points—Team A's sales performance and retention issues with its salespeople—you end up with a disjointed, noisy scene that's harder for your audience to follow.

Individually, each story point isn't noise, but each can interfere with another's signal if they occupy the same scene. To reduce this macro extraneous noise, you'll want to be selective; only use multiple charts when they are truly necessary for understanding an intended insight. If you're ever in doubt, it's better to assign the visuals to their own unique scenes to avoid adding clutter.

At a *micro* level, you can also introduce extraneous noise by the design choices you make with your data visualizations. Edward Tufte is attributed with saying, "clutter and confusion are not attributes of data—they are shortcomings of design." In 1983, Tufte coined the term *chartjunk*, which refers to all the nonessential visual elements in a chart that aren't required to understand its information and may even detract from its perception or comprehension (Tufte 1983). Since Tufte introduced this concept, it has sparked much debate in the data visualization community about how far to take it. Rather than strictly adhering to a minimalist design philosophy, it's important to weigh how the design elements are helping or hindering your message. Table 8.1 shows examples of common forms of chartjunk that can add extraneous noise to data stories.

Table 8.1   Examples of Chartjunk

	More Chartjunk	Less Chartjunk
3D effects: Adding a three-dimensional perspective to a chart can distort its information and make it harder to interpret. If you're trying to facilitate comparisons, 3D charts should be avoided at all costs.		
Dark gridlines: Dark or thick gridlines can compete with the information in the foreground. Gridlines can serve a valid purpose and assist people in evaluating data. However, they should be subtle (thin, light color) so they don't overpower the core information.		

	More Chartjunk	Less Chartjunk
Nonstrategic use of color: Color is a powerful tool in your data storytelling toolbox, but too often it is used carelessly or randomly in charts. Instead, color should be applied purposefully to convey key points within your chart (see Principle #5).		
Granular scales: Rather than your data being too complex, the scale of a vertical or horizontal axis may be too detailed for what's needed. It may be helpful to simplify the scale so it doesn't overwhelm your audience with unnecessary detail.		
Artistic effects: Different design effects such as shading, beveling, or gradients are sometimes used to give charts more "visual impact." However, these effects should be avoided if they're distracting and make comparisons more difficult.		
Overuse of labeling: While it may be necessary to attach labels to data points, systematic labeling can add a significant amount of textual noise. Instead, it is better to focus labeling strategically on key values that matter to your story.		

Unfortunately, when you're working with different analytics tools, the chart defaults in these products often include various forms of chartjunk. When you're exploring the data, you may be able to look past the extraneous noise created by these nonessential visual elements. However, as you prepare to share your insights with other people, you may need to edit or recreate the visuals. You don't want chartjunk encumbering your audience with unwanted noise that can interfere with your message. While extraneous noise can be subtle, it can add small amounts of mental friction to your data communication. Poor visual design burdens your audience with unnecessary cognitive load, which could prevent them from following your message.

Principle #5: Focus Attention on What's Important

A person who is gifted sees the essential point and leaves the rest as surplus.

—Thomas Carlyle, philosopher and writer

Even after you've removed noise from your visuals, your audience may still find it challenging to absorb all of the rich information you have to share with them. Nobel Prize–winning economist Herbert Simon noted that information "consumes the attention of its recipients. Hence, a wealth of information creates a poverty of attention" (Simon 1971). A critical task of any data storyteller is to direct the attention of the audience to what really matters in each visual. Your data isn't going to be equally important. Some data points directly tie to your conclusions or arguments while others are simply present for context or comparative reasons. You need to establish a hierarchy of information so the audience knows where you want them to focus their attention. In this section, I'll examine four effective methods of directing your audience's attention to what matters: *color contrast, text, typography,* and *layering.*

Color Contrast

As a preattentive attribute, color is one of the most powerful tools that you have at your disposal. When color is used strategically, it can help an audience notice things they might not otherwise see. However, it's less about color and more about color contrast. For example, if you were to count the number of eights in each set of numbers, it would be the easiest with the middle set due to the color contrast (see Figure 8.7).

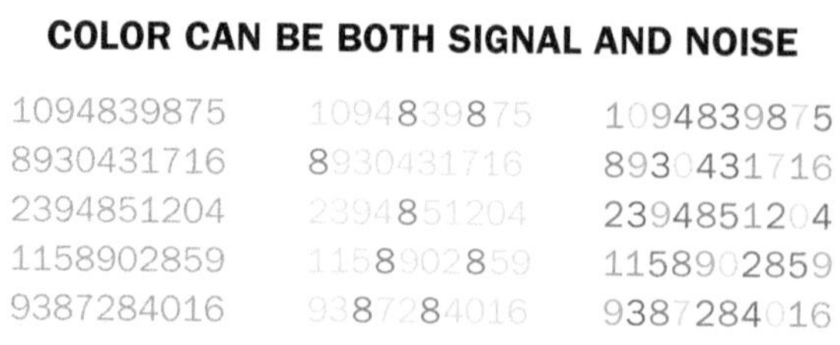

COLOR CAN BE BOTH SIGNAL AND NOISE

1094839875	1094839875	1094839875
8930431716	8930431716	8930431716
2394851204	2394851204	2394851204
1158902859	1158902859	1158902859
9387284016	9387284016	9387284016

Figure 8.7 The color contrast between the blue and light gray numbers in the middle set of numbers makes it easier to notice and count the number of eights.

As the director of your own data stories, color contrast enables you to control what is featured in the foreground and background of a visual. You can use a distinct color to highlight certain data points—thereby placing them in the foreground—and then use grayscale to move everything else that is less important to the background. For example, in the previous leads-by-campaigns chart (see Figure 8.5), you could color a key campaign that you want to feature but use grayscale on the other campaigns to preserve them as relevant context (see Figure 8.8).

As you use color strategically in your visuals, it's important to be mindful of how colors can encode information into your charts. In Figure 8.8, orange is now associated with Campaign D. Throughout the rest of the data story, you need to use this same color for Campaign D; otherwise, inconsistent color usage will add unnecessary cognitive load. If you were to focus on a different campaign (Campaign A) in subsequent charts, a different color should be used so your audience can easily recognize the shift in focus. Color can be powerful for highlighting specific points, especially if it's used consistently and purposefully. However, you need to be mindful that using too many colors at the same time can quickly turn into noise. If you use bold colors sparingly, they're going to stand out when you use them.

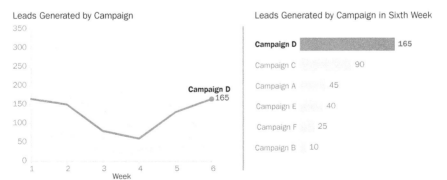

Figure 8.8   By highlighting the main insight with color and using grayscale for the less-important information, you can establish what is in the foreground and background of your visuals.

Power of the Palette

By Alan Wilson, Data Visualization Designer

Color is often misused in data visualizations. And yet, it can be a powerful tool that can draw your audience in and help them better understand your data. The key is to understand the type of data you're visualizing and how color can improve audience cognition. There are three primary ways in which color can represent information, and if you understand what they are, you can avoid most of the pitfalls created by poor color use.

Sequential color palette: When you have a range of numbers (like revenue or item count), you can either assign them a color that is on a continuous gradient scale or one that is broken into bins (see Figure 8.9). The large and small values will be at opposite ends of the color scale. In this scenario, be mindful of the following:

- Map larger values to the darker side of the scale (darker numbers are associated with density and bigger amounts).
- Shift the color's hue and not just its lightness. This will make your colors more beautiful and will also make your data easier to read, as any two parts of your scale will be distinct from one another.
- Use naturally darker (cooler) hues like blue and purple on the dark side of the scale and naturally lighter hues like green and yellow on the light side.
- Don't use a rainbow scale with too many colors. Research has shown these scales do a poor job of accurate representation.

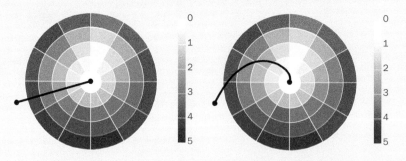

Single-Hue Sequential Color Scale   Multi-Hue Sequential Color Scale

Figure 8.9   The color scale on the left uses only a single hue, whereas the one on the right blends together two unique hues.

Diverging color palette: This scale is used to represent a range of numbers with a meaningful mid-point (e.g., Return on Investment) (see Figure 8.10). Many of the rules for sequential color apply here—with some additional considerations:

- Approach the range as two sequential scales that share a low value (light color), which becomes the mid-point of your diverging color palette.
- Be sure the hues of each scale don't get too close to one another, or the distance from the mid-point will be hidden instead of accentuated.

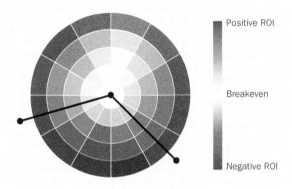

Diverging Color Scale

Figure 8.10 The diverging color palette can be useful with a range of values in which the mid-point is meaningful.

Categorical color palette: When you have nominal or categorical data (like customer types or sales regions), different colors can be used to distinguish the groups from each other (see Figure 8.11). While useful, this particular palette is the most often abused, so you need to consider the following:

- Use as few colors as possible—research shows that human cognition is best at three to four colors and begins to seriously break down after six.
- Pick colors that are unique hues that aren't difficult to tell apart. The primary objective of categorical colors is to allow

(*continued*)

(*continued*)

users to separate one category from another, so the hues need to be distinct.

- Arrange the colors by hue whenever possible. Aligning them to the natural order of colors (like a rainbow) will enhance their appearance.
- Assign colors the same relative lightness/luminance; they should feel like a "family" of colors.
- Be careful with sequential color schemes, as the audience may associate the darker colors with larger numbers.
- Avoid palettes that are difficult for people with color blindness to read, such as red/green.

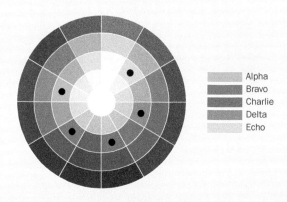

Categorical Color Scale

Figure 8.11 With the categorical color palette, you want to have distinct hues that stand out from each other.

Proper use of color is difficult—even experienced designers spend time making sure their colors are in-line with their message. Fortunately, there are a number of great color tools you can leverage in the visualization of your data. Check out the following resources: ColorBrewer 2.0, Chroma.js Color Scale Helper, Viz Palette, and Colorgorical.

Text

Even though it may feel like text is of secondary importance to your graphs, words can serve as critical guideposts and help lead your audience in the right direction. Text can be used strategically to drive attention in two key ways: *titles* and *annotations*.

The title of a chart is one of the most prominent but often misused sections of a data visualization. We often squander this valuable real estate by labeling charts with descriptive—*not explanatory*—titles. For example, you'll see descriptive but generic titles like "sales reps by monthly revenue," "annual budget expenditures," or "number of complaints by location." For general purposes, these labels are functional. However, when you're telling a story with your data, you must capitalize on the titles as an opportunity to reinforce the main point of each visual. Instead of "sales reps by monthly revenue," you would highlight the main point of the chart: "Northwest region has 7 of the top 10 sales reps" (see Figure 8.12). In data storytelling, the titles can reinforce your narrative and help frame what you want the audience to focus on.

EXPLANATORY TITLES CAN HELP TELL THE STORY

DESCRIPTIVE   EXPLANATORY

Figure 8.12 While you could figure out the point of the left chart, the explanatory title helps the audience to quickly orient themselves to the intended takeaway from the visual. Because "Northwest region" is colored blue, the legend is optional.

In addition to chart titles, annotations are another means of using words to guide your audience down the right path. In a data journalism study of more than 130 news-related charts, researchers found annotations fell into two primary categories: *observational* and *additive* (Diakopoulos 2013). An observational annotation draws attention to interesting features of the data. For example, an observational annotation might highlight a specific outlier or set of extreme values in the data that the audience should notice. In contrast, an additive annotation provides relevant context that is not depicted in the data. For instance, this type of annotation may explain why there was a sharp decrease in a metric due to a data-collection issue. In some cases, you may use a hybrid annotation that offers both an observation and additional context.

Every annotation should include text with some kind of connector that ties it to a specific data point or set of points (see Figure 8.13). "Floating" or disconnected annotations can be confusing if the audience isn't clear which part of the visual the comments are referring to. In some cases, you can use color to more strongly tie annotations to specific color-coded parts of a visualization. The annotations shouldn't obscure any data or be too far removed from the actual data. It's important to be intentional about what is annotated because overzealous commentary

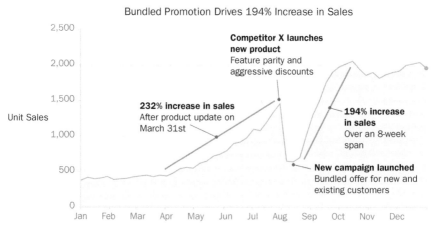

Figure 8.13 In this area chart, a mix of observational (194%), additive (competitor X, new campaign), and hybrid (232% increase after product update) annotations guide the audience through the most salient parts of the data.

can quickly turn into noise. In general, you'll want to keep annotation text as concise as possible, but it may be longer if you're delivering your data story indirectly to an audience.

As you position annotations within or around a chart, you'll want to ensure there's a logical flow or visual hierarchy to them so they're easy for your audience to follow. Typically, people will scan a visual for focal points beginning at the top-left position, moving across to the right and back diagonally in a series of "Z" movements. If you don't want your audience to follow this flow, you may have to apply other visual techniques to lead them down the desired path (numbering, size differences). If you're not sure how someone will follow your annotations, ask a colleague for feedback on how they would read the content in your chart.

Typography

Because text is an integral part of all visuals, typography elements can be used to highlight essential information so it catches the attention of your audience. In particular, the font type, size, weight, and color can be used to emphasize certain text so it stands out from the rest of the content (see Figure 8.14). The goal of modifying one or more of the typographical elements is to create a *noticeable contrast* between the

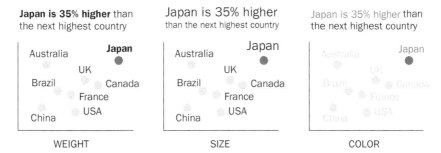

Figure 8.14   Typographic elements such as weight, size, and color can be used to focus attention on specific information within a data visualization. You can also combine these elements to add even more contrast if needed.

highlighted words or numbers and the rest of the text. The strategic use of typography can make your visuals easier to scan so your audience can quickly get the essence of your story point. However, in order for the modified text to catch your audience's eyes, there must be ample contrast. As such, typographical treatments should be used selectively and reserved only for the critical content you want to highlight. For example, if all of the text in a chart is **bolded**, nothing is unique or special. Because it doesn't encode any meaning, the bold text just adds chartjunk to the visual.

Layering

Some data visualizations are going to be unavoidably complex. With these visuals, it will be challenging to steer people down a particular path and help them interpret the data the right way. Before you even have a chance to highlight your insights, the complexity or richness of the information could leave your audience overwhelmed or distracted. Rather than displaying the entirety of a detailed data chart, you can break it up into more manageable layers or sections. The information can be revealed in a controlled manner so the audience can more easily absorb it layer by layer. You gain the benefit of ensuring the audience grasps each new layer before proceeding to the next layer of information.

The layering approach can be especially helpful if you're introducing an unfamiliar chart type or calculated metric. You can slow down and make sure they soak it in before moving to the next chunk of information. In Figure 8.15, the loan application data has been divided up so it doesn't overload the audience with too many details at one time. The scene builds as each new layer is introduced. Eventually, you'll reveal the complete data visualization to the audience. The magic of layering is that you maintain attention and lose fewer people along the way to your main points. However, layering can be more difficult for indirect communications (static reports, infographics), in which you have less control over how people consume your content.

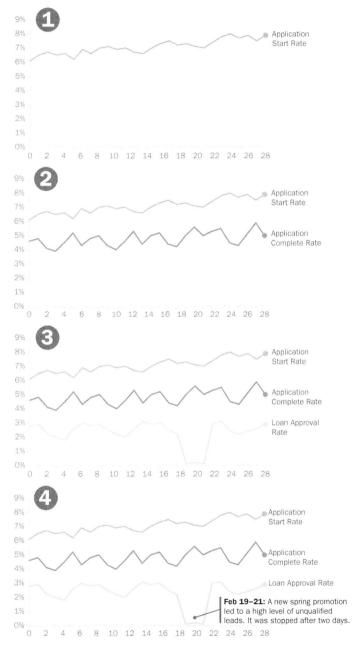

LAYERING CAN BREAK UP A COMPLEX CHART INTO MANAGEABLE CHUNKS

Figure 8.15 With layering, you can turn a complex data visualization into more manageable chunks of information that are easier for an audience to follow and understand. All of these layers would still form a single scene.

Principle #6: Make Your Data Approachable and Engaging

People react positively when things are clear and understandable.
—Dieter Rams, industrial designer

In the late 1970s, German industrial designer Dieter Rams grew increasingly concerned about the sloppy state of design, which he described as "an impenetrable confusion of forms, colors, and noises" (Few 2011). Reflecting on his renowned design work at Braun, he crafted 10 principles of good design. While Rams focused primarily on industrial design, two of his design principles apply well to visual storytelling:

#4. Good design makes a product understandable. It clarifies the product's structure. Better still, it can make the product talk. At best, it is self-explanatory.

#8. Good design is thorough down to the last detail. Nothing must be arbitrary or left to chance. Care and accuracy in the design process show respect toward the user.

In visual storytelling, good design will make your products (data stories) more readable and understandable. While design can't reduce the complexity of a given topic, it can streamline how easy it is for the audience to follow your ideas and insights. If you respect your users (audience), you'll pay attention to details that may at first seem subtle or insignificant. You'll quickly discover they can have a meaningful impact on the effectiveness of your visuals. Even after you've minimized the noise and highlighted the key information in your visuals, polishing the design elements can go a long way to streamlining and enhancing your data story.

A good visual design can both reduce potential cognitive friction and make your data more engaging. As a data storyteller, you want to make your content approachable and easy to evaluate for a wide range of people—from a CEO to a data scientist to your grandmother. In this section, I'll examine how design can enhance the usability of your charts in four key areas: *labeling, reference lines, formatting,* and *convention adherence.*

Labeling

Imagine traveling by car if there were no road signs (and no GPS). Even though you have all of the road infrastructure in place, it would be very chaotic to navigate to unfamiliar destinations without any signage. Labeling is equally important to good chart design. While too much labeling can add noise to a chart, a minimal level of labeling will always be required to describe what information is being shared. The tips in Table 8.2 can help to streamline the readability of your charts.

Table 8.2   Tips to Streamline Readability of Charts

	More Challenging	Less Challenging
Axis labels: In order to make sense of the data in a chart, it's critical that all axes are clearly labeled. If an axis or its scale is ambiguous, then it will only slow your audience's ability to understand the information in your chart. An exception to this rule might be date units such as months or years that are straightforward and easy to understand without labels.		
Direct labels: Whenever possible, it's better to directly label values and avoid forcing the audience to reference a legend that is further removed from the data. Although looking back and forth between data values and a legend is less efficient, in certain situations, it may be the only option (grouped column charts).		

(*continued*)

Table 8.2   Tips to Streamline Readability of Charts (*continued*)

	More Challenging	Less Challenging
Legible text: It is harder to read text that is at a vertical or diagonal angle than text that is horizontal. For categories or values that require longer labels, you may consider using a bar chart instead of a column chart because it is easier to accommodate longer labels in a horizontal format.		
Simple increments: You want to use scale increments that are natural and easy for the audience to process. For example, increments of 1, 2, 5, or 10 are less awkward to navigate than increments such as 3, 6, or 12.		

Reference Lines

If you've ever tried swimming long distances, you know how important it is to have a point of reference to ensure you're traveling in a straight direction. For visual comparisons, reference lines can help your audience more easily make comparisons within your charts—as long as the lines are subtle and used strategically. The tips in Table 8.3 reveal different ways in which reference lines can be used to support various types of comparisons.

Table 8.3   Tips for Using Reference Lines

	More Challenging	Less Challenging
Guidelines: When you have a long list of values in a bar chart or table, your audience may struggle with comparing individual items. By adding thin guidelines between groups of three to five items, you make it easier for the audience to locate and compare different items, especially when the value labels are justified to the same spot.		

	More Challenging	Less Challenging
Anchor lines: When you highlight a point in a scatter plot, you may want to add thin lines for the point's x and y positions. These horizontal and vertical lines can better support comparisons between key data points. Anchor lines can also be used in bar, column, and line charts to provide more context in a visual (mean value, target).		
Trendlines: With line and scatter plot charts, you may consider adding a "line of best fit" that displays the trend of the relationship between the two variables. It also helps to communicate the positive or negative relationship through the slope of the line.		
Shaded regions: In some cases, you may want to highlight a certain range or band of values within a chart. For example, you may use a shaded area to indicate the negative territory or a targeted outcome. The regions can help the audience more quickly interpret the data by having additional visual context.		
Gridlines and sections: Thin gridlines in a bar, column, or line chart can assist the audience in making comparisons between different values. A bar or column chart can also be broken into comparable sections, which can achieve a similar effect but is less common than using gridlines.		

Formatting

Even though you may have the right content and chart type, your choice of format or structure for your data can enhance how readable it is for your audience. The formatting considerations in Table 8.4 can help make your information more approachable.

Table 8.4   Tips for Formatting

	More Challenging	Less Challenging
Color scheme: By default, many analytics tools employ multiple colors in their chart defaults, which can be distracting. A monochromatic scheme that uses various shades of a single hue may require less effort to process.	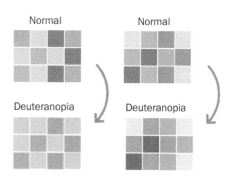	
Colorblindness: About 8% of men and 0.5% of women have color vision deficiency (CVD), making it harder for them to distinguish between green and red hues. You may want to ensure that these individuals can still interpret your charts correctly by using colors such as blue and orange that are easier to differentiate. In the example on the right, you can see the difference that color choice can make to someone with deuteranopia (a green-blind type of CVD that causes individuals to only see two or three hues—compared to the usual seven hues).		
Sorting: Arranging the items by rank from largest to smallest can make your data easier to read and follow. However, in some cases, it still may be more important to maintain a specific order (alphabetical) to facilitate looking up certain values.		

	More Challenging	Less Challenging
Aspect ratio: In order for your data to communicate effectively, you may need to adjust the width-to-height ratio so the audience can more easily discern the key trends or patterns in the data. With a little more breathing room between the data points, a detailed line chart may be easier to examine and understand.		
Smoothing: When you provide granular data, the jaggedness caused by short-term fluctuations in the data can make it harder to assess overall patterns in column or line charts. If you apply a weighted average to smooth the data, the resulting curved lines will make the general movements in the data more visible.		
Transparency and jittering: In "overplotting" situations where multiple values are plotted on top of each other, it can be hard to ascertain the density of the data points. Making the dot points more transparent can help rectify this problem. For some dot plots, you may want to "jitter" the data (randomly assign them a horizontal position) so the points are more spread apart to further clarify the density.	 A B	 A B

Convention Adherence

Designers often have an awkward relationship with conventions and norms. On one hand, they may seek to challenge certain conventions to gain attention with their designs, but on the other hand, they often embrace these common practices to make their designs more straight-forward and easier to consume. Unless you have good reasons, I would recommend adhering to established conventions with your chart designs. The following examples in Table 8.5 illustrate some conventions you should consider.

Table 8.5   Tips for Convention Adherence

	More Challenging	Less Challenging
Color polarity: If your data shows a positive or negative result, you may consider assigning an appropriate color to it (green = good, red = bad). If you assign the wrong color, your audience will be confused by your chart. To avoid color blindness issues, you can use dark and light hues or redundant symbols to clarify the differences.		
Color association: Some items may already be associated with certain colors (countries, companies, political parties, etc.). Rather than assigning random colors to them, you can strengthen the encoded information with familiar, corresponding colors.		
Independent variable on *x*-axis: A common practice is to put the independent variable ("cause" variable) on the *x*-axis and the dependent variable ("effect" variable) on the *y*-axis. For example, it's customary to measure time along the horizontal *x*-axis since it is not changed by the other factors you're measuring.	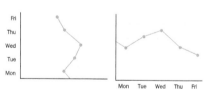	
Direction: Typically, we associate the left and downward directions with negative values and the right and upward directions with positive ones. In a quadrant analysis, the top-right quadrant is frequently seen as the most desirable location.	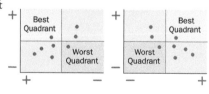	

	More Challenging	Less Challenging
Starting position: In the case of radial charts (pie, donut, radar), the 12 o'clock, or zero-degree, position is a natural starting point for these types of data visualizations. Generally, the largest slice is located at this 12 o'clock position, and then the rest of the slices follow it in clockwise fashion, sorted by size.		

While the careful treatment of the design elements can make your information more approachable, design also gives you an opportunity to make your visuals more engaging for your audience. For more than 130 years, the *National Geographic Society* has been a leader in fact-based visual storytelling. According to its Chief Marketing Officer, Claudia Malley, *National Geographic*'s success at engaging more than 730 million people on a monthly basis comes down to its "relevant, relatable, and timely content" (Stein 2016). In your own stories, the relevance and timeliness of the content are attributes of the actual data, but your design approach will influence how relatable your content is. The more relatable your information is, the more it will resonate with an audience on a deeper, emotional level. To make your data more relatable, I suggest two complementary techniques: imagery and real-world examples.

Imagery

Some people may dismiss imagery as just another form of chartjunk since images are not essential to understanding the underlying data. From a rational perspective, they would be correct—but not from an emotional one. In Chapter 2, the *Picture Superiority Effect* highlighted how images are more memorable than words alone. Images in the form of icons, diagrams, and photography can add visceral clarity to your information and increase the likelihood that your insights will be remembered. Just like the other visual elements, when images are used strategically, they can bring the scenes of your data story to life. For example, icons can be used to communicate information more quickly and memorably than text. Pairing an insight with an evocative photo can amplify its emotional impact and make the data feel more real (see Figure 8.16).

USE ICONS AND PHOTOS SELECTIVELY TO ENGAGE YOUR AUDIENCE

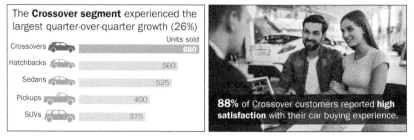

Figure 8.16 Both icons and photos can help make your content more engaging for your audience.

At a major consumer brand, an analytics director found that his team could better capture the attention and interest of the various product teams if they incorporated product images into their data presentations. In a work culture that was more creative than quantitative, the analytics team had to adapt how they shared insights with internal stakeholders in order to get the buy-in they desired. Rather than offering data visualizations about nondescript product SKUs, they discovered product images could draw the product managers into the data. Depending on your audience, you may consider integrating photos of products, employees, or locations into your visuals to increase engagement (see Figure 8.17). The images should only be used if they add meaningful color to the subject matter. If they will only be viewed as incidental decorations, leave them out to preserve the focus on the insights.

THREE HOTTEST WOMEN'S SHOES FROM THE FALL COLLECTION

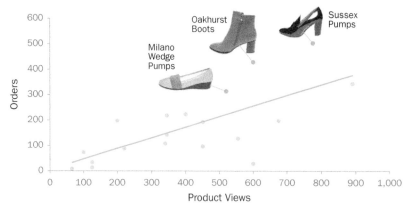

Figure 8.17 The three product images call attention to the key data points in this chart.

Real-world Examples

In its 2012 Olympic coverage, the *New York Times* did a masterful job of revealing the significance of Bob Beamon's 1968 Olympic record-setting achievement in the men's long jump event (Quealy and Roberts 2012). Recognizing that most people would lack perspective on Beamon's record-setting jump of 29 feet and 2.5 inches (8.9 meters), they compared the distance to jumping past an NBA basketball court three-point line (see Figure 8.18). By making the distance more relatable, they ensured Beamon's accomplishment was less ambiguous and more impressive.

USE RELATABLE COMPARISONS

29 feet 2½ inches
(8.9 meters)

Figure 8.18   To make the 1968 Olympic record-setting long jump distance of Bob Beamon more relatable, the *New York Times* compared it to leaping beyond the NBA basketball three-point line.

When your audience is presented with unfamiliar information, they may lack the necessary context to completely grasp what your insights signify. In addition, when you're sharing very large or small numbers, people may struggle to fully fathom the magnitude or minuteness of what the data represents. Rather than leaving your insights somewhat abstract in their minds, you can connect the data points to real-world examples that are more relatable. If you use recognizable, real-life items on a scale that humans can imagine, your examples will resonate more readily. However, beware of being too generalized in your approach. For instance, the problem with using "reaching to the moon" or "circling the Earth" analogies is very few people can truly appreciate these distances—maybe just astronauts and pilots. Try to find examples that are both familiar and conceivable.

To make your data points more concrete, you may need to recast them so they are on more relatable terms for your audience. For example, a paid search consultant was working with a company on managing its large paid search budget. Each month, he noticed they were paying for generic industry keywords that *never* converted into any online sales. When he shared how removing these nonperforming keywords could save the company $10,000 monthly, his recommendation was just "a drop in the bucket" for a marketing team that was spending millions of dollars on paid search advertising each year. So instead, he tried a different approach. He annualized the cost for continuing to pay for these keywords (12 months × $10,000 = $120,000) and highlighted how the savings could be used to hire two college graduates *to perform more analysis like what he was providing*. Even though the marketing team didn't hire two new analysts, the problem was framed in such a way that caught their attention, and they stopped advertising on the nonperforming, generic keywords.

Principle #7: Instill Trust in Your Numbers

There are two goals when presenting data: convey your story and establish credibility.

—Edward Tufte, statistician and author

When you're trying to catalyze change with your data stories, the audience needs to trust your numbers. Because potential change can be uncertain and threatening, people will look for any reason to dismiss or discredit your findings. Assuming the data foundation of your data story is sound—minimal bias, acceptable data quality, thorough analysis, and so on—your visuals must also establish credibility with the audience. A simple oversight in your visuals can undo hours of analysis work and close a window of opportunity that may never re-open. For example, misspellings, typos, and bad grammar can convey carelessness to your audience, which may cause them to question how detail-oriented you were in the analysis phase. Human errors such as having parts of a whole chart not add up to 100% or even mislabeling an axis can derail your message. Make sure you take time to review and proofread all of the scenes of your data story before sharing it. In addition, consider having someone else review your charts to avoid simple mistakes that could hurt your story.

While attention to detail will always be important, you also need to be aware of how data can be visually manipulated in charts—*and not inadvertently mimic those tactics*. Even when your intent isn't to distort the data, you must be mindful of how certain visualization practices may be perceived as "lying with statistics." Table 8.6 illustrates practices you should try to avoid, as they may be perceived as being deceptive.

Table 8.6   Deceptive Practices to Avoid

	Potentially Misleading	Not Misleading
Truncated axis (column/bar): Whenever you truncate the *y*-axis of a column or the *x*-axis of a bar chart, the lengths of the bars are no longer representative of the actual values. This approach can be misleading, as it can exaggerate small differences between values.		
Truncated axis (area): Similar to column charts, the shaded region of an area chart shouldn't have a truncated *y*-axis, as it distorts what is displayed. However, it is generally accepted that line charts don't require a zero baseline in the same way that column and area charts do.		
Overstated axis scale or aspect ratio: To manipulate the data in a chart, the axis scale can be inflated, or the aspect ratio (width-to-height ratio) can be stretched disproportionally. In general, your chart should be wider than taller, and the data should occupy about two-thirds of the chart's scale range.		

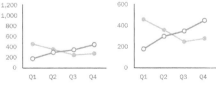

(continued)

Table 8.6   Deceptive Practices to Avoid (*continued*)

	Potentially Misleading	Not Misleading
Inconsistent date intervals: If the dates in a time series do not follow regular intervals, then plotting them at equal intervals can be misleading. Some audience members may question why the dates are irregular and not consistent. You should use a proportional scale on the *x*-axis rather than one with equal intervals.		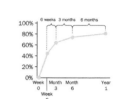
Limited date ranges: Generally, it's not a good idea to "cherry pick" a timeframe so that you can mask results that could undermine a desired narrative. While it's fine to limit the amount of data you show, you shouldn't hide relevant context, especially if it could materially influence how people perceive and interpret your data. In the left example, big shifts in prior time periods are material. In the right example, they aren't as substantive, so they could be left out.		
Irregular binning: How you aggregate or bin the data can shape what a data visualization communicates—whether it's a map, bar chart, or histogram. Unusual or unexpected binning approaches may be viewed skeptically by your audience as attempts to skew the results.		
Erroneous proportions: Some analytics tools give you the option to create bubbles that are proportional by diameter or radius length rather than by area. While the differences are more dramatic, they are also inaccurate and misrepresentative of the values.		

	Potentially Misleading	Not Misleading

Missing sources: Anyone can make up a statistic or tout a data point from a questionable source. Whenever a key statistic doesn't list a clear source, it can come across as evasive and deceptive. However, once you've stated the source, it doesn't need to be highlighted in every subsequent chart unless the source changes or you anticipate individual visuals being shared independently from the rest of the data story.

57%
of teens fear a shooting could happen at their school

57%
of teens fear a shooting could happen at their school

Source: PEW RESEARCH Survey of US teens ages 13 to 17 conducted March 7-April 10, 2018

You don't want to give your audience any reason to doubt your numbers or insights. It's important to be aware of how people might question the veracity of your data due to how you visualize it and what you communicate (or ignore). To build credibility with the audience, you must ensure they understand your intent is to inform and enlighten, not deceive. If you anticipate any concerns, you'll want to be explicit about why you visualized the data in a particular manner. Leaving the audience to make assumptions about why you grouped the data a certain way or why you trended only so many months could weaken their trust in your message. However, if you're forthright about the logic behind your design choices, they won't feel misled even if they don't agree with your approach.

A Principled Approach to Visual Storytelling

The purpose of visualization is insight, not pictures.
—Ben Schneiderman, data scientist

Even though the visuals of your data story will receive the most attention from your audience—the data storytelling process begins by establishing a data foundation that is both relevant and trustworthy. It continues with organizing and structuring the insights into a meaningful and compelling narrative. In the final step of this process, you visualize your insights in a clear and concise manner so the information is easy for your audience to follow and understand. The seven principles shared in this and the previous chapter can guide your visual storytelling, transforming your key findings into a powerful series of visual scenes.

Before you start visualizing your story, you'll need to clarify two things. First, you need to determine how many scenes your story will have and the flow of your content. The narrative storyboarding, that was discussed in Chapter 6, can help identify the main points and organize them into a coherent narrative. When you're ready to visualize your data, the storyboard serves as an indispensable roadmap for directing your data visualization efforts. Second, you need to determine how you're going to deliver the data story to your audience—directly or indirectly. The delivery method will influence your story's visual design. For example, if you're not telling your story in person, more explanation or annotations will be required for each scene. The three-step process in Table 8.7 can help you plan and design the scenes of your data story.

Table 8.7 Three-step Process to Plan and Design Your Data Story

Sketch. Before you start creating any charts in an analytics tool, you might find it helpful to sketch a mock-up for each story point, especially if your story has multiple scenes. You can use a notepad, sticky notes, or a whiteboard to create a rough vision for how you're going to visualize the information. Because you're only investing a small amount of time to create each sketch, you're freed up to iterate quickly until you identify the best visual approach for each chart. The act of sketching your entire data story also gives you an opportunity to step back and ensure that your visuals are not too repetitive and that you have the right flow. You can also walk a colleague through your story to gather feedback and make modifications before you spend any time building charts.

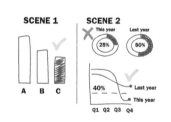

Design. Once you're happy with the rough visual outline of your data story, you can start designing the data visualizations. At this stage, you're focused on making sure the charts are aligned to your story points and convey the information in an effective manner. As you work with the actual data, you may discover you need to modify your charts from what you planned in the sketch phase. It's important to be flexible and defer to whatever approach will best communicate your insights.

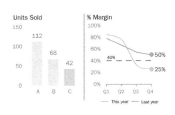

Refine. After you've created the initial charts for your data story, you should evaluate how well each one supports your storyline. You may find small edits to your charts can dramatically enhance their overall effectiveness. For example, you may add direct labels to make a chart easier to read or realign the colors used in a chart to be more consistent. These kinds of simple but important refinements can add polish to your final scenes and help them resonate with your audience.

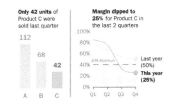

Many people perceive storytelling as a *passive* experience in which the audience just listens or watches as the narrative is told to them. However, data storytelling is an *active* experience in which you invite the audience to join you on a guided tour through your insights. A data story enables the audience to participate in a simplified, focused discovery process—examining the charts and comparing the numbers for themselves. The easier you make the visuals to follow and process, the more likely your audience will understand, retain, and agree with your main points. The late Hans Rosling compared data storytelling to music when he said,

> Most of us need to listen to the music to understand how beautiful it is. But often that's how we present statistics: We just show the notes; we don't play the music. (Reynolds 2007)

Effective visual storytelling is about getting your audience to hear how wonderful your music sounds—not just read the notes. Only when the signal is strong and clear will they be able to fully appreciate the beauty of your numbers. If you've done a good job with your visual storytelling, you'll have an attentive audience that is excited to begin tackling the problems or opportunities you've identified. In the final chapter of this book, I'll walk through some different examples that effectively combine the data storytelling elements—*data*, *narrative*, and *visuals*—to form powerful stories that are both meaningful and memorable.

References

Diakopoulos, N. 2013. Storytelling with data visualization: Context is king. September 17. http://www.nickdiakopoulos.com/2013/09/17/storytelling-with-data-visualization-context-is-king/.

Few, S. 2011. Dieter Rams' ten principles for good design. *Visual Business Intelligence* (blog), December 15. https://www.perceptualedge.com/blog/?p=1138.

Quealy, K., and Roberts, G. 2012. Bob Beamon's long Olympic shadow. *New York Times*, August 4. http://archive.nytimes.com/www.nytimes.com/interactive/2012/08/04/sports/olympics/bob-beamons-long-olympic-shadow.html?_r=0.

Reynolds, G. 2007. Hans Rosling: Don't just show the notes, play the music! Presentation Zen, September 18. https://www.presentationzen.com/presentationzen/2007/09/data-is-not-bor.html.

Simon, H.A. 1971. Designing organizations for an information-rich world. In *Martin Greenberger, Computers, Communication, and the Public Interest*. Baltimore, MD: Johns Hopkins Press.

Stein, L. (2016). A look around Social Media Week, New York. https://www.brandingmag.com/2016/02/29/a-look-around-social-media-week-new-york/ (accessed 24 May 2019).

Tufte, E.R. (1983). *The Visual Display of Quantitative Information*. Cheshire, CT: Graphics Press.

Wong, D.M. (2010). *The Wall Street Journal Guide to Information Graphics: The Do's and Don'ts of Presenting Data, Facts, and Figures*. New York: W.W. Norton & Company.

Chapter 9

Crafting Your Own Data Story

When we dream alone, it's just a dream. But when we dream together, it is the beginning of a new reality.

—Brazilian proverb

A few years ago, my wife and I had the amazing opportunity to visit Italy with another couple. One of the highlights of our vacation was a tour of the beautiful Amalfi Coast, which included a short visit to the ancient Pompeii site. Because we were on a cruise ship, we could spend only a few hours at Pompeii before we needed to head back. The tour company arranged a private tour guide for our small group so we could maximize our time at the excavated Roman ruins.

Our guide, a young Italian named Marcello, turned out to be an archeology student who had worked on the site's ongoing excavations. With more than 170 acres at Pompeii to explore, it was extremely helpful to have an expert guide take us directly to some of the most interesting parts of the archeological site. While many tourists were walking around the ruins—somewhat aimlessly—we were able to target specific areas with the limited time we had. Our guide was able to enrich our experience of Pompeii with background information that helped bring the ancient ruins to life.

On several occasions, I noticed other tourists lean in or linger to hear what Marcello had to say about the buildings, frescoes, and artifacts. Even though other tourists were able to see many of the same sights we did, having a guide meant we were able to gain a deeper appreciation for the history and culture behind the ruins. I'm sure many of our fellow tourists would have relished the opportunity to have someone like Marcello who could have skillfully led them through the site's maze of ancient streets and structures.

Similarly, in a work environment, people will be equally keen to gain insights into the business—potential problems, risks, and opportunities. They may feel overwhelmed or even numbed by the wide array of information available to them. However, because humans are innately curious, they'll welcome the opportunity to learn of new insights from others, especially in the form of narratives. As a data storyteller, you act as a guide for your audience through the data you've gathered and analyzed. In this important role, you'll seek to achieve three key objectives as you prepare to tell your data story:

1. **Explain.** Based on your deeper knowledge of the data, you'll determine which information will be most relevant and salient to share. You'll tailor the data story to the needs and interests of your audience. You'll spend time clarifying concepts and providing ample context so your insights are clear and understandable for them.

2. **Enlighten.** Using the data visualization tools at your disposal, you'll produce visuals that help your audience to see the significance of your findings from a graphical perspective. You'll point out key attributes of the data in the charts so the audience knows where to direct its focus and how to interpret what they see. They'll discover new insights they wouldn't have seen without your help and direction.

3. **Engage.** You'll seek to combine all of the elements—numbers, words, and visuals—into a meaningful, cohesive narrative that will resonate with your audience. Whenever possible, you'll humanize your data by relating it to people your audience cares about. The passion you display for your subject matter will also help you to connect with your audience.

These three guiding objectives—*explain, enlighten,* and *engage*—will determine your insight's fate and whether it is acted on. Even when an insight has great potential upside, that doesn't guarantee it will be embraced and adopted by others. If it isn't clear or doesn't resonate with the intended audience, it's unlikely to go anywhere. The primary reason why you invest time in building a data story is to give your insight a better chance at fulfilling its potential.

When you satisfy your three objectives as a data storyteller, you end up communicating more than just facts and figures. Your data stories have the power to change what people think and how they act. As a data storyteller, you are not only guiding an audience through the data to key insights but *seeking to inspire change.* Once you're practiced in the art of data storytelling, your impact will only be limited by the magnitude of your insights.

Through the chapters of this book, we've explored the importance of storytelling, what a data story is, and what its different components are. After closely examining each of the data storytelling pillars—data, narrative, and visuals—you're ready to see how they can be combined to create compelling data stories. In this final chapter, I'll share examples of different data stories, starting with one shared by the late, great data storyteller Hans Rosling.

Learning from a Master Data Storyteller

The world cannot be understood without numbers. But the world cannot be understood with numbers alone.

—Hans Rosling, physician, professor, and statistician

In 2010, the British TV channel BBC Four produced a one-hour documentary with Hans Rosling called *The Joy of Stats.* Within this program, there's a short segment known as "200 Countries, 200 Years, 4 Minutes" in which Rosling reveals how the health and wealth of countries have evolved over the last 200 years (Gapminder 2019). However, rather than having him present his insights using a standard projector, they simulate an interactive bubble chart that hovers in augmented reality in front of the master data storyteller. In this unique setting, Hans Rosling's genius and passion leave us spellbound as he demonstrates how data can be made to sing.

From this short segment, we have an opportunity to study the various storytelling techniques Rosling employed to craft and deliver his data story. In a play-by-play manner, I'll break down the different tactics he used to develop his narrative and engage his audience. Before you read my analysis of Rosling's data story, I highly recommend watching his four-minute video to see this insightful Swedish storyteller in action (http://bit.ly/200countries200years). Through the lens of the concepts within this book, you'll better understand what made Rosling such an effective and engaging data storyteller.

Figure 9.1   Rosling orients the audience to the axes and quadrants in his virtual bubble chart.
Source: Used with permission ©Wingspan Productions.

0:34—Key Tactics: Labeling, Annotation, and Axis Scaling

At the beginning of his story, Rosling adds labels to the axes (lifespan, income) and clarifies what the two main quadrants are (lower-left: poor and sick; upper-right: rich and healthy) using annotation (see Figure 9.1).

You'll notice his *y*-axis didn't begin at zero years (approximately 20 years to 75 years), and the *x*-axis has a logarithmic scale ($400 to $40,000). As a general rule, starting axes at zero and using a linear scale is preferred. However, in order to maximize the space and spread the data points apart, you might need to make similar adjustments to enhance a scene in your data story.

Figure 9.2   Rosling explains what the bubble sizes in his chart represent.
Source: Used with permission ©Wingspan Productions.

1:00—Key Tactics: Time Period, Label Sizing, Categories, Chart Elements (Bubble Size)

To establish the Setting, he shares the starting point of his time-line (1810). The larger size of the year label is indicative of how important it will be to the overall story. Rather than positioning it at the top of the chart, the year label is located prominently within the chart, where it is closer to the country bubbles—and therefore in the audience's line of sight. Interestingly, Rosling didn't create a color legend for the country categories. To reduce noise, he probably decided a legend wasn't necessary after he initially explained what each color represented. Finally, he also made sure to explain upfront the size of the bubbles is relative to the size of a country population (see Figure 9.2).

Figure 9.3 Rosling uses a reference line to emphasize that average lifespans are below 40 years of age.
Source: Used with permission ©Wingspan Productions.

1:18—Key Tactics: Reference Line, Selective Labeling, Highlighting

As he finalizes the Setting, he uses a reference line to show how all of the countries in 1810 have average lifespans that are below 40 years of age (see Figure 9.3). Instead of labeling all of the countries, which would have been overwhelming, he only references the top two countries at the time: the UK and the Netherlands. To make these two countries stand out, he labels them and brightens the intensity of the selected bubbles to differentiate them from the rest of the European countries.

Figure 9.4 Rosling physically reacts to the downturn in 1918.
Source: Used with permission ©Wingspan Productions.

1:30—Key Tactics: Animation, Additive Context

After the initial setup, Rosling uses animations to progress through the years to show how the countries evolve in terms of health and wealth. With this unique animation process, aside from a few close-ups of the chart, only the year labels and country bubbles change. At different stages, he provides additive context to explain how the Industrial Revolution helps the European countries to become healthier and wealthier while the colonized countries in Asia and Africa remain sick and poor. He also highlights how the effects of World War I and the Spanish Flu epidemic cause all the countries' average lifespans to drop around 1918. He even mimics the downward movement of the data with his body while emphatically proclaiming, "What a catastrophe!" (see Figure 9.4). He also notes when a major event such as the Great Depression in the early 1930s occurs but doesn't impede the upward march of the Western countries.

Figure 9.5 Rosling pauses the time progression and uses selective labeling to highlight several key countries.
Source: Used with permission ©Wingspan Productions.

2:22—Key Tactics: Personalization, Selective Labeling, Highlighting

Rosling pauses the time progression at 1948 to show the wide spectrum between the Western and colonized countries. He personalizes the data by highlighting his homeland of Sweden and emphasizing the upcoming shifts all occurred after his birth year—that is, in his life-time. This subtle gesture helps to humanize the data and him as the presenter. Rosling again uses selective labeling to highlight a few key countries of interest and their current position (United States, Brazil, China) (see Figure 9.5). He then prepares the audience to notice the massive shift that occurs as former colonies gain independence and improve their living conditions. His story culminates with the rise of the emerging economies (Argentina, Mexico, South Korea, Malaysia, Brazil, and Taiwan) that reach the upper-right quadrant in the 1970s. He also highlights African countries that were negatively impacted by civil war and the HIV epidemic (Congo, South Africa).

Figure 9.6   Rosling breaks apart the China bubble to compare its different provinces with other nations.
Source: Used with permission ©Wingspan Productions.

3:30—Key Tactics: Zoom, Selective Labeling, Drill-Down, Explicit Comparisons

When he reaches the last year in his dataset (2009), Rosling zooms into the middle section to show where most of the countries are located. He then highlights the disparity among countries by calling out two nations at opposite extremes of the bubble chart (Congo—worst, Luxembourg—best). He also acknowledges how country averages can mask inequalities within individual countries. He then proceeds to break apart China to compare different provinces with other nations at similar health/wealth levels (see Figure 9.6). For example, he compares Shanghai to Italy and the rural parts of Guizhou to Ghana. Through these comparisons, we can see the inconsistencies between regions within a single country.

Figure 9.7 Rosling narrates the final segment of how all countries can move to the top-right quadrant.
Source: Used with permission ©Wingspan Productions.

4:00—Key Tactics: Summary Animation, Trendline

At the end of his data story, Rosling summarizes the entire progression of countries in an "action replay." This animation effect reinforces his central insight (Aha Moment) that the gap between "the west and the rest" is closing, and we're entering "an entirely new converging world." He overlays a trendline/arrow to highlight the path that he believes all countries can follow to the upper-right quadrant of health and wealth (see Figure 9.7). He ends his data story by underlining how aid, trade, green technology, and peace can help all countries achieve better living standards.

Even though more than 120,000 data points were plotted for this four-minute data story, you never feel overwhelmed by what's being shared. Hans Rosling holds our hands as he guides us through the data, giving us a new appreciation of the global health and wealth trends that have occurred over the past 200 years. Throughout the process, we notice what he wants us to see, and he provides timely, relevant context as the patterns shift.

As you contemplate your own data, you may be thinking to yourself, "My [fill the blank] data isn't as cool or impactful as Rosling's data. I can't present my data in augmented reality!" Technology wasn't what made this video clip special—it was the narrative that was delivered by someone who believed strongly in its importance. George Lucas stated, "A special effect is a tool, a means of telling a story. A special effect without a story is a pretty boring thing." From this example, we learn how integral both the storyteller and narrative are to the overall data story. Rosling's insights would have been bland if he hadn't taken the time to craft a powerful narrative around them. While we may not be able to replicate his passion, witty sense of humor, or augmented reality graphs, we can apply many of the same techniques that Rosling used to enrich our own data stories.

Behind the Scenes with Hans

Figure 9.8 Hans Rosling filming the data story for *The Joy of Stats* in London in 2010. Creative Director Archie Baron is on the bottom left, and Director Dan Hillman is second from the right.
Source: Used with permission ©Wingspan Productions.

When Creative Director Archie Baron at Wingspan Productions first saw one of Hans Rosling's TED Talks, he was blown away by the engaging Swedish statistician. The elegance and significance of Rosling's storytelling helped Baron "see the world in a different way." When his television production company approached Rosling about *The Joy of Stats* project, Baron knew the showcase of the entire one-hour program would be capturing the energetic Swede sharing one of his inspiring data stories. However, Baron believed the audience's comprehension would be diminished if the video had to cut back and forth between the storyteller and the graph.

His team decided they would have Rosling conjure up the data out of thin air and have it hover in front of him in augmented reality. Similar to the virtual displays used in the Tom Cruise movie *Minority Report* (2002), this approach would keep Rosling and his animated bubble chart in the same frame. "The idea was that by putting Rosling in the graph," says Baron, "he completely owns it and the story it tells." When the Wingspan team pitched the idea to Rosling, the professor was initially skeptical about whether it would work. He hadn't always been satisfied with past attempts at filming his data storytelling and never wanted infographics to be purely for show. However, after showing him a brief demo of how the virtual chart might work, they were able to convince him to take a leap of faith with them.

Even though the data story segment was only four minutes long, it consumed 25–30% of the production time for the 60-minute show. During many long days of scripting and storyboarding, Baron witnessed how Rosling paid meticulous attention to every detail and was determined to develop a script that would be clear and compelling for the viewers. Director Dan Hillman noted, "I loved the technical precision which he applied to finding the best way to tell a story, tell a joke, show a number, and make a point." For the filming location, they decided it should be in a real location with some depth rather than a bland TV studio. This is why you see Rosling entering a warehouse building at the beginning of the video. *(continued)*

(continued)

On the day of the filming, Rosling was incredibly focused throughout the entire day—even though it was one of the hottest days of the year in London. With only limited reference points to orientate himself, he had to act as though the graph was directly in front of him (see Figure 9.8). Baron said, "Every eye line, gesture, and finger wag had to be exactly in the right place or else it wouldn't work. We couldn't make the data fit the shot; the shot absolutely had to fit the data." Hillman and Baron recognized Hans's unique personality would be an integral part of his storytelling. They were able to bring it out in key moments when he joked about the 1948 Winter Olympics and physically accentuated the downward movement of the data when the Spanish Flu and WWI occurred. Even his closing statement of "Pretty neat, huh?" captured his magnetic charm.

After filming multiple takes, Rosling put his trust in the production team to add the virtual charts to the live footage. Rosling's normal visualization tool for displaying his animated bubble charts, Gapminder's Trendalyzer (developed by his son Ola Rosling), had to be adapted to work with television animation software, which required extensive coding to achieve an accurate integration. In addition to the animation work, an entire lexicon of sounds was created to represent the different interactions with the data. Rosling was a strong advocate for iterating toward a final product. At one point, Baron remembered receiving an email from Hans with 17 comments on just the first two minutes of an early cut of the video. At the end of a lengthy editing process, Baron knew they had something special but had no idea what its impact would be. He stated, "Normally, people aren't going to want to watch a 60-something Swedish statistician present public health data, but Hans was a unique showman."

The video clip went instantly viral two weeks before the show aired on BBC Four and has gone on to generate nearly nine million views. In 2011, *The Joy of Stats* won a Grierson Award for Best Science Documentary. Reflecting on his seven-year partnership and friendship with Rosling, Hillman said, "What made his message always exhilarating to hear was that he gave us all confidence in our potential. Confidence that we could, despite everything, change our world for the better.

Deconstructing a Data Story

One of the underestimated tasks in nonfiction writing is to impose narrative shape on an unwieldy mass of material.

—William Zinsser, writer

In this book, I've covered various principles and guidelines on how to develop and build an effective data story. My goal was to provide you with enough direction and structure to help you transform your facts and figures into communications that resonate with your audiences. However, not all of your data stories are going to neatly align with every concept and framework in this book. You're going to need to use your judgment on what will work best in each unique situation. Likewise, the same data story may need to be modified to accommodate different circumstances or situations.

For example, being able to present your story in person will change its shape and format. If you deliver your story to diverse groups of people, you may need to alter its design and emphasis to match each unique audience. If you have a short amount of time to share your insights, you'll compose your data story differently than if you have a longer window of time. Since each new scenario will be unique, you'll need to be flexible and adaptive with your data storytelling. The concepts and principles in this book are meant to *guide your approach, not restrict it.* When you need to deviate from a best practice, do so in an informed, calculated manner, knowing what you're sacrificing to achieve a specific aim with your storytelling.

One of the most effective ways of learning new techniques is to see them in action. To illustrate how the different elements combine to form a data story, I'll share an example focused on the US education system that I presented at a conference. After you've read the entire data story, I'll review some of the key design decisions I made as I was building it. To make it easier to review later, I've divided the story up into three main sections, or acts. As you read the following data story, do your own evaluation of the interplay of different elements—data, narrative, and visuals. Even when you use good practices in your data storytelling, there is usually more than one way of telling each data story, and each storyteller will have his or her own unique style and preferences.

Act I: The Setting

Welsh industrialist and social reformer Robert Owen (1771–1858) stated, "To train and educate the rising generation will at all times be the first object of society, to which every other will be subordinate." Education is essential to a country's development and growth. Much of the United States's success as a nation can be traced back to having one of the best education systems in the world. However, over the past few decades, concerns have risen that the United States's educational advantage may be eroding.

In 1983, a landmark report titled "A Nation at Risk" outlined the deteriorating quality of the US education system. The report authors lamented, "If an unfriendly foreign power had attempted to impose on America the mediocre educational performance that exists today, we might well have viewed it as an act of war" (US Department of Education 1983). After the report sounded the alarm on America's school system, US politicians came to the stark realization their country may be losing its competitive edge in the global labor market.

In 1989, US President George H. W. Bush gathered together 50 state governors to create a set of national educational goals, including ranking first in the world in mathematics and science by 2000. However, at the turn of the millennium, the country was no closer to being top ranked in either discipline. In 2000, the PISA (Program for International Student Assessment) results revealed American 15-year-old students ranked 14th in science and 18th in mathematics among 27 OECD (Organisation for Economic Co-operation and Development) countries (see Figure 9.9). Not only was the United States not first, but its results were below the OECD average.

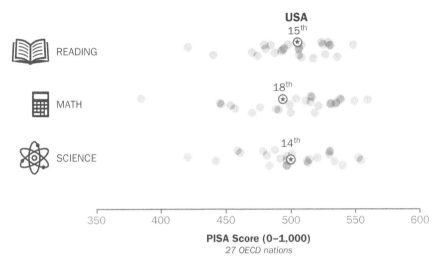

Figure 9.9 Based on PISA data, the United States didn't rank highly in any of the three core subjects.
Source: PISA.

Act II: The Build-up

In 2002, with bi-partisan support, President George W. Bush introduced the No Child Left Behind (NCLB) Act, which marked a more involved role in K-12 education for the federal government than ever before. It had the bold objective to ensure all students were proficient at their respective grade level by 2014, including disadvantaged subgroups—racial minority, low-income, and special education students. A core emphasis of the new law was to introduce more transparency and accountability into school performance through expanded standardized testing. For third through eighth grades, annual testing for reading and math was introduced. Each state was allowed to establish annual achievement targets, and punitive sanctions were imposed on schools that did not achieve "adequate yearly progress." As FiveThirtyEight.com noted, NCLB fundamentally "changed the way the American educational system collects and uses data" (Casselman 2015).

Essentially, NCLB initiated a data revolution within the US education system. It occurred almost a decade before many enterprises began recognizing the importance of being data-driven. Being armed with more data than ever before, NCLB proponents believed state politicians, administrators, and teachers would be better equipped to address key gaps in their respective education systems with better-informed decision making. To measure the overall impact of NCLB, the National Assessment of Education Progress (NAEP) conducted national and state-level testing every two years in reading and math in the fourth and eighth grades.

If we focus on math proficiency—a key skill in today's data economy—we see NCLB missed its 100% proficiency goal by a large margin (see Figure 9.10). By 2015, only 40% of fourth-grade and

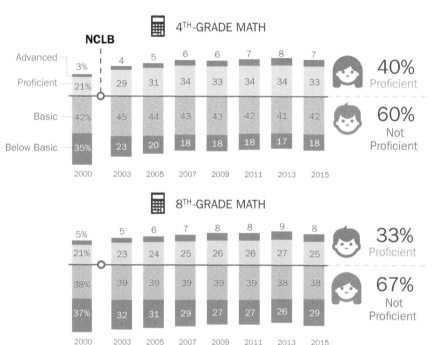

Figure 9.10 NCLB had the goal of achieving 100% proficiency in math and reading. While math proficiency levels increased marginally for fourth- and eighth-grade students, a majority of them are still below "proficient" at their grade level. *Source:* NAEP.

33% of eighth-grade students were considered "proficient" in math. In the pre-NCLB years (1990–2002) for both groups of students, the proficiency gains in math were greater. For example, from 1990 to 2003, the math proficiency level of fourth-grade students improved 20%, but only 7% with NCLB. It's also important to note neither US political party that was in power—Republican or Democrat—was successful at addressing this problem when in power. From 1990 to 2015, two Republican (Bush, Bush) and two Democrat (Clinton, Obama) administrations were unable to make any significant progress in this area.

The other goal of NCLB was to close the performance gap for disadvantaged students. However, it achieved only minor gains for Hispanic and Black students in math and reading (see Figure 9.11). To put these meager gains in perspective, if we were to hold this same rate of improvement constant, it would take another 72 years and 108 years for Hispanic and Black fourth-grade students, respectively, to close the achievement gap with white students in math proficiency. This glacial pace probably wasn't what the NCLB authors envisioned for the education reforms they introduced.

While NCBL didn't achieve its ambitious education goals, did the influx of testing and data help politicians, administrators, and teachers improve the American performance on the world stage? Sadly, the United

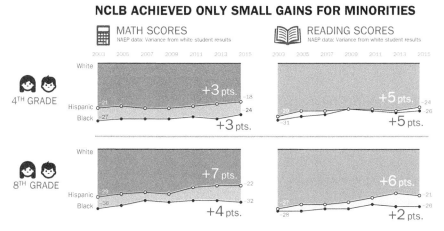

Figure 9.11 Hispanic and Black students experienced only minor gains in math and reading compared to their white peers.
Source: NAEP.

States slipped further behind in the international PISA rankings, especially in math—where it dropped from 18th in 2000 to 29th in 2015 (see Figure 9.12). If 30 points on the PISA test is the equivalent to a year of schooling, US students' math skills (470) are about two-thirds of a grade level behind the OECD average (490) (*The Economist* 2016). If mathematics is the foundation for data science and artificial intelligence, the United States can't afford to let its skills erode in this critical subject area.

FROM 2000 TO 2015, THE UNITED STATES FELL FURTHER BEHIND—PARTICULARLY IN MATH

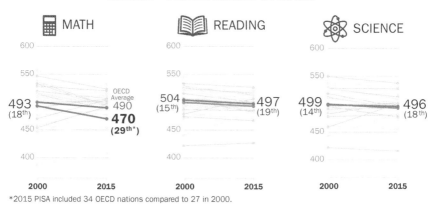

*2015 PISA included 34 OECD nations compared to 27 in 2000.

Figure 9.12 After NCLB, the United States slipped further behind other OECD countries, especially in math. With math skills being foundational to data science, the nation can't afford to fall behind more math-savvy countries. *Source:* PISA.

Act III: The Solution

Esteban Bullrich, a former minister of education in Argentina said, "PISA is like an X-ray of a country's education policy. It is not a full picture of your health, but it can help you spot where things are sickly" (*The Economist* 2016). One of the key challenges the United States faces within its education system is child poverty. Among the high-income countries, one in five children (21%) live in poverty, which is defined as households with an income 60% lower than the national median. Based on 2014 data from UNICEF, a shocking 29.4% of US children (aged 0–17) live in poverty (see Figure 9.13) (UNICEF 2017).

In order to understand how child poverty affects student performance, we can evaluate PISA scores based on how much US public

FOR A WEALTHY COUNTRY, THE UNITED STATES HAS A HIGH % OF CHILD POVERTY

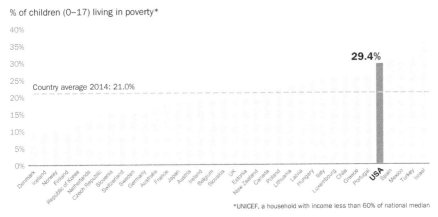

Figure 9.13 For a wealthy nation, the United States has a disproportionately high amount of child poverty compared to other OECD countries.
Source: UNICEF.

schools participated in free or low-cost lunch programs (see Figure 9.14). Poorer students will rely more heavily on subsidized meal programs than richer students who don't require the same meal assistance.

SCHOOL LUNCH PARTICIPATION REVEALS HOW CHILD POVERTY IMPACTS MATH SCORES

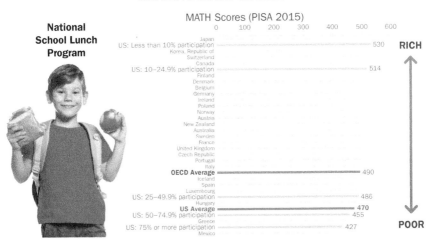

Figure 9.14 When you examine the influence of school participation in lunch programs, you can see wealth played a key role in shaping PISA math scores in the United States.
Source: PISA.

In the more affluent schools, where less than 25% of the students relied on the meal subsidies, the math scores were comparable to those of the best-performing countries such as Japan, South Korea, and Canada. However, at the other end of the spectrum, schools with higher concentrations of poor students who depended more heavily on the lunch programs performed far below the OECD average, with math scores similar to those of Hungary, Greece, and Mexico. The income disparity between the top and bottom segments of US students clearly influenced the nation's PISA math scores.

In the global education race, there are signs that the United States is steadily falling behind. It may be time to reexamine *how* and *where* the country is spending its education dollars. In terms of education spending per student in 2015, the nation spent the fourth highest amount of all OECD countries (US$15,494 per student). However, it found itself in the worst quadrant (see Figure 9.15)—one of only two countries that outspent the OECD average (US$10,220) but underachieved the OECD average (490) for PISA math scores. Unfortunately, the achievement gap between wealthy and poor students in the United States

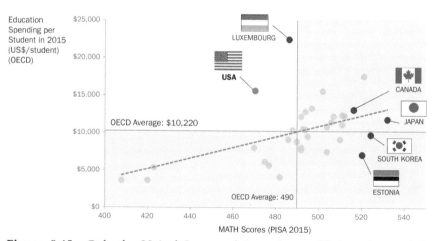

Figure 9.15 Only the United States and Luxembourg fall into the top-left quadrant as countries that surpassed the OECD average for education spending but achieved only below-average math scores in PISA testing.
Source: OECD, PISA.

will continue to widen when school funding is heavily influenced by property taxes—rich neighborhoods have the funds to excel, and poor ones struggle to provide the basics.

What can be done to address this growing problem? In December 2015, the Every Student Succeeds Act (ESSA) replaced the NCLB Act. This act offers the US states more flexibility to govern how they deliver education to their respective students. Education equity was a core focus of the new act, and the responsibility now rests with each state in how it chooses to educate its students. Canada's highly successful education system relies almost exclusively on its provinces to administer equitable education. So, in principle, the state-led approach has the potential to succeed without heavy federal oversight and intervention. Under ESSA, the following levers can help US states advance equity in education for all students:

- **Greater accountability and transparency.** All 50 states had to submit accountability plans to the US Department of Education for approval, and the ESSA requires states to report on per-pupil spending to increase transparency across school districts.
- **State funding to offset local inequity.** State governments need to invest additional resources to counteract the fiscal inequity created by disparities in local funding for education.
- **Early childhood education.** Underprivileged students can quickly fall behind their peers academically as they begin kindergarten. Providing quality preschool to low-income children can help prepare them to learn and keep pace with other students.
- **Community schools.** Low-income students often face difficult circumstances at home that can make focusing on learning more challenging. The community school approach can address the problems happening at home by offering social services to the low-income families (healthcare, food, school supplies, tutoring, counseling, etc.).
- **Qualified teachers.** Low-income schools and districts often have a disproportionate number of inexperienced, ineffective, and out-of-field teachers. States must monitor and evaluate the quality of their teachers and ensure all students have access to skilled instructors.

With the introduction of ESSA, the success of the US education system now rests on the united efforts of the country's 50 states. Americans must now hold state legislatures responsible for ensuring equity remains a key focus of their education plans. If the states fail to intervene on behalf of underprivileged students, the nation will witness more countries leaping ahead of its education system. Greater equity in education will pay dividends as millions of disadvantaged students won't be left behind but instead invited to lead and shape the nation's future. Who knows what socioeconomic background the next Thomas Edison, Marie Curie, or Albert Einstein could come from?

NCLB Data Story: Behind the Scenes

This US education data story used a variety of data from different sources, as well as an assortment of data visualizations to convey its key messages. It also followed the data storytelling arc across the three main sections. To give you a deeper understanding and appreciation of how this data story was formed, I'll share some of the key design decisions that occurred in each section.

Act I Review

The first section introduces the topic and focus of the data story. After providing a brief background on the US education system in the Setting stage, I used a visual Hook—the United States's mediocre PISA scores in 2000—to draw the audience into the story. Here are some of the tactics I employed in this section (see Figure 9.16):

ACT I - VISUAL HIGHLIGHTS

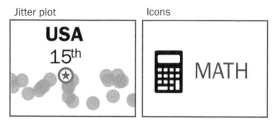

Figure 9.16   In Act I, I used a jitter plot and icons as key visual storytelling tactics.

- **Starting point.** Rather than beginning my data story with a comprehensive overview of education trends in the United States, I jumped right into an indicator of the problems facing the nation—its subpar ranking among countries in terms of its international PISA scores.
- **Quotes.** To set the stage and provide context for my data story, I employed a couple of quotes. In some cases, an astute quote can be just as effective as a good visualization at grabbing people's attention.
- **Jitter plot.** For the PISA scores, I used a jitter plot (see Figure 9.9) to spread out the results of the other OECD countries. When the data points were overlapping, it was harder to see the spread of the various nations.
- **Selective labeling.** Aside from the United States, I didn't label any other countries on the chart, so the audience wouldn't be overwhelmed by too much noise. At this stage, labeling the other data points wasn't important to the message.
- **Icons.** In the visual, I used icons to place more emphasis on the three core subjects. I could then reuse these icons throughout the rest of the data story to reinforce which subjects I was focusing on. I decided to use star dots to highlight the US scores in the chart and add a little patriotic flair to the visual.

Act II Review

The next section introduced the NCLB Act and evaluated whether it was able to reverse the declining educational performance in the United States. A couple of Rising Insights were used to share how ineffective NCLB was at achieving its objectives. The Aha Moment revealed its weak impact on turning around the United States's PISA scores or its international ranking. Here are some of the tactics that were used in this section (see Figure 9.17):

- **NCLB background.** Even in the second act, I still provided context on the NCLB Act. You don't need to restrict contextual information to just the Setting phase if it's essential to your storytelling.

ACT II -VISUAL HIGHLIGHTS

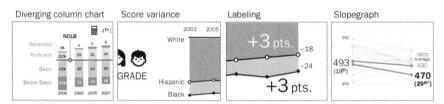

Figure 9.17 In Act II, these close-ups highlight some of the visual design decisions that were made in this section.

- **Selective focus.** To avoid overwhelming the audience, I focused on just the math scores. However, I chose to show both the fourth- and eighth-grade proficiency results to demonstrate how similar they were to each other. Choosing what data to include and exclude is a crucial step in forming your data story.

- **Diverging column chart.** For the proficiency-level data, a diverging column chart (see Figure 9.10) is effective at displaying a rating scale because the negative and positive can be situated on either side of a common baseline. This chart was inspired by a similar chart created by Pew Research (Desilver 2017). However, I decided to color-code the negative and positive values with red and blue respectively. To highlight how the final proficiency levels fell short of the 100% targets, I used child icons to draw attention to the 2015 figures on the far right.

- **Score variance.** Rather than just trending all of the racial group scores in a line chart, I thought it would be better to emphasize the variance over time for each group compared to the white students.

- **Panel area charts.** In Figure 9.11, I decided to include both math and reading scores for fourth- and eighth-grade levels to show how the four trends were similar—small increases in test scores over the 12-year period.

- **Labeling.** Instead of expecting the audience to calculate the shift in scores from 2003 to 2015, I added the score improvements to each panel chart. I also removed the x-axis labels from the panel charts on the bottom row (eighth grade) to reduce unnecessary noise.

- **Extrapolation.** To emphasize the slow pace of change, I extrapolated out the duration of time it would take fourth-grade Hispanic and Black scores to close the gap (72 and 108 years). Sometimes, it can be helpful to roll up results into larger amounts so people can better appreciate the cumulative effects.
- **Slopegraph.** This chart type (see Figure 9.12) can be effective for situations in which you're highlighting key shifts between two time periods. As the climax or Aha Moment of my data story, this chart shows NCLB did little to slow the United States from falling further behind other OECD nations, especially in math.
- **Highlight colors.** Rather than labeling individual countries in Figure 9.12, I only highlighted the US and OECD average scores. I could have focused on just these two lines, but having other country results in the background as grayscale provides useful context.

Act III Review

In the final section, the story turns its attention to uncovering what can be done to address the declining ranking of the US education system. To weigh potential solutions, more supporting information must still be presented to the audience at this stage. Here are some of the final tactics used to complete the data story (see Figure 9.18):

ACT III - VISUAL HIGHLIGHTS

Figure 9.18 In Act III, these close-ups represent some of the visual design decisions that were made in this section.

- **Chart versus statistic.** Figure 9.13 shows the United States is the fifth-worst OECD country for child poverty. I could have just shared this single statistic (29.4%), but I felt as though displaying the data for all the OECD countries added more weight and context. In other scenarios, you may elect to share a single figure, and it can be impactful without necessarily having to graph it.

- **Axis label orientation.** You may have noticed I violated the visualization best practice to keep text horizontal and not at an angle. In this case, using a horizontal bar chart instead of a column chart took up too much vertical space on the page. I opted to put the country names at a diagonal angle so I could use a column chart that required less vertical space.
- **Reference line.** In Figure 9.13, the average percent line (21%) provides a useful reference line to identify which countries are experiencing higher- or lower-than-average child poverty rates. The audience can easily see which countries have lower rates of child poverty and which ones are struggling like the United States.
- **School lunch program data.** This subset of PISA data enabled me to infer how poverty affected math scores. It provided more clarity into what was influencing the weaker math scores in the United States.
- **Highlight colors.** In Figure 9.14, I highlighted the different US segments in blue with the rest of the OECD countries in grayscale to push them to the background. The OECD and US averages are also featured for benchmarking purposes.
- **Student image.** On the left of Figure 9.14, I included an image of the student holding food to connect with the school lunch program data. By including the stock photo of the young boy, I wanted people to remember this data is about real kids who struggle with having adequate nutrition on a daily basis. Essentially, I tried to humanize the data and make it more relatable.
- **Scatterplot.** To show the relationship between two variables (education spend per student, PISA math scores), I created a scatterplot (see Figure 9.15). I added reference lines for the OECD averages on both axes to create for four quadrants. I also included a trendline to help the audience more quickly discern which countries were under- or overachieving in terms of education spend and math scores.
- **Flag images.** For this chart, I labeled some of the better-performing countries with flags. I could have just added

the country names, but I found the flags helped the selected data points stand out more. I debated whether to add the Luxembourg flag because it wasn't central to my story. However, when I tested the chart with various audiences, I found they always ended up asking which country shared the same quadrant with the United States. Adding the Luxembourg flag removed this needless question.

- **Background gradient.** In Figure 9.15, I also added a gray gradient background to three of the quadrants to draw attention to the top-left quadrant, where the United States was situated. It was important that people realized this was the least efficient and undesirable quadrant.

- **Recommendations.** The solution or next steps must be tailored to the ability or power of the audience to act on the information. In this case, my insights were geared toward the general public, not policy makers. My goal (*telos* appeal) was to create more awareness for both the weakening math skills within the US education system and for what Americans could do to ensure their state governments don't overlook the importance of increasing equity under ESSA.

As you reviewed this NCLB data story, you may not have realized how much thought and preparation went into the selection of the data, formation of the narrative, and design of the visuals. Aside from it being a useful example, there was also a secondary purpose in sharing this particular story. Even though NCLB introduced unparalleled levels of data into the US education system, it had a negligible impact on student performance. A former school principal Simon Rodberg noted, "Better instruction won't come from more detailed information, but from changing what people do . . . convincing teachers of the need to change and focusing where they need to change" (Rodberg 2019). As organizations amass more and more data, it's important to remember that all the data in the world will accomplish nothing if it can't be used to inspire change. No matter what position, function, or industry you're in, the ability to communicate insights effectively will be essential to turning insights into beneficial enhancements.

Everyday Data Stories Come in All Shapes, Sizes, and Flavors

"Good story" means something worth telling that the world wants to hear. Finding this is your lonely task. . . . Your goal must be a good story well told.

—Robert McKee, screenwriting expert and author

Many successful data stories aren't prepared by well-known data journalists or data visualization experts. You won't find them posted to popular media sites or shared at prominent conferences. Their authors also don't receive any industry accolades or recognition. However, these data stories can have a tremendous impact on the teams, departments, and companies where they're shared. I'd like to turn the spotlight on a couple of these everyday examples of data storytelling.

Based on a True Story #1: An Editor Must Retain a Skilled Writer

At a major media company, Sarah, a senior editor, cringed when she found out that one of her young, up-and-coming writers with a good social media following had just received a job offer from a competitor. After joining the company less than two years earlier, the junior writer would be receiving a significant pay increase—from $30,000 to $60,000. Sarah knew that if she lost this rising star, her team would struggle to hit its targets the rest of the year. However, she was also apprehensive about going to the lead editor and requesting a major out-of-cycle pay increase.

After spending a couple of hours with her analytics team analyzing the incremental contributions of this specific writer, Sarah was shocked to discover the young writer was worth more than $1.5 million to the company in annual advertising revenue! Rather than building an elaborate data story, Sarah sent a simple email to Jim, the lead editor, in the format of a data trailer (see Figure 9.19).

Rather than providing her busy manager with all of the data from their analysis of Wendy's contributions, Sarah limited her data story to just a simple data trailer: *Setting* (two-year tenure, 30,000

DATA TRAILER IN AN EMAIL

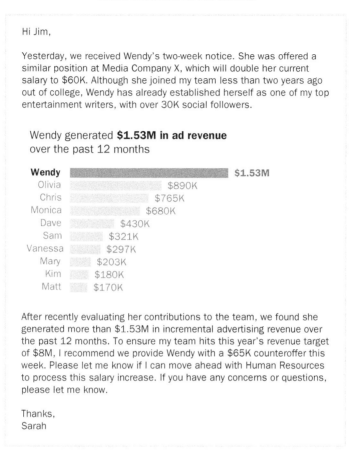

Hi Jim,

Yesterday, we received Wendy's two-week notice. She was offered a similar position at Media Company X, which will double her current salary to $60K. Although she joined my team less than two years ago out of college, Wendy has already established herself as one of my top entertainment writers, with over 30K social followers.

Wendy generated **$1.53M in ad revenue** over the past 12 months

Wendy	$1.53M
Olivia	$890K
Chris	$765K
Monica	$680K
Dave	$430K
Sam	$321K
Vanessa	$297K
Mary	$203K
Kim	$180K
Matt	$170K

After recently evaluating her contributions to the team, we found she generated more than $1.53M in incremental advertising revenue over the past 12 months. To ensure my team hits this year's revenue target of $8M, I recommend we provide Wendy with a $65K counteroffer this week. Please let me know if I can move ahead with Human Resources to process this salary increase. If you have any concerns or questions, please let me know.

Thanks,
Sarah

Figure 9.19   Sarah emailed her boss, Jim, a modified data trailer to save one of her high-performing team members, Wendy.

social followers), Hook ($60,000 job offer), and Aha Moment ($1.5 million in revenue). In this case, the data trailer included the proposed Solution ($65,000 counteroffer), as it was an urgent request that needed attention. If Jim wanted to dive deeper into the revenue calculations, Sarah could prepare a more robust data story for him. In this case, the $1.5 million in incremental ad revenue made the counteroffer decision a no-brainer for Jim, and he quickly approved Sarah's recommendation. Five years later, Wendy still works at the same media company and probably has no idea just how valuable she is to her employer. Wendy's version of Sarah's data story could have concluded with a different recommendation—forget $65,000, try $125,000.

As this example illustrates, every data story doesn't need to be a major production. A simple chart with a concise narrative may be all that is required to drive a quick decision and targeted action. In this case, the visual helped emphasize Sarah's Aha Moment to her boss. While you may not always need a chart in shorter communications, a simple visual may be just the tipping point you need to influence a key decision like this one.

Based on a True Story #2: A Manufacturer's Need for a New Pricing Strategy

After being acquired by a private equity firm, a major packaging manufacturer was given the aggressive goal of significantly improving its profitability over the next three years. Rather than continuing to expand its customer base, the investors wanted the leadership team to focus on optimizing its existing business. The analytics team went to work identifying potential areas in which the manufacturer could optimize its financial performance. Exploratory analysis into their pricing approach produced the most promising findings. To initiate a potentially difficult shift in its current sales strategy, their analytics manager, Kevin, needed to obtain buy-in from the senior leadership team. He crafted a data story to help explain and contextualize the financial opportunity of adopting a new pricing approach.

Setting and Hook: Almost a Third of Customer Accounts Weren't Profitable: Kevin's first goal was to educate the leadership team on its current customer portfolio in terms of both revenue and profitability. The manufacturer generated approximately $75 million in profits from $720 million in annual revenues. With the help of a scatterplot with a gradient scale to indicate the gross margin percent, the executives could see a significant red cluster of customer accounts with low or negative gross margin. To service this segment of customers, the company was mostly losing money. Approximately $250 million of its total revenues—a third of its business—came from accounts with a gross margin ratio under 5%. Using a filtered version of the scatterplot graph (see Figure 9.20), Kevin was able to draw attention to this group of underperforming accounts. The chart became the crucial Hook for the rest of his data story.

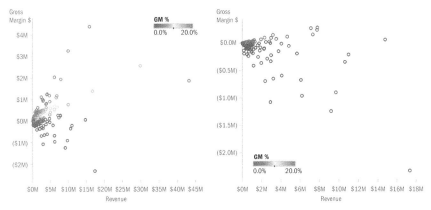

Figure 9.20   The left-side scatterplot shows customer accounts based on their gross margin and revenue. The color gradient highlights the profitability or gross margin % for each account. The right-side scatterplot has been filtered to highlight only the accounts with less than 5% gross margin.

Rising Insights: Increasing Gross Margin Instead of Generating Incremental Sales:

Kevin then showed the leadership team how bringing the accounts with less than 5% gross margin up to just 5% would generate an additional $27 million in revenue and profit. This action would be the equivalent of an incremental sales increase of $270 million at 10% gross margin. Furthermore, if the manufacturer could get the less-profitable accounts to reach the company average of 10% gross margin, it could generate a total of $40 million in revenue and profit. It would be the same as landing an additional $400 million in sales at its current 10% average gross margin (see Figure 9.21). The 5% in gross margin was viewed as an achievable target, while reaching 10% might take two or three years.

For one key reason, optimizing the existing business as opposed to winning new business was viewed as a more viable option. Even if the manufacturer was able to generate the incremental sales, it wouldn't have the production capacity to service additional work without

SIGNIFICANT BENEFITS FROM INCREASING GROSS MARGIN FROM WEAK ACCOUNTS

Figure 9.21 If the manufacturer increased the gross margin (GM) percentage for its worst customers, it could generate incremental profits of $27 million (5% GM) and $40 million (10% GM). These two gross margin amounts were the equivalent of incremental sales increases of $270 million and $400 million respectively.

significant capital expenditures, as they were already operating at full capacity year-round. If it simply focused on raising its prices to improve gross margin, it could maintain its current capacity.

Aha Moment: Pricing Adjustments for "Worst of the Worst" Accounts: Kevin then focused on the "worst of the worst" accounts as the biggest, immediate opportunity. The company had $170 million in business that was at or below zero gross margin. If they could get these accounts to zero gross margin, it could generate $16 million in incremental revenue and profit. Essentially, if the company lost this segment of customers, it would make an additional $16 million *by not selling to them any longer.* Additionally, it would free up capacity to take on more profitable work. If these accounts wouldn't consider reasonable price increases, the manufacturer had to consider ending its relationship with them.

Kevin's team was able to build the case that the risk of losing these customers was fairly low. It was unlikely that their competitors could offer better prices, as their company was a major player in the industry with advantages in terms of raw material buying power and cost structure. If it was unprofitable work for this major manufacturer, it would also be for their competitors. If their rivals were willing to take on these accounts, they would fill their plants with poor margin production, which would mean higher margin opportunities could come to Kevin's organization due to capacity constraints in the industry.

Solution and Next Steps: Delivering a Tough Message Supported with Data: Effective communication and sales execution were critical to the success of introducing this new pricing strategy. While the leadership team was prepared to lose customers, their preference was to retain them. Aside from changing the sales team's commission structure from focusing on revenue to profitability growth, the salespeople were given a copy of the scatterplot chart, along with a very basic sales and profitability one-pager for each of their "worst of the worst" accounts. Equipped with this information, the sales representatives were able to discuss with customers the manufacturer's negative gross margin issue in a calm, factual manner and deliver the message with confidence.

In Figure 9.20, you'll find a customer at the far bottom right of the scatterplots—deep in negative-gross-margin territory. When the information was shared with this major customer, they responded by saying, "Having you at negative margin is not a good thing. That doesn't help either of us." The pricing strategy actually ended up strengthening the relationship with this customer—helping the manufacturer to increase margins significantly (–$3.2 million to $0.2 million gross margin) in a year and to nearly double the business in two years ($17 million to $32 million). After two more years, the account grew to $50 million with $5 million in gross margin—an incredible four-year turnaround.

Overall, the manufacturer's profits grew from single digits to over 20% within three years. The new pricing strategy was instrumental to this success. Data storytelling not only enabled the analytics manager to gain buy-in from his leadership team, but it also informed how the sales team negotiated better pricing with their negative-margin customers.

These two real-world data stories illustrate how effective data storytelling can transform the fortunes of a team or an entire organization. Neither example required an excessive amount of data or visuals to tell their stories. If you take and apply the concepts and principles in this book, you'll be positioned to achieve similar success with your own "everyday" data stories—no matter what shape, size, or flavor they come in.

Data Storyteller: A Guide and a Change Agent

No one ever made a decision because of a number. They need a story.
—Daniel Kahneman, psychologist, behavioral economist, and author

Data storytelling is transformative. Many people don't realize that when they share insights, they're not just imparting information to other people. The natural consequence of sharing an insight is change. *Stop doing that, and do more of this. Focus less on them, and concentrate more on these people. Spend less there, and invest more here.* A poignant insight will drive an enlightened audience to think or act differently. So, as a data storyteller, you're not only guiding the audience through the data, you're also acting as a *change agent*. Rather than just pointing out possible enhancements, you're helping your audience fully understand the urgency of the changes and giving them the confidence to move forward.

In an age of rapid digital transformation, organizations are going to need more data-savvy change agents than ever before. People who can find insights and turn them into improvements and innovations will be highly valued in the marketplace. The power of data storytelling can't be limited to just a handful of data professionals. Since data is no longer the limited domain of certain functional areas such as IT, finance, or accounting, it's now critical that employees in all departments from Human Resources to Sales know how to communicate with data effectively. Every organization—start-up, enterprise, nonprofit, or government agency—needs to invite more of its people to engage in data conversations. The telling and sharing of data stories can serve as a much-needed catalyst in developing a stronger, more diverse data culture. In the journey to becoming a data-driven change agent, each individual must progress through the following three stages (see Figure 9.22):

THREE KEYS TO BECOMING A
DATA-DRIVEN CHANGE AGENT

Figure 9.22 To become a data-driven change agent, you need to be sufficiently data literate so you can understand and interpret the data correctly. Next, you need to be curious and free to explore the data to find meaningful insights. Last, you need to acquire data storytelling skills so you can communicate your insights in an effective manner.

1. **Data literacy.** First, as I mentioned in Chapter 1, you need to gain a foundation in basic numeracy skills such as being able to process and interpret a standard data table or chart. You'll also need to be familiar with basic statistics (mean, standard deviation, correlation) as well as the domain-specific metrics of your role, function, and industry. For many people, it may have been a while since they last took a math or statistics class in college. It may be important to refresh these skills so you can understand and interpret the data correctly. A potentially good data story will quickly unravel if it's based on a poor or erroneous interpretation of the numbers. Fortunately, data literacy skills can be developed through training and hands-on experience.

2. **Data curiosity.** The next important step is to develop the desire and capacity to be curious, ask questions of the data, and seek to expand your knowledge. While some people may be more inquisitive than others, curiosity is an innate trait shared by all human beings. Aside from the time constraints that may be placed on our inquisitiveness, our environment and mental state can also influence how curious we are. External factors such as limited data access, poor quality or irrelevant data, or difficult-to-use data tools

can curtail curiosity. Likewise, internal factors such as apathy, a fear of failure, overconfidence, or close-mindedness can also prevent us from exploring data. If these types of barriers can be minimized or removed, you'll be more inclined to venture into the data and seek answers to key questions. The magnitude and value of the insights you discover will dictate whether they deserve to be crafted into data stories so they can be fully actualized.

3. **Data storytelling.** The last step is to learn how to effectively communicate your insights so they can be clearly understood by others. No transformation will occur if your message is unclear, overwhelming, or convoluted. Your data communications also must be persuasive and memorable if they're going to stick with your audiences. If you've done a good job preparing and telling your data story, the audience will embrace your insights as their own and be motivated to act on them.

If you're reading this book, you are most likely already data literate and somewhat curious about data. At this moment, you're probably interested in augmenting your existing data storytelling skills. However, if you'd like to start telling data stories but don't feel you have a good grasp of the underlying data, you must first spend time strengthening your numeracy skills. Because data is the foundation, a weak insight will always compromise the integrity of a data story, no matter how well it is structured or visualized. If you have the necessary data literacy skills but lack curiosity, I'd recommend evaluating what internal or external factors may be holding you back. The growing amount of available information is begging to be explored by an inquiring mind that isn't stuck in neutral.

American folklorist Jack Zipes observed, "The role of the storyteller is to awaken the storyteller in others." Due to the circular nature of this process (see Figure 9.22), an interesting relationship is forged between the data storyteller and audience. Before you build a data story, you need to be aware of how data literate your audience is and tailor your content to their level. As an audience is repeatedly exposed to new insights, the data literacy level of the participants will be enhanced over time. Just like regular reading can improve someone's literacy skills, consuming data stories on a continual basis will boost their data-literacy abilities. Furthermore, data stories may spark interest among the audience members to explore the data for themselves and build data stories based on their own findings. Gradually, more change agents will be created through the act of data storytelling, and their voices will be added to an increasingly vibrant exchange of data conversations.

Your mission as a data storyteller is to ensure each meaningful insight that crosses your path receives a fair shot at having its story heard. You may already have several insights in mind that are begging to have their tales told. Your skill in telling a compelling data story may be the difference between a problem being resolved or overlooked, an opportunity being seized or missed, or a risk being mitigated or exacerbated. Poet Dr. Maya Angelou said, "If you want what you're saying heard, then take your time and say it so that the listener will actually hear it." With data, you not only want your message heard—you want the audience to see and understand the insights as clearly as you do. If you've uncovered what appears to be a significant insight (and it falls in the Story Zone from Chapter 4), you must invest the time and effort to craft a data story that is commensurate with its weight and importance. If you produce anything less, you do a disservice to the insight and put it at risk of being discounted or ignored.

Even though the way in which we tell stories has evolved significantly over the centuries, stories still possess an almost mystical power over us. They still play an integral role in how we process and store information. Hopefully, through reading this book, you've gained a new appreciation for narrative's potential in enhancing how you share your insights. From Florence Nightingale to Hans Rosling, different data storytellers have been able to successfully combine data visualizations with narrative to inspire and drive positive change. Based on the data storytelling principles I've shared in this book, you should be better prepared to follow a similar path with your own data discoveries.

The Hopi Indian tribe is attributed with the saying "Those who tell the stories rule the world." Today, with our increasing reliance on data, the people who tell data stories effectively will be the ones who influence and rule our digital world. But to paraphrase one of my favorite storytellers of all time, the late comic book icon Stan Lee, "with great power comes great responsibility." While data storytelling can rescue insights that would otherwise be lost in a sea of data, it can also be used to distort truth and mislead people. As truth-seeking data storytellers, our responsibility is to ensure our data stories lead to enlightenment, not deception. The art of data storytelling is still at a formative stage in its development, and it is our shared duty to ensure this digital craft is held to a high standard and conducted with integrity.

No matter how sound your facts are, how compelling your narrative is, or how stunning your visuals are, data storytelling will be challenging at times. Because new insights represent change, you're going to be confronting the status quo, accepted traditions, common practices, and institutional norms on an ongoing basis. While data storytelling can strengthen the delivery of your key points, it doesn't guarantee difficult decisions will be easier for your audience to make.

Dr. Martin Luther King Jr. said, "Change does not roll in on the wheels of inevitability, but comes through continuous struggle." Your unrelenting efforts to provide the numbers with a clear, compelling voice will make a demonstrable difference—whether it's to your team, organization, community, or cause. As this is a relatively new field within the ancient discipline of storytelling, we'll continue to see new innovations and approaches in data storytelling as our capabilities and creativity evolve. Just as I've shared some of the key learnings from my journeys in data storytelling, I look forward to hearing of your triumphs and trials in crafting stories from data. Regardless, may your data stories *end happily ever after* by inspiring audiences to act and embrace change. Nuff said! (Thanks, Stan.)

For more information and resources on data storytelling, go to Effectivedatastorytelling.com.

References

Casselman, B. 2015. No Child Left Behind worked. *FiveThirtyEight*, December 22. https://fivethirtyeight.com/features/no-child-left-behind-worked/.

Desliver, D. 2017. U.S. students' academic achievement still lags that of their peers in many other countries. Pew Research Center, February 15. https://www.pewresearch.org/fact-tank/2017/02/15/u-s-students-internationally-math-science/.

The Economist. 2016. What the world can learn from the latest PISA test results. December 10. https://www.economist.com/

international/2016/12/10/what-the-world-can-learn-from-the-latest-pisa-test-results.

Gapminder. 2019. 200 Countries, 200 Years, 4 Minutes. https://www .gapminder.org/videos/200-years-that-changed-the-world-bbc/ (accessed May 25, 2019).

Rodberg, S. 2019. Data was supposed to fix the U.S. Education System. Here's why it hasn't. *Harvard Business Review*, January 11. https:// hbr.org/2019/01/data-was-supposed-to-fix-the-u-s-education-system-heres-why-it-hasnt.

UNICEF Office of Research. 2017. Building the future: Children and the sustainable development goals in rich countries. Innocenti Report Card no. 14.

US Department of Education. 1983. A nation at risk. https://www2 .ed.gov/pubs/NatAtRisk/risk.html (accessed May 25, 2019).

About the Author

B rent Dykes has spent more than 15 years in the analytics industry, consulting with some of the world's most recognized brands, such as Microsoft, Sony, Nike, Amazon, and Comcast. Currently, he is the senior director of Data Strategy at Domo. As an analyst, manager, and technology evangelist at companies such as Omniture, Adobe, and Domo, Brent witnessed firsthand the challenges of communicating data effectively. With an educational background in marketing (SFU BBA, BYU MBA), he brings a unique perspective to data storytelling that blends both qualitative and quantitative skills. While honing his data storytelling frameworks and techniques over the past several years, Brent has shared his insights at multiple data conferences and corporate workshops around the world.

After creating a popular PowerPoint blog (Powerpointninja.com) with more than 100 articles, Brent shifted his focus to data-related topics. In 2012, he published his first book, *Web Analytics Action Hero* (Adobe Press), and then a follow-up ebook, *Web Analytics Kick Start Guide*. He is a regular *Forbes* contributor with more than 30 published articles on various data topics. In 2016, he was honored to receive the *Most Influential Industry Contributor Award* from the Digital Analytics Association (DAA).

After growing up in New Zealand and Canada, Brent settled with his family in Utah. Besides learning the language of data, he is also trilingual in English, Portuguese, and Spanish. When he's not telling stories with data, Brent enjoys traveling with his family, cycling, reading, and watching films. You may run into him at triathlon events, where he often serves as a race sherpa for his Ironman wife. He's an avid Vancouver Canucks fan and enjoys collecting rare comic books, which further reflects his passion for visual storytelling.

About the Website

To help you with your own data storytelling efforts, I've prepared some assets you can download from the book's companion website www.wiley.com/go/effectivedatastorytelling.com. The password for this site is: Dykes2020. These files will show you how different charts in the book were created, and others feature diagrams that can be printed for your own reference and inspiration. Here are some of the files that will be available online:

1. **EDS_ch7-8_figures.xlsx:** This Excel file contains all of the charts that were featured in the figures found in Chapters 7 and 8. If you have questions about how a chart was created, you can review the chart settings and formatting in this file. You'll find one or two worksheets that correspond to each of the figures from these two visuals-related chapters.

2. **EDS_ch7-8_figures.pptx:** This PowerPoint file contains all of the chart figures from Chapters 7 and 8. I shared this file so you can see how I had to augment some of the Excel charts in PowerPoint to create the final versions that appear in the book. I converted the Excel charts to images to simplify the PowerPoint file. Normally, the charts are just embedded objects.

3. **EDS_reference_diagrams.pdf:** This PDF file contains some of the key diagrams from the book that may be useful as reference material. Based on reader feedback, I may expand the diagrams that are included in this file. Please let me know if there's a diagram from the book that you'd like to see added to this reference file.

Index